Heart to heart, are there any enemies?

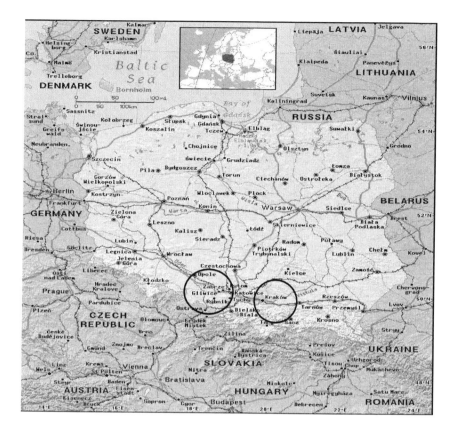

Map of Poland

Note the circled location of Krakow, which is also known as "Cracow" on some maps. Note, too, the circled location of Gliwice. Both cities are relevant to *The War Within, The Story of Josef.*

Public Domain map

Cover Photo Credit: Walter Walkow

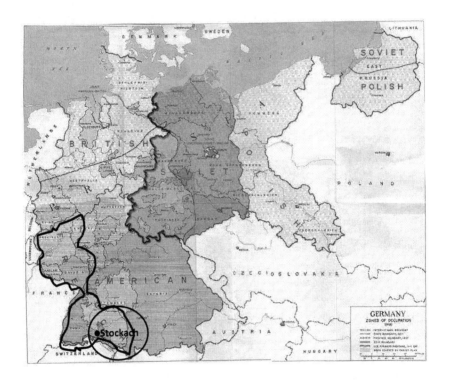

Allied Occupation of Germany

When the war ended, Germany was divided into Allied Zones of Occupation: Soviet, British, French, and American. The French Zone, where the events in this book took place, is in the western part of Germany, just north of Switzerland. The body of water between Switzerland and Germany is Lake Constance, which is also known as the Bodensee. The town of Stockach was in the French-Occupied zone of post-war Germany, and is the setting for much of *The War Within, the Story of Josef*.

Public Domain Map

Map of Modern Germany

Notice the locations of Stockach in the southwest and Bremerhaven in the north, the port from which most displaced persons emigrated from post-World War II Germany.

Source: CIA, The World Factbook, 2004, in the Public Domain

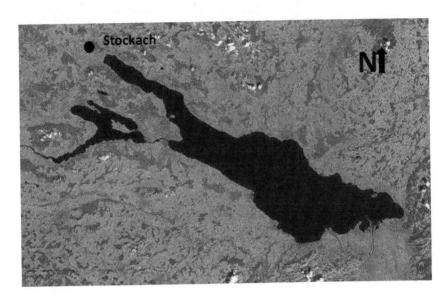

Satellite Image of the Lake Constance Area

On the south shore of the lake is Switzerland; Austria is to the east, and Germany is to the north. Stockach, in Germany, is about fifteen kilometers from the lake. It is a picturesque area, and many people spend vacations at or near the lake. Stockach's proximity to neutral Switzerland and its semi-rural locale made it less likely to be bombed by the Allies, although some skirmishes occurred.

Photo credit: Stritti, German Wikipedia.jpg, in the Public Domain

Germany has concluded a Non-Aggression Pact with Poland...We shall adhere to it unconditionally... we recognize Poland as the home of a great and nationally conscious people.

Adolf Hitler, May 21, 1935

I HAVE ISSUED THE COMMAND - AND I'LL HAVE ANYBODY WHO UTTERS BUT ONE WORD OF CRITICISM EXECUTED BY A FIRING SQUAD - THAT OUR WAR AIM DOES NOT CONSIST IN REACHING CERTAIN LINES, BUT IN THE PHYSICAL DESTRUCTION OF THE ENEMY. ACCORDINGLY, I HAVE PLACED MY DEATH-HEAD FORMATIONS IN READINESS - FOR THE PRESENT ONLY IN THE EAST - WITH ORDERS TO THEM TO SEND TO DEATH MERCILESSLY AND WITHOUT COMPASSION, MEN, WOMEN, AND CHILDREN OF POLISH DERIVATION AND LANGUAGE..ONLY THUS SHALL WE GAIN THE LIVING SPACE (LEBENSRAUM) WHICH WE NEED. WHO, AFTER ALL, SPEAKS TODAY OF THE ANNIHILATION OF THE ARMENIANS?

Adolf Hitler, August 22, 1939
According to reports received by the Associated Press
Bureau Chief, Louis Lochner

Inscription from the United States Holocaust Memorial Museum in Washington D.C.

Poles will disappear from the world... It is essential that the great German people should consider it their major task to destroy all Poles.

Heinrich Himmler, after Aug. 22, 1939

The War Within, The Story of Josef

by

Patricia Walkow

Josef Walkow

Josef Walkow, in his early twenties, after the war. Approximately 1946-1948.

Courtesy Monica Walkow Dudzinski

Table of Contents

Preface

Born just a few years after the end of worldwide hostilities, I grew up in the shadow of World War II. In those days, American children included in their nighttime prayers a special "thank you" to God for ending the war, and for letting them live in America, the best place on earth.

My Friday night memories included my father's card games. His buddies frequently came to the house to play poker and engage in friendly conversation. Yet inevitably, discussion turned to "The War," the defining event of these young men's lives. They talked about their own wartime experiences, friends they lost, and brothers killed on Omaha Beach, or somewhere in the South Pacific, Germany, or Italy. They reminisced about their sweethearts who anxiously waited for them, and they remembered buddies who returned, injured, from the war.

The war saturated my home, not in blood, but in the poignant memories of these men.

The sad stories of my father's friends were greatly tempered by the diet of war movies consumed through the 1950s and 1960s. They stereotypically depicted the unforgivable single-mindedness of "goose-stepping" Germans and the glory of epic sea, air, and land victories over both Germany and Japan. For the casts of handsome movie stars and beautiful actresses, love was allowed, but duty and honor always prevailed. Of course, the Allies were victorious, and the bravest of all were the Americans. We youngsters believed everything. Un-nuanced, these movies narrowed my understanding of World War II, but I did not know it then.

Though I am not Jewish, my childhood was spent in a predominantly Jewish neighborhood, in Midwood, Brooklyn, and I attended a college with a significant Jewish faculty and student body, Brooklyn College of the City University of New

York. I knew about the Holocaust. A girlhood friend who lived on my block had a dear grandmother who was a concentration camp survivor. The kindly, elderly woman had a tattoo on her arm. Fascinated, we kids were told to avoid looking at it, and we were forbidden to ask her any questions about it.

As a teenager and young woman, mostly everything I had read about World War II and its victims focused on the horrific experience of the Jews, and the systematic plans to annihilate them.

When I met my Polish Christian father-in-law, Josef, and my German mother-in-law, Ella, I learned a great deal more about the wartime subjugation of Polish people, both Jewish and Christian. It wasn't until I knew my in-laws for some years that I appreciated both their fear of hunger and the joy they had in their contented lives, far away in time and distance from past horrors. They never spoke at length of the war. Their words were usually succinct, and they almost always quickly steered the conversation in a different direction. Their handling of the subject was puzzling, yet I was fascinated by anything they shared about the World War II years and their early years in the U.S. Slowly, the seeds of their story planted themselves within my mind. I just was not ready to nurture the seeds then.

Hitler occupied Poland in September of 1939, when Josef was almost fourteen. The teenager was taken from his home and forced into a life of slave labor in service to Germany. He served through the war in work camps and parts of concentration camps in Poland, and then in factories in southern Germany. A tragic event almost forced him to lose his life at one of his conscripted jobs, but a young German man, not too much older than he, intervened. Through his relationship with this young German man, he met a young German girl, Ella.

My in-laws were not people who reveled in their victimhood, which is such a ubiquitous *modus operandi* of life today. They always looked to the future, and made sure their children did, too. Perhaps to a fault; because they rarely spoke of the war years or the years immediately afterwards, their children were unaware of some of their own history. Whether Josef and Ella used their silence to push the war away from their consciousness or to protect their children, I do not know; perhaps it was both.

After I visited the D-Day landing beaches at Normandy and several European war cemeteries, I better grasped the vastness and depth of the war's human tragedy, not only among Allied and German soldiers, but also among civilians of all nationalities and religions. What a toll on humanity, youth, and cultures!

The seed inside me had finally germinated. It was time to tell Josef and Ella's story, and the seed grew deeper and deeper roots.

I discreetly asked them questions over the years I knew them, but as usual, their answers were taciturn. A few sentences were uttered, at most, and grudgingly. Sometimes, things surfaced unexpectedly, if not through word, then in behavior. These moments were windows into the past, and they offered a view of what it was like back then, and how past experiences affected them many years later. Their reactions to everyday events sometimes uncovered old scars, deep fears, valid grievances, and genuine current happiness.

I listened to the remembrances of their children, relatives, and friends in the U.S., Poland, and Germany. The scenarios and conversations in this story are invented within the context of the experiences I know Josef had during and after the war, from the period 1943 through 1954. Josef and Ella did not die like the soldiers whose graves so moved me at Normandy, yet they both had their youths obliterated, and their lives changed forever.

My research process involved reading dozens of books and countless articles in both paper and online format. Many written accounts by slave laborers, ordinary German citizens, and soldiers—both Allied and Axis—helped develop this story. I learned more about World War II's impact on people than I ever saw in any film. The research relentlessly broadened both my perspective and my understanding. It revealed another holocaust—a silent holocaust—just as real as the one perpetrated against the Jews, but not as visible, not as prolifically documented. It was about the systematic death-by-labor of Eastern European people.

I hope the reader will gain insights into this quieter holocaust while reading about Josef, but the story does not overly focus on the cruelty of one people against another people. It does not provide endless dates of battles, descriptions of killing machines, or conquests of countries. It does not cite endless casualty statistics, which are factual, dry, and easy to find. In this story, war is simply the necessary and accurate setting for the human events that unfold within it. But the human stories are not dry. They are not just about statistics. The human stories are about real people living through sometimes unimaginable events. *The War Within, The Story of Josef*, uses milestones of the war to give form and meaning to the intertwined lives of five people who each fought the war internally.

After researching, and then writing and re-writing Josef's story, I know a lot more now, not only about war itself, but also about people caught up in an unfolding history they could not control. Despite loss of freedom, loss of loved ones, and loss of basic human dignity, people have the capacity to choose their reactions to their life situations.

This story is about understanding the hearts of enemies.

Corrales, New Mexico
June 2016

Acknowledgements

My foremost gratitude goes to my father-in-law, Josef, and mother-in-law, Ella, for their love over all the years I knew them. They never wished to burden their children or their children's spouses about World War II or its aftermath.

My husband Walter, his brother Franz, and sister Monica, have offered their own memories, as well as those their parents shared with them; they also offered artifacts from the past. Their input into this book has been beneficial beyond words.

Their first cousin, Józef Walków (my father-in-law's nephew), living in Poland, offered family history unknown to his cousins living in the U.S. Our correspondences, converted from English to Polish and then Polish to English, helped broaden the knowledge of my husband's paternal family.

Luzia Rimmele, from the same town in Germany where my in-laws lived, was able to fill in some gaps in my understanding of events and people. Members of my writing group, as well as beta readers, offered vital suggestions.

Dozens of books and articles written about Germany during and after the war have been enlightening. Books about slave laborers, displaced persons, and refugees offered insights into the motivations for post-war migration from Europe. Books about the Marshall Plan and Catholic Relief Services explained aid, relocation, and industrial recovery programs, as well as the humanitarian, ideological, religious, and political motivations that underpinned them.

And finally, to all who survived the war and moved on to build new lives, I am humbled by the experiences you endured, and I salute you for your courage and determination. Thank you for everything you have taught me.

You are true heroes.

1- Awakening

What is that scent? Flowers? No, bleach...no, flowers.

Josef slowly became hazily aware of something he had not experienced in a long time. It was a gentle brush of air teasing his face, and the delicate, subtle, flowery scent of crisp, clean, perfumed sheets, with an undertone of bleach. The fragrance was somewhat familiar, but he could not recall where he had smelled it before.

There were voices, too. He couldn't make out what was being said, and he fell back to sleep.

When he awakened again, Josef noticed the sheets were still there, but no voices. He stubbornly refused to open his eyes.

My leg!

He searched for his left leg and expected it to be in its normal place, as it had been for almost eighteen years. For the eighth day in a row, he found an alien space below his knee. While he had been resigned to the loss of his leg when he was taken to the hospital, he now felt his face flush with heat...anger. He was angry at the Germans, angry at the world, and angry at the doctor. Mostly, at the doctor.

He could have saved my leg if he wanted to. How am I going to work with just one leg?

Still not wanting to open his eyes and face another day as an amputee, Josef replayed the moment when his leg was injured. It was all he thought about, and he recalled the unfortunate event many times a day. A large, heavy, wooden barrel was positioned on the loading platform in the factory where he worked. It was almost five feet tall, with very dark, rough-grained wood, and shiny brass metal bands and rivets. The barrel wasn't placed securely on the platform and it tumbled onto the factory's concrete floor. The metal band encircling its widest part snapped, sailed twenty feet across the concrete floor, and sliced

Josef's left leg between his ankle and knee. Bright red blood stained his dirty pants. His brother Michael, who was working next to him, ripped his own undershirt from his body, tore it into a rectangle, and wrapped it around Josef's leg to stem the bleeding. At the same time, they both looked around to be sure no one at the factory saw how bloody Josef's leg had become.

They both knew it was a serious wound. There was no way to clean it except with water, and they cleaned it as best as they could. In normal times, they would have asked for medical help. But these were not normal times, and despite his pain, Josef continued to work for several days. He tried to hide his injury as it became red, filled with pus, and increasingly painful.

In the days following the accident, Josef shivered with fever. His brother felt helpless, but they both knew if the Germans found out about the injury, they would most certainly execute Josef. The two brothers measured time not by hours and days, but by the terrifying advance of infection in a deep and dirty wound.

As the pain became more severe, Josef longed for his mother. As a Catholic, he exercised the tradition of saying morning and night prayers. But now, he prayed quietly to himself while working throughout the day. Rather than asking God to remove the pain, he asked for the strength to endure it, and to be able to face whatever may come. And he prayed his leg would heal on its own. Yet, despite his yearning for his mother to be with him, despite his prayers, the left leg festered, turned gray, and then black.

Even now, flat on his back in bed and minus his leg, Josef thought he smelled its decay. He didn't want to open his eyes. If he kept them closed, he could block the entire world. He didn't know why, as a captive of Germany, his life has been spared. It made no sense to him. It wasn't the norm, and he didn't believe in luck or miracles.

As a Polish laborer, he was an expendable slave, taken from his home by the Nazis. Slave laborers were kept alive only as long as they were able to do the work the Germans needed. There was no medical care, no extra rations to feed a wounded body, no period of light duty.

Slave laborers who couldn't work were usually executed.[1]

He had seen it several times. Slackers and sick workers were simply hauled outside and taken away, then either executed or sent to a re-education camp...a concentration camp.[2] For some reason, he was an exception, and the only reason he could think of for the special treatment was his ability to fix some of the machinery used in the factory. He was convinced his talent for understanding machines had saved him.

Perhaps, if I just think it all through, it will make sense. Perhaps, if I don't open my eyes, it will all go away.

But he could no longer sleep. He wanted to know why his life was spared.

He opened his eyes to gentle morning sunlight coming through the window a few feet beyond the foot of the bed, to his left. The starched, white curtains on the open window were gently moving with a soft breeze that he felt against his forehead. The sun was bright and the curtains lightly filtered the shadows of leaves from a nearby tree. They seemed to dance on the adjacent wall. The curtain, the sheets...everything seemed so clean, so fresh, so normal.

The room was very different from the stark, antiseptic hospital room. The sheets were different—thick, smooth. This was someone's home, and it certainly bore no resemblance to the stables or barracks where he lived, cramped and dirty, with the other laborers. He had not been inside a home since 1940, three years ago.

Josef was discharged from the hospital the previous night. Willie had picked him up and taken him into his own house to recuperate from the surgery.

How could I have forgotten that?

Turning his head away from the window, Josef saw Willie asleep in a blue, yellow, and white, striped upholstered chair

3

next to a round table on the right side of the room. Willie's left hand rested on the table's white linen cloth, a newspaper half in his lap, and half on the floor. Josef could see the wristwatch he wore. It was the one he had fixed for Willie a few months ago, before the barrel accident.

Willie was an ambulance driver and medic in the small southern German town where the factory Josef worked in was located. Willie was German, and had a good friend who worked in the factory's office. From time to time, Willie, who seemed to be just a few years older than Josef, came to the factory to visit his friend, have a cigarette, or share a bite to eat.

On one of those visits, Willie was complaining to his friend that his watch wasn't working well and that he did not know how to fix it. He grumbled that anyone who knew how to fix it was no longer around, and that it would be hard to replace it. All kinds of things were scarce during the war. Wristwatches, and people to repair them, were no exception.

Josef overheard this conversation. He had a limited yet functional understanding of German, as well as the ability to make himself understood. He decided to offer to fix the watch. The thought was spontaneous, and it both surprised and annoyed him.

Taking a chance, he walked to Willie and said, "If you can get me the tools I need and some solvent, I can try to fix that for you."

Willie scoffed, "You?"

"Yes, I fixed wristwatches before I came here."

"You're just a kid. How did you learn to fix watches?"

"My father taught me."

"How do I know you won't steal it?"

Josef wanted to sarcastically yell, *Because you'll shoot me if I do, you obnoxious Nazi,* but he remained silent.

"Well, watch me fix it."

Willie hesitated, but then said, "I'll come by after work tomorrow."

Willie found the labor detail leader at the factory, and told him about the conversation he and Josef had. The leader glanced over at Josef, and shook his head in consent.

The following day, Willie returned with the necessary tools and solvent, and Josef went to work on the watch.

He took the watch from Willie, and as he placed it on a nearby table and opened its case, thoughts of his father overwhelmed him.

Papa had a talent for repairing almost anything, even inventing small machines at times. When Josef was nine years old, his father invited him to come outside on a cool autumn afternoon, when the smell of fallen, damp leaves infused the air. Bundled in sweaters, Papa sat at a small, uneven wooden table behind the house, not too far from a fire burning in an old, rusted, metal tub.

"Josef, come here," Papa called, as Josef looked out the back door.

"Why?"

"Just come here. I want to show you something."

Josef put some warm clothes on and went to his father, sat next to him, and leaned against him.

"Stand here, Josef," Papa said, and pointed to the space between his legs. Josef did as he was told and stood between his father and the table, as Papa worked on a wristwatch. The man was content, though encumbered by his bundled-up middle son in his embrace. Several times Papa had to dodge Josef's head so he could see what he was doing. Josef peered over the large hands that cradled the wristwatch and he studied how Papa removed the back case. Papa showed him how the gears interconnected and how the movement of one affected the movement of another. Young Josef understood the concept immediately, and from then on, he was always invited to help Papa repair things and create whatever gadgets were needed around the little farm. He rarely turned down these invitations from his father. Like his father, he had an innate understanding

5

and appreciation of machinery, which was honed with each gadget he repaired. He enjoyed figuring out how things worked, he loved helping his father, and he adored having his father all to himself.

In the bittersweet warmth of his memories, Josef examined the gears in Willie's watch. He quickly got lost in the machinery, where the laws of physics and mechanics were predictable and unbiased, and where he felt closest to his father.

Willie seemed interested in the watch's gears and asked a few questions about what Josef was doing. Josef's explanations included a few words and phrases in German, and many hand motions. Somehow, the two young men were able to have a discussion about the watch.

After about thirty minutes, the watch was working. Josef reassembled the parts, put everything back in the case, and handed it back to Willie. It was an easy fix, mostly just cleaning dirt-encrusted gears.

Willie gave a crooked, surprised smile, a smile Josef found condescending. After uttering a curt *"Danke,"* he tossed a few coins on the table for Josef, returned to his ambulance, and drove off.

Months had passed since that day. Now, Willie's watch was fixed, Josef had lost a leg, and Willie was asleep in a chair in this beautiful bedroom, his glasses still on, looking after Josef.

There was a teapot, teacup, and saucer on the linen-covered table next to Willie, along with some thick-crusted bread and a jar of purple-colored jam. There was a folded white cloth napkin. The teapot was white porcelain with red and yellow roses on it, and the spout was trimmed in gold.

Civilized, beautiful.

Josef's stirrings awakened Willie. He came over to the bed, and asked Josef how he felt.

"I need to use the bathroom."

At the hospital, he had learned how to use crutches to get to the bathroom. But Willie helped him anyway, since it was the first time Josef was using the bathroom in Willie's house. When he returned to bed, Willie offered him some hot tea, and bread with jam.

"There is no butter for the bread, Josef. It is rationed and we use it for cooking rather than just spreading it on bread."

"I don't need butter."

Josef ate the bread slowly, savoring each bite of the dense loaf and relishing the sweetness of the jam, hoping not to do anything to upset his stomach.

Neither young man spoke. They eyed each other intently, each equally amazed that Josef was in Willie's house.

Willie saw the questions forming on Josef's lips.

"We'll talk later. Rest today, and get used to being in my house. You are safe here, and the doctor told me how to care for you so that you get stronger and better able to move around. I'm certified in first aid and will contact the doctor if necessary."

He showed Josef a little brass bell on the nightstand next to the bed.

"If you need something, just pick up this bell and ring it. Do you understand?"

"Yes, but who will come?"

"My mother will come if you need help and she'll bring you something to eat later. Please call her 'Frau Mirz,' Josef."

"That's your family name? Mirz?"

"Yes."

Willie made no inquiry as to Josef's last name—he had it in writing anyway on the papers that certified Josef's removal from the factory. Willie checked the bandage, and gave Josef a couple of pills, "For pain and infection," he said, and Josef swallowed them.

"Who lives in the house besides you and your mother?"

"No one."

"Are you leaving now?"

"Yes, I need to get back to work for a few hours. Remember to use the bell if you need anything."

7

"What time is it, Willie?"

Willie glanced at his watch—the one Josef had fixed. Josef noticed Willie wore a silver signet ring on the same hand as the watch, and also saw his fingernails were incredibly clean.

"It is ten in the morning. After you settled into this room last night, you went straight to bed and slept through until now."

"The transfer from the hospital to the house took a lot of energy, and I guess I just couldn't fight the tiredness."

"That's understandable."

Josef had many questions for Willie, including the most nagging one—*Why did you help me?* He wanted to know if it had really been necessary to amputate his leg, or if it was just the fastest, easiest way for the doctor to deal with him. He wanted to know what was going to happen to him.

He started to say something, but Willie held his hand up to stop him, stood up, turned abruptly, and left the room.

Josef's questions would have to wait until he saw Willie again. He was offended at Willie's hasty departure, as though Willie could not tolerate being in the same room with him.

He was also confused about Willie's behavior. Willie had defied the rules of Germany's wartime social order to help a slave laborer, but when presented with an opportunity to have a real dialogue with one, he fled.

Josef did not have the strength to sort this out, at least not right now. He looked around the room again and saw how clean and pleasant it was. He felt for his leg again, and still, there was an empty space where it once had been. That hadn't changed.

He missed his brother Michael, and his home back in Poland. And Willie's behavior baffled him.

Josef did not know Willie Mirz was even more perplexed.

2 - Bewilderment

Willie had brought the ambulance home the previous night because he was on call to handle emergencies. He climbed into the driver's seat and issued a long, tired sigh. He just sat for a while, tightly clutching the steering wheel, staring straight ahead at nothing in particular, brooding. For a few moments he closed his eyes, as though in conscious sleep, then reopened them. It had been an exhausting week.

He was glad Josef would probably live, but he was confused by his own actions. He had never helped a prisoner before.

Why had he helped this one?

He reminded himself of something important—slave laborers were inferior to Germans, just about everyone was. Willie found this particular view of the human pecking order comforting and was relieved he was born a German, rather than someone less than German.

"But," he thought, "we are all human beings. Blood is blood; pain is pain; a leg is still a leg. If a patient in my ambulance had his body covered, and only the legs were exposed, how could anyone tell if the person was German, Polish, English, or Russian?"

Willie relaxed his tight grip on the steering wheel and released the tension in his arms. He ran his fingers repeatedly over the polished, metal steering wheel, feeling the solidity in its German engineering, thinking how he had to find some legitimate work for Josef. The teenager had made a name for himself as someone with an uncanny talent for repairing, and even fashioning machinery. Despite this talent, the authorities at the factory could replace Josef with another worker, even if the new laborer didn't have Josef's skills. Willie convinced them he had genuine work for a slave laborer amputee.

Convincing his mother had been another matter.

A few days before he brought Josef home, he assured her Josef would be assigned work in service to the German people, and he would stay with them only until he had recuperated sufficiently to go elsewhere. He told her Josef would expect no payment except a place to sleep and a little food, and he would not be in the way, interrupting her daily routine, once he was able to get around.

Sonya was unhappy her son had brought home a stranger—let alone a sick one, and the enemy! She had insisted Josef be disinfected for lice and be cleaned up, or he was not going to be sleeping on any of her sheets, in any of her beds, or in any of her bedrooms, no matter how sick he was. She was adamant about cleanliness and wanted him out of the house quickly.

Willie rested his head on his hands, still holding the steering wheel. Had it really been a week ago when Josef was doused with insecticide outside the hospital and then washed before surgery? It felt much longer as he relived the afternoon he brought Josef to the hospital and the days following the teenager's surgery.

Willie had not called the hospital ahead to inform the staff he was bringing in a slave laborer with a potentially fatal injury. He just showed up with Josef in the ambulance—an emergency case. Willie knew any German who unjustifiably helped captives could be punished, usually with imprisonment. Those who did help, did so with fear. For the authorities, it was easier and cheaper to kill a prisoner and replace him, rather than heal him.

The government was known to punish doctors for offering help to Jews and slave laborers of any nationality, and Willie knew the surgeon would feel uncomfortable treating Josef. But Josef was a useful laborer and could serve Germany. His work record showed he could not only perform hard labor and fix watches and other machines, but also do carpentry.

At the hospital, Willie spoke quietly to the doctor outside the exam room where Josef was waiting, and outlined all the work Josef could do. Those who ran the factory considered him a talented and versatile laborer and were willing to allow him to get some medical attention. Willie showed the doctor the transfer papers the labor detail leader had drawn up with the labor camp commander to remand Josef into Willie's oversight.

The graying doctor pondered what Willie told him about Josef for a minute. He looked down at the floor and focused on his worn black shoes, slowly shaking his head in silent consent. But before he and Willie entered the exam room to see Josef, the doctor raised his eyebrows at Willie and stared directly at him, as though to say, "I hope you know what you are doing."

While the doctor examined Josef, Willie waited in the hallway and hoped the leg could be saved. The leg looked exceptionally bad, and he didn't want to second-guess the doctor's decision to amputate, if that was the only course of action.

When Willie returned to the exam room, the doctor told Josef he could not save the leg. Josef trembled and grimaced, fighting back tears. He was not only angry. He was terrified, had a high fever, and was in pain.

"Can you give him something for the pain?" Willie asked the doctor.

"That's exactly what I was going to do."

Looking at his patient, the doctor reassured him, "Josef, this injection will dull the pain. It will make you drowsy, too, and we are going to operate soon—hopefully within the hour."

"Who will do the operation?" Josef asked.

"I will."

"And afterwards, what happens?"

"You'll be here in the hospital until you are well enough to leave." The doctor briefly glanced at Willie.

"What am I supposed to do after I leave the hospital?" Josef asked.

"You will need to be rehabilitated and learn to live with one leg."

His eyes now wide, he looked questioningly at Willie and the doctor, and asked "What does that mean?"

11

"You will need to exercise your muscles to get them as strong as possible," said Willie, helping to clarify what the doctor meant by Josef having to be rehabilitated.

The doctor prepared the pain killer injection and administered it to Josef, helping him lie down first.

Within just a few minutes, Josef was more relaxed and sleepy. He said the iconic Catholic "Hail Mary" prayer to himself. It was a prayer he repeated many times a day:

Hail Mary, full of grace, the Lord is with thee. Blessed art thou among women, and blessed is the fruit of thy womb, Jesus. Holy Mary, Mother of God, pray for us sinners now....

Josef lost consciousness with the remainder of the prayer unsaid.

When the doctor was sure Josef was not aware of anything, he turned to Willie.

"An amputation is tragic for this young man. Can you stay with him for a few minutes until the staff gets him prepared for surgery?"

"Of course, Herr Doktor."

The doctor left the room, and Willie sat down on a hard, wooden chair. He did not have much time to think about the situation, since the nurse came into the room a moment later to prepare Josef for surgery.

Willie returned to his ambulance when Josef was wheeled to the operating room. During his workday, he thought of Josef, and at the end of his shift, he visited the teenager and found him sound asleep.

The doctor told him the surgery went well, and Josef would need to stay in the hospital for about a week. Willie thought a week was too short an amount of time for Josef to recuperate, but did not say anything about it to the doctor. He knew most amputees spent weeks in a hospital, but it wasn't up to him to make recommendations to a physician about how long Josef should remain in the hospital after the amputation. And it was wartime. The very act of helping Josef was highly unusual.

It was more than just unusual. It was criminal.

People could talk. He and the doctor could be reported to the authorities. They could be disciplined. Their families could be interrogated.

Josef was a Pole, and that made him the enemy.

Seven days after the surgery, the hospital discharged Josef. The doctor advised Willie about what would be normal and abnormal for Josef, and provided a package of appropriate medicines and bandages. He told Willie he would make a home visit to check on his patient, but he also made it clear that he preferred not to see Josef in his office or operating room ever again. Although he did feel sorrow for the teenager who had just lost his leg, the doctor was afraid to appear overly sympathetic. He was unyielding in his position—Josef would not recuperate in the hospital. So, Willie took him to his own home to recuperate.

Having relived the past week or so, Willie raised his head from the steering wheel, turned the key in the ignition, and drove forward. Recounting what had happened did not give him any new insights or peace. He was confused by his own actions. He knew he had saved Josef's life, but he didn't know why.

Something was churning in his soul, but he could not identify what it was, and he could not shake his discomfort. "Maybe it is just the war," he thought. "It seems to go on and on. Will it ever end?"

He had never believed much of the political propaganda glorifying the German successes in the war. He knew there was a chance Germany may not win the war. There were no guarantees of victory, and he couldn't picture his future if Germany lost the war. Yet, he needed to appear optimistic, because it was expected of German citizens.

He also knew he needed to find some real work for Josef.

"What work doesn't require legs? What can he do?"

Surrounding communities used slave laborers in the agricultural fields. Josef could not do field work now, with only one leg, and so soon after the amputation. He probably could not go back to the barrel factory, either. Used to transport food and munitions as well as age wine, those barrels were huge, bulky, and heavy. Willie, or anyone else, could not expect Josef to perform this kind of work anymore for six or seven days a week.

Preoccupied, Willie didn't see the hospital, and drove past it. As he turned the ambulance back, he wondered, "Josef can fix watches. What else can I find for him to fix?"

Willie had a busy day transporting people, mostly civilians, but the question niggled him all afternoon and into the early evening. He was tired when he got home. He washed up and ate a little soup. Sonya, his mother, told him Josef seemed to be stable and she had given him the medications the doctor provided.

Willie went to bed early that night, more tired from the day's normal workload of ambulance calls than he should have been.

3 - Josef and Willie Talk

Josef was disappointed, and a little worried, because Willie did not return to see him that afternoon or evening. But as Willie had mentioned, his mother did prepare a small meal for Josef—a soup with vegetables and grain, some bread, an apple, and more tea. Josef hadn't had such a feast in a long time. The laborers were given meager rations, and it was not uncommon for a healthy boy to waste away and even die within a few months of being placed into forced labor.

Josef sensed Frau Mirz—Sonya—disliked waiting on him.

She had rapped on the door with a single, commanding knock, and entered the bedroom without waiting for an answer. Sonya did not look directly at Josef. Instead, she appeared preoccupied with other items in the room while she talked to him.

Frau Mirz was taller than Josef, and her blonde hair was tied back tightly from her face. There were a few streaks of gray in her hair and they complemented the simple gray dress she wore. Her eyes were a piercing blue. She was neither thin nor heavy, but solid. One could call her stately.

"Here is your supper." She placed the tray of food on the nightstand.

"*Danke.*"

"Eat it all—I am not going to waste scarce food on you."

"Yes."

"Do you need to use the bathroom?"

"Yes."

"Here are your crutches. I'll help you."

"*Danke.*"

Sonya helped Josef to the bathroom, waited in the hall, and then took him back to his room.

"Did you wash your hands?"

15

"Yes."

"You'd better stay clean. I don't want any problems with lice."

"Yes, Frau Mirz."

"Get back in bed, and I'll give you your tray of supper."

Josef got back into bed, and had to stretch to cover himself with the blanket. Sonya made no effort to help and turned her head away from him, instead.

When he was settled in bed, she gave Josef his tray and told him to ring the bell when he was finished, so she could pick it up and take it back to the kitchen.

When she left, Josef's slow, growing rage filled his chest, welled up into his mouth, and stung his eyes. He wanted to scream how he resented everything, and how furious he was. He wanted to throw the food across the room, and rip the curtains from the window.

But he didn't. He simply ate his supper of thick vegetable soup and rye bread while his eyes burned with tears of fury, grief, and gratitude.

He needed to talk to Willie. Now.

But it wasn't until the following afternoon when Willie appeared at his bedside, a cuckoo clock in one arm, and a toaster in the other.

Josef was sitting up in bed, reading the only material available to him—a Bible. It was in German so he was really glancing at the illustrations more than reading it. But he knew all the stories, anyway.

"*Guten Tag*, Josef, how are you?"

"I am better, thank you. Your mother gave me a fresh nightshirt to wear."

"Are you in pain?"

"It's bearable. The medicine does help."

Willie smiled, "Good! Josef, I brought you a few things to see if you can fix them. The cuckoo doesn't come out of its house fully, and only one side of the toaster works. My mother really loves that cuckoo clock. Can you take a look at them in a day or two and see if you can fix them?"

"Yes, I will do that." Josef motioned for Willie to hang the clock on the wall. He needed to see what it did when it struck the hour. Willie got a nail and a hammer from another room, hung the clock, and set it.

"Let me know what tools you will need."

"Willie, *warum*...why?" asked Josef.

"Why what?"

"Why did you save my life?"

Anticipating this question, Willie had rehearsed his answer.

"At the factory, they say you fix all the machinery they have, and you have a real talent for it. In addition, this village needs someone who can fix all the household appliances, as well as repair farm and factory machines that have broken. Carpentry work is unfinished, plumbing needs to be mended, electrical projects have stalled, and on and on. So many things have not been completed, or totally ignored on account of the men being away fighting, or killed. We Germans are accustomed to everything working well, and when they don't, we have to get them operating smoothly as soon as possible. It is part of how the German people live normal lives."

Josef bit his lip and swallowed, indignant at the arrogant implication only Germans would like to live normal lives.

"How do you know I can fix all these things you say are broken?"

"The master at the barrel factory told me how adept you are at repairing machinery. You fixed my watch, didn't you?"

"Yes, but a watch, a toaster, a cuckoo clock, and even something like a water pump are not the same." Again, Josef asked, "Willie, why did you save my life?"

Willie kept his gaze on Josef for a moment, then sat down in the chair next to the table. He was reticent, incapable of answering Josef's question. As he nestled into the chair, he realized he simply didn't know the answer.

"Josef, when I stopped to see my friend at the factory last week, I noticed you were limping. I know slave laborers who can't work are usually killed. Do you remember I asked you to lift up your trouser leg so I could see what was wrong?"

"Of course I remember."

"I could see the blood stain, and before you lifted your trouser leg, I could smell the wound. When I saw it, I knew it was serious, and you needed medical attention right away."

"I was trying to hide my leg from the labor detail leader. As long as I was working, he would ignore me!"

"Yes, Josef, I know that."

Josef remembered the moment at the factory when Willie ordered him to show him the injured leg. He was painfully rolling a barrel to the loading dock, and when he stepped outside just for a moment to finish positioning the barrel inside the frame of the large loading doors, Willie saw him. Immediately, Willie shifted his gaze to Josef's leg, demanding to see it. He crouched down and intently examined the leg while Josef stared at the sunlight bouncing off the steep, gabled rooftops in town. Beyond, through a break in the buildings, clouds passed over rows of tidy spring green vineyards marching over rolling hills oblivious to war. Snow still tipped the mountains far to the south. It was an idyllic fairy tale scene and mocked the bleak lives of young slaves.

"You need to see a doctor," Willie had said in an authoritative voice. He made a slicing motion with his hand and said, "Your leg is really bad. I don't know if it can be saved—the doctor will decide. I am taking you to the hospital. Get into the ambulance."

"They'll kill me!" Josef screamed.

"*Nein*, I have need of a laborer like you. The work I have does not require legs."

Willie led him to the passenger side of the ambulance and told him to wait for him inside the vehicle. Josef craned his neck, searching for one other laborer, in particular, to let him know what was happening. But he did not see his brother, Michael, anywhere. Josef thought Willie might be tricking him into believing he was being taken to see a doctor, but, instead, was planning to shoot him and dump his body. He had no reason to trust Willie. None at all. Resigned, Josef got into the passenger's seat, still trying to spot his older brother.

Josef wanted to live, to survive this war, and to go home. He wanted to see his parents, his younger brother, his boyhood friends, and his house. He wanted to go back to school to study engineering. He wanted a girlfriend. He wanted to live long enough to have his life back.

Willie talked to the labor detail leader. Every slave laborer had to be accounted for in the morning, and again in the evening. After some discussion between the two of them, Willie returned to the ambulance and asked Josef for his identifying papers—a booklet called the *Arbeitsbuch Für Ausländer* (Workbook for Foreigner) Josef had to carry on his person at all times.[3] It tracked all of his assignments. Josef handed it to him, and Willie returned to the labor detail leader. The transfer was recorded in Josef's booklet, and on other papers the labor detail leader kept. Willie returned to the ambulance, handed the booklet back to Josef, examined the injured leg again, and turned the key in the ignition. Josef knew his fate was in Willie's hands, and it infuriated him.

And what does Willie mean that the work he has for me does not require legs?

But that was a week ago. Just a week.

Now they were face to face, in Willie's house, having a real conversation.

Josef looked directly at Willie and asked one of the questions that hounded him.

"You said something very interesting the day you took me to the hospital."

"What was that?"

"What did you mean when you said the work you have for me does not require legs?"

19

"I mean there are repair jobs you can do sitting down. There are a lot of them around the town."

"But Willie, *why*? Why did you help me?"

Willie was silent for an uncomfortable minute. He placed his elbows on the table and clasped both his hands together, resting his chin on them, closing his eyes.

Josef did not interrupt Willie's silence. He wanted Willie to say he helped him for no other reason than he was hurt, for no other reason than he was another human being, that it was the compassionate thing to do, that he was young and had a full life to live.

Willie opened his eyes, looked intently at Josef and slowly shook his head from side to side.

"*Ich weiss nicht warum*...I don't know why I helped you, Josef."

Now it was Josef's turn to stare silently at Willie. There was no real relationship between them. They weren't friends. He had simply fixed a wristwatch. It didn't make sense, and Josef decided not to press the question any more at that moment.

He changed the subject. With his limited German and a lot of pantomime, he said, "Bring me a few screwdrivers, pliers, a hammer, a file, some glue, some copper wire if you can find it, and some screws. I will examine the clock and toaster in a couple of days. Please tell your mother I will need her to take the clock off the wall at some point."

He paused and took a breath, "She doesn't like me, you know."

"Right now, I am quite certain she does not like me either," Willie laughed, "but I will try to get you the tools you will need."

4 - Willie and Sonya

Willie left the bedroom and headed for the kitchen where Sonya was whipping some eggs for an omelet supper.

"How is he?" she said.

"He seems to be coping and he appreciates what you do for him."

"He should," she said. "When do you think he can go elsewhere?"

"I don't know for sure, Mother, but it will be a few months. Does he give you any real trouble?"

"No, he just interrupts my routine, and I don't want the neighbors to talk," she said tersely.

"Does he ring the bell a lot?"

"No—only when he needs help getting to the bathroom, but then once in there he can stand enough on crutches to do what he has to do, and to wash himself. He washes up a lot."

"That make sense, I think. These laborers are not kept in the cleanest conditions. He probably appreciates the fresh running water."

"He is always very polite, as he should be."

Willie looked at Sonya. Her head was cocked over the mixing bowl she held in the crook of her left arm. He noticed she was agitated, beating the eggs into oblivion.

Surprising even himself, Willie said "I hope someone would take care of me as you do Josef if Germany was invaded by another nation. I could be a slave laborer in another country."

Sonya almost dropped the bowl, but managed to place it on the counter. She turned and glowered at her son.

"Nonsense! Just nonsense!" she emphasized, with an uneasy laugh, holding on to the counter. The thought of it was ludicrous. Ludicrous and terrifying.

Willie had not meant to frighten Sonya.

In was almost the summer of 1943. Germany was no longer winning every battle, although the German media made it seem so. No radio transmissions were allowed other than state-sponsored stations, but brave souls used short wave to hear BBC and other non-German stations. As a result, the previous winter's German defeat at Stalingrad was common knowledge, even before it was officially broadcast.

Amid increasingly bad war news for Germany, Willie felt he needed to reassure Sonya that his chances of being taken prisoner were practically zero. He was sorry he even said anything about it. Sonya was already anxious about having a recuperating enemy in the house, so Willie assured her Josef would be busy fixing things, and he would not be in her way during the day.

"It is very unlikely I will be made a slave laborer anywhere. I am sorry I frightened you, Mother."

She didn't say anything, but gave a shallow sigh of relief.

"Mother, I am beginning to collect all kinds of small items Josef can probably fix. With the war, things remain broken. Please look around to see what needs attention. Small things, at first...until he can get around a little better. See if the neighbors have any items to be repaired, too."

"We have a lamp that flickers on and off. The doors on the outside garden shed are off their hinges, and they need to be re-hung. I'm sure I can find more!" Sonya, however, wanted to know something.

"Willie, why are you helping this boy?" Her throat tightened when the word "boy" left her lips.

Willie knew his mother would eventually demand an answer to that question, and he had prepared one.

"Our country needs his skills right now. It's not only toasters and clocks. It is also lamps and stoves. He may be able to fix farm machinery, auto machinery, well pumps, broken windows, and the like. He has no choice, and we can give him any assignment."

22

"Are all his papers in order? Can you get in trouble for what you're doing?"

"Yes, they are in order. I took care of them even before I took him to the hospital. I have all the right signatures. It's fine, Mother."

Sonya glared at her son.

"So you are doing this for Germany?" she asked.

"Yes, for Germany."

"There is no other reason?"

"What do you mean, Mother?"

"Do you still believe in the goals for our country?"

Willie paused a moment and caught his breath. He gave Sonya a patronizing look. "I most certainly do!"

"Don't lie to your mother," said Sonya sharply, as she shook her right index finger. "Your father would not have liked it."

"Mother, I am not lying."

"Just be very clear as to why you are helping the boy."

"I've made it clear, Mother. When will supper be ready?"

"In about fifteen minutes."

"May we eat in about an hour? I want to take a walk. I've been sitting in the ambulance most of the day."

Sonya placed the bowl with the beaten eggs in the icebox, and slammed its door in annoyance.

"Go!"

"I'll be back in an hour. I promise."

Willie left the house through the front door, leaving Sonya alone in her kitchen. She thought of her husband, Hans, killed early in the war, and her younger son, Gunter, who was killed, blown apart by a grenade just last year at the age of nineteen. It was hard for her to believe they were both gone. So many men had died. So many of them were just boys.

She met Hans at a village picnic when they were in their late teens. They were both smitten with each other from the start, and after Hans completed his tour of duty in World War I, they settled down to a quiet life. But it was hard. Germany had received harsh penalties for its instigation of World War I, but things got better toward the late 1930s as Adolf Hitler put Germany to work.

Hans had a good job. It offered his family a comfortable, though not extravagant living. He worked his way from a bank clerk to an assistant bank manager, receiving regular promotions over the years. The world was at peace, and life seemed promising for the young family.

As they got older, Gunter and Willie were expected to register for obligatory national service, often collecting blankets, clothing, and other items for German troops. But the two boys never expressed a desire to become deeply active in any youth associations. Both Sonya and Hans were relieved, since they felt the Hitler Youth Organization undermined their authority as parents to raise their boys with their own values.[4]

Hitler and his Nazis initiated World War II. It commenced with the incorporation of Austria into Germany, and then the takeover of Czechoslovakia. The conquest of Poland followed. Sonya and Hans could not believe Germany was going to war again, barely a generation after World War I. Being good citizens, they showed their support by attending rallies and flying banners.

They expected the war to be over quickly.

Hans was summoned to military duty. In his adolescent zeal, Gunter was not unhappy to be conscripted into the infantry. Willie was exempt from military service because his eyesight was very poor without glasses.

Sonya knew Hans would have been proud of the young man their eldest son had become. Now twenty-three, Willie was tall, handsome, blond, had blue eyes, and was working in the community as an ambulance driver and medic. The girls were wild for him. Despite his current military service exemption, Sonya knew it could be revoked, and she treasured every moment with her son. He had a quick sense of humor and appeared at ease with everyone he met. He considered being

German a gift, and she was certain he understood and appreciated the idea of Aryan Germans being a superior race.

But the attention he was expending on this slave laborer surprised her, and made her a little fearful for her son.

"This slave laborer," she said aloud, slowly.

Josef was just a boy, and Sonya saw how thin he was when she put her arm around his waist to help him to the bathroom. Willie's words haunted her—suppose he had been a slave laborer in a foreign country, instead?

Without intending to, she wondered how old Josef was, and how his mother was coping with his being taken from her, possibly not even knowing where he was, or if he was alive.

She took a loaf of her homemade rye bread from the breadbox. As she reached for two plates from the cupboard to set the table, she hesitated with her hand in mid air. As though an unseen force was commanding her, she took three plates, instead.

Arbeitsbuch Für Ausländer
(Foreigner's Work Book)

Slave laborers were required to carry a work assignment booklet on their person at all time. Their jobs were documented in the book. Josef had one like this. Also, the "P" patch had to be worn on the outside of the clothing...sewn on. It indicated the person wearing it was a Polish slave laborer. The Nazis required undesirables to wear patches, and the letter or image on the patch varied with nationality, worker status, religion, sexual orientation, health, and other criteria. Most people are familiar with the mustard-toned Star of David that Jews were required to wear, but many other groups were also targeted.

Image is in the Public Domain

5 - One is Resolute, One is Unsure

While Sonya set the kitchen table, Josef hobbled with his crutches to the round table in his room. He examined the toaster from the outside and saw nothing amiss. Willie hadn't brought him any tools yet, but he wanted to start the repairs.

The longer I can make myself useful, the longer they'll keep me alive. I've been working for the Germans for three years now. I must be doing something right.

Josef had turned fourteen a few days after Hitler invaded Poland in September of 1939. During the following year, he, along with many other Polish young men and women, were dispersed throughout Germany and any territory it conquered to work in service to the Third Reich. All the forced laborers experienced wrenching, tearful goodbyes with their mothers and fathers. Josef also had to say goodbye to Pyotr, his nine-year-old brother, who remained at home.

Josef was allowed to take a few items of clothing in a knapsack, and food for a few days. Packed into cattle cars, the laborers were sent to their assignments. Josef was to stay in Poland to work in the mines near Gliwice, then help erect buildings and improve roads that led to camps for people deemed undesirable by the Germans. These camps turned out to be concentration camps. Josef's brother, Michael, was in the Polish Army and was captured as a prisoner of war. After he finished his time in a prisoner of war camp, he was transferred to Stockach, Germany, as a slave laborer.

After having made some inquiries about his sons, their father, Leon, learned Michael and Josef were not together. He had some money and some cigarettes, and bribed an official to get Josef transferred to the barrel factory in southern Germany where

Michael worked. Leon could have been shot for his action, but the official kept his word, and Josef was eventually assigned to the barrel factory and joined Michael there.

~~~

As he fiddled with the toaster, Josef's mind wandered to Michael. He missed him, and feeling comfortable at Willie's house weighed on him, knowing Michael was nearly starving. Josef needed to ask Willie for a favor, an added favor, beyond saving his life.

Subject to relentless injustice, Josef had a choice—to crumble or become fearless. He resolved to become fearless, and to directly ask for what he wanted.

But Willie was not so resolute. After the tense conversation with Sonya, he walked on the outskirts of his town, Stockach, hoping to enjoy the rolling hills and vineyards as a distraction.

It was early evening, cool and clear. As the sun set, the apple blossoms lost their color, but relinquished their sweet scent to Willie. The vineyards faded from green to a dusk-induced gray. Stars appeared. Indifferent to war, the earth smelled sweet.

So many times he and Gunter had ridden their bicycles on these roads, daring each other to go hands-free, to race, and perform stunts they knew would have upset Sonya.

One autumn they had a contest as to who could swipe the most apples from the trees arched over the road. The rule was they couldn't stop the bicycle, even for just a second, to pluck an apple. They would stuff their shirt, jacket, and pants pockets with as many apples as they could pick. Whoever had the most apples when they got home, won. Gunter usually excelled at this game, and Sonya was faced with an unexpected day's work of baking apple cakes and putting up applesauce.

Now there would never be another bicycle ride with Gunter.

Willie walked fast, almost out of breath, sweating despite the brisk evening air.

When his mother advised him to be clear about why he was helping Josef, he realized it certainly was possible even he, a German citizen, could become a slave laborer in some other country. It was possible he could lose a leg. It was possible he could be removed from his home and never see his mother or home again. There was no guarantee Germany would win the war. Willie was certain there had to have been a better path for Germany, a path that didn't devour other countries and enslave people.

And now he had responsibility for Josef.

He upbraided himself, "What was I thinking?"

In his heart, he knew Josef was just a kid, a kid who had a right be angry and frightened.

Willie returned to the house, un-rejuvenated. Neither the walk, the vineyards, the view, nor the fresh air eased his turmoil.

Sonya cooked the omelet as soon as Willie returned.

"How was your walk?" she asked.

"Fast."

"You seemed preoccupied and a bit annoyed when you left. Is there something wrong, Willie?"

"No."

"Are you certain, Son?"

"Yes."

Sonya wasn't convinced, but she knew better than to continue this particular conversation with Willie. He was reluctant to talk when he felt pressured.

"Well, then, why don't you help Josef to the table?"

Willie took a deep breath, "What did you just say, Mother?"

"I said, 'Why don't you help Josef to the table?' Don't you see I have three plates set?"

"Are you serious? You want him to sit with us at supper?"

"Yes, I'm serious. I'm tired of going down the hall all the time to wait on him. He can sit with us."

Willie went to fetch Josef, but Josef was wearing a nightshirt. He didn't want to sit at anyone's kitchen table in just a nightshirt.

Willie grabbed a bathrobe from his own room and helped Josef put it on.

"What took you so long?" Sonya asked as they both came into the kitchen. But she answered her own question when she saw Josef wearing Willie's robe.

Sonya greeted Josef by pointing to a chair.

"Sit."

Josef sat down and watched the two of them. Sonya was slicing bread while Willie was pouring some beer into two glasses, and water into a third glass. The table was set with white dishes, white napkins, and a blue table runner. Sonya served the food. She gave Josef a portion, a little smaller than hers or Willie's, and sat down. Willie gave Josef a glass of water.

No one talked. Knives sawed against plates as they cut their omelets. The guttural sounds of gulps of water and beer seemed amplified. Jam slithered across bread with a gentle whoosh. Forks clinked. Josef never realized how noisy a silent meal could be.

When they were finished eating, Josef thanked Sonya, told her how delicious it was, and got up with his crutches to bring his plate to the sink.

"No, you'll drop it. Willie, please take his plate," said Sonya.

Willie placed the dish in the sink and turned to Josef, "I'll help you back to your room."

"I'd like to go in the garden and get some fresh air, if it is acceptable to you."

Sonya and Willie looked at each other, a little startled Josef would be so brazen, asking for something not offered to him. But Willie agreed, and helped him outside.

The backyard had some newly greening rose bushes, a swath of unkempt grass, a large storage shed with windows, a newly planted vegetable garden, and a wooden table and chairs. A rough-hewn, wooden, post and rail fence separated Willie's yard from the house behind it. The fence was little more than a boundary marker. It offered no privacy and no security. Josef could see the skeleton of last year's vine on the fence. He loved nature—the sky, the birds, the trees. He did not know the names of many plants, but he knew a beautiful flower when he saw it, and he knew the sweet smell of honeysuckle vine. He hoped this dry, brown vine curling around the fence was honeysuckle. It was his mother's favorite, and she embroidered the flowers on her blouses. He wondered if he would be at Willie's long enough to see the vine bloom, and if he would ever see his mother again.

Josef noticed the yard on the other side of the fence had a well-tended lawn and a very large vegetable garden. Bushes, possibly roses, reached to the bottom of the first floor windows. The house was larger than Willie's, and Josef wondered who lived there. It appeared prosperous, and he assumed they had servants.

Josef turned to Willie and said, "Willie, I need to help Michael."

"Who is Michael?"

"My brother. He is my older brother. I should have told you."

"Where is he?"

"He's in the same factory where I worked. He needs to know I am alive. I can't imagine what he's thinking. He may think I died."

Willie was taken aback at this news. "Do you expect me to make myself seem even more suspect by talking to your brother, too?"

"I don't expect anything. I can never repay you for saving my life. But I am asking you to tell him I am alive. And, I plan to save some of the bread your mother gives me. Can you get it to him? Will you tell him I am alive and recuperating? I am sure he thinks I died."

"I cannot take him into my house or any other house."

"I am not asking you to take him in; that is not what I said. I am asking you to find an excuse to take him aside and let him know about me, plus give him my share of bread."

Willie could not believe what he was hearing.

31

"How forward of this fellow!" he thought. Yet, he was touched by Josef's concern for his older brother. He made no promise to Josef, and spent some of the night tossing restlessly in his bed, envisioning how he would let Michael know Josef was alive. He had to force himself not to think about how worried or heartbroken Michael might be.

Willie whispered to himself, "It's an awful thing to lose a brother."

6 - Sonya

The next morning, Josef put aside half of his bread for Michael. He wanted to be sure Sonya thought he ate it, so he hid it from her in the nightstand drawer. A few days later, on a warm but cloudy morning, Josef had the toaster and the cuckoo clock with him in the backyard. He was sitting at the wooden table, and he had figured out the toaster just had a disconnected wire. When he opened it, some crumbs fell out. He caught them in the palm of his hand and ate them. Though no one witnessed him do it, he was embarrassed. Frau Mirz fed him well, but he just couldn't waste even a tiny crumb.

While he was outside, Sonya decided to give Josef's room a thorough cleaning.

Since the house and everything in it was her business, she opened the nightstand drawer and saw several pieces of bread, some almost hard. She wondered if Josef was saving it for a snack. She didn't want bugs or mice in the house and had to tell Josef right away she would not tolerate food being stored anywhere in his room.

She went outside and sat on a chair by the wooden table where Josef was working.

Immediately, Josef was at the receiving end of a barrage of questions.

"Josef, why do you have stale bread in the nightstand? Are you hungry still? Do you realize the bread can bring bugs and mice into the house? How can you eat it anyway when it gets hard? Why are you wasting good food?"

Sonya didn't let him answer the questions, but just fired them rapidly at him one after another. Finished with her inquest, she sighed and gently asked, "Why are you saving bread and letting it get stale, Josef?"

Josef noticed she had softened her tone.

Does she know how strident she sounded? He decided to tell her the truth. In the long run, it would be easier than creating a story and sticking with it.

"My older brother still works at the factory. I try to save him some of the bread you give me so he does not starve. No one has been able to get it to him, but I save it anyway."

"You receive ration stamps, don't you?"

"Yes, but it does not allow me to purchase much at all."

"How much do you get?"

"We've been told our rations are sufficient. I have heard it amounts to a little less than 700 calories of food a day."

Sonya was perturbed by the news both Josef and his brother received such meager rations compared to about 2,500 calories a day for Germans, although that amount had been reduced as the war continued.[5]

She understood 700 calories were insufficient, and certainly, they were woefully inadequate for a teenager working at hard labor six or seven days a week.

Josef continued, "I asked Willie if he could get the leftover bread to Michael at the factory, but he made no promises to help Michael, or to even to let Michael know I am alive. Your son needs to stay out of trouble and not cause any suspicion."

Josef opened his mouth to say something else, but an agitated Sonya interrupted him.

"Josef, how old are you?"

"Seventeen. Eighteen in a few months."

"And how old were you when you started working for Germany?"

"I was almost fifteen when I was sent to work for the Reich."

Sonya took a deep breath, and asked, "And what of your parents?"

"What do you mean?"

"Are they alive?"

Until Sonya asked that question, he didn't know there were some questions capable of causing physical pain.

"I don't know. I have not seen either of my parents or my younger brother in three years." His eyes filled with hot tears.

"Do they know where you are?"

"At first, yes, they knew. We were allowed to communicate with letters, but eventually the authorities where I was working in a Polish mine either stopped mail delivery, or never distributed the letters and packages sent to us. I don't know if they know where I am now. My brother wrote to them and told them we were together here in Germany, but we never heard from them. We don't know if they received his letter, but I must say the barracks rules here are little more lenient about contacting family than some other camps I have been in."

"Do you ever hear anything about your family through hearsay—from other Poles arriving here to work?"

"In the beginning, when I worked in the coal mines in Silesia, I heard news about my town in Poland from new workers, but only rarely of my parents. Once in a while, someone had information. But I never knew what was accurate, or what was just rumor. As time passes, there is less and less news, and there are fewer and fewer people who may have lived where I used to live."

He stopped for a moment. He swallowed. Hard. *Don't cry, don't cry in front of Frau Mirz.*

"I don't really know anything now about my mother, father, and younger brother. Michael hasn't had news from them, or about them, either."

"How old is your younger brother?"

"Pyotr is five years younger than me."

"He was allowed to stay home with your parents, in Poland?"

"I think so. But I don't know if he was taken to work in a camp or factory once he got older. It has been a few years since I've been away from Poland. I don't know what the Nazis do now."

Sonya looked at Josef, a little more softly now, "Do you have any sisters?"

"No, just brothers."

Sonya tapped her right foot up and down on the ground. The more Josef talked, the harder she tapped. She hoped Josef's younger brother was not part of the slave labor force. She hoped Josef's parents were alive.

"Wait here, Josef."

She returned to the house, curious about Josef's seeming remoteness from the tragedy he was living, as though he was talking about some fictional person, and not himself. She didn't know if he was too sad or too hardened to show emotion, or if he was afraid to seem vulnerable in front of her, or any German.

Sonya opened the door to Gunter's room and unlocked a steamer trunk where some of his boyhood toys and civilian clothing were stored. She swooped up a bundle of his clothes, caressed them, and inhaled their scent. This was as close as she could ever be to hugging her youngest boy. He was gone. Gone.

Gunter had been shorter than Willie, and she guessed Josef was about Gunter's height, but thinner. It was time to let Josef have some clean clothing. She selected a few items and took them outside, along with a tray of bread, tea, a precious pat of butter, and a piece of ham.

She placed everything on the wooden table.

"These clothes belonged to my son, Gunter. You need to wear something other than nightshirts! While you are here, please wear them."

Josef cocked his head, "I didn't know you have another son."

"He was killed in the war. He was nineteen, with a physique like yours. He had blond hair—not light brown like yours. And while your eyes are light blue, his were deep blue."

Josef didn't know what to say. As far as he was concerned, there was one less German on earth to worry about. But he could see Sonya's grief was real.

Josef put his tools down and made eye contact with Sonya. He wanted to touch her hand, but didn't dare.

"I am sorry about your son." He said it gently.

She said hoarsely, in a raspy whisper, "There is nothing to be done. He's gone. So is my husband. He died early in the war."

Again, Josef didn't know what to say. There had been so much loss for everyone. There were no words he could offer her.

Sonya stared at the garden, and Josef thought it was as though she saw the garden as it used to be, with a full family, laughing and talking, as families do. Finally, she turned her head towards Josef, "Would you like some tea?"

He didn't really want any tea, but he saw she needed the company.

"Yes, please."

"Do you see those double doors on the shed, the ones off their hinges?"

He leaned to the right to see them, careful not to unbalance himself in the chair.

"Yes."

"It will take two men to fix those doors. Willie is a wonderful son, but he is not handy at all."

Josef had surmised Willie's lack of handyman skills when he saw how clean the young man's fingernails always were.

"If you can help fix them, I can ask Willie to get another worker here to help."

Josef looked directly at Sonya and gently nodded his head. He understood this would be Willie's excuse for getting Michael a pass to work outside the factory.

Sonya poured two cups of tea. Even though she preferred to use her butter ration for cooking, she lightly buttered the bread, placed a piece of ham on it, and handed it to Josef.

"Please, eat it, Josef. Eat it all."

Josef took the snack.

"Frau Mirz, this is very kind of you...the tea, the clothes, Michael."

Then she sliced a unusually generous piece of her freshly baked rye bread, wrapped it securely in a napkin, and put it aside.

A Surviving Strip of Ration Stamps for Poles

Food and common goods were rationed during the war, and, as an occupied land, Poland was no different. The strip on the left is a set of German-issued ration stamps used for purchasing household goods, textiles, soap, cigarettes, alcohol, leather goods and steel goods. The image on the right is a closer detail. Rations were unequal, with Jews receiving the fewest, Germans receiving the most, and non-Jewish Poles receiving a paltry amount, but more than Jewish Poles.

Photo credit: Walter Walkow

7 - Progress

When Willie returned from work in the early evening, Sonya called him into the kitchen after he had washed his face and hands in preparation for supper.

He leaned nonchalantly against the counter, with a mug of beer in his hand. Sonya was wearing a crisp white apron with straps crisscrossed down her back, and was seated at the kitchen table, slicing cabbage, onions, and lettuce.

"How was your day, Mother?"

"Fine, thank you. I need to talk to you about something."

"What is it, Mother?"

"Josef."

"What about Josef?"

"I gave him some of your brother's clothing today. He has nothing to wear."

Willie's jaw dropped. He placed his beer mug on the counter. "Why?"

"I told you, Willie. He has nothing to wear."

"I know, Mother, but why *Gunter's* clothes?"

"Willie, they are closest to his size. You know our ration allotments don't allow us to buy new clothes often. It is just a few items."

"I don't agree with this!"

"Why, Willie?"

"I don't know." He paused and sighed. "I miss Gunter. And I miss Father, too."

Sonya nodded her head.

"I also miss them, and always will."

Willie pleaded, "If you let Josef wear Gunter's clothing, please save some items for me. Maybe, someday, when the war is over, I will get married and have a son. I'd like him to have something that once belonged to my little brother."

"I've already put aside some of his clothing, as a keepsake. And we still have his bicycle, a few of his boyhood toys, and some of his books."

Resigned to Sonya's decision, Willie asked, "Is this the reason you needed to talk to me? Gunter's clothes?"

He waited for her to respond, but she did not answer him.

"Mother, should I help Josef to the table now?"

"Not yet. I have to finish making the salad, and I want to talk to you about something else."

Willie rolled his eyes, clueless about her next topic. If he knew anything about Sonya, he knew she could be full of surprises.

Sonya walked to the breadbox, wiped her hands on a kitchen towel, and opened the cloth napkin with the slice of bread she had cut earlier in the day. She added a thin slice of cheese atop the bread, wrapped the snack in butcher paper, and tied the package with some string. She handed it to Willie.

"Willie, please see if you can get this to Josef's brother tomorrow. Just put it in the icebox for now. Josef told me about his brother today."

Willie slumped his shoulders.

"His name is Michael, Mother. He's Josef's older brother."

Irritated, Willie explained, "I've already discussed this with Josef. They're captives, remember? I just can't go down to the factory and give the impression I am helping a laborer for no good reason."

"Of course you can't," she soothed. "But I am sure Josef has some other clothing in the barracks where the laborers are housed. He has ration stamps, too, I'm certain. We could use them while he is with us. Don't you think it might be fair for him to share them with us? Willie, I thought that you could bring the bread and cheese to Michael, and ask him to get Josef's clothing. Josef has only two sets of clothing. That way, Michael will know his brother is alive and safe."

Willie wished he had been given the chance to hear that phrase—alive and safe—about Gunter.

40

He surrendered. "Mother, you amaze me. You always get your way, and I wind up doing your bidding even when I have my doubts. Did you charm Father like this, too?"

"Maybe," she said coyly, and smiled broadly. "Make certain Michael washes Josef's clothing. I don't want any bugs in the house."

Sonya prepared the salad dressing and set the table, while Willie went to Josef's room to help him walk to the kitchen.

As he walked down the hall to fetch Josef, Willie was pleased to find his injured charge had already made it halfway to the kitchen, using the crutches.

The three of them sat at the table, and though little was said, Josef felt it was more relaxed than the first time they had supper together.

Willie addressed Josef. "Mother gave me some bread and cheese to give to your brother. I should be able to get it to him tomorrow, and I will ask him to give me your clothing. He will have to wash it all first."

Josef raised his eyebrows and nodded his head. He was surprised Willie had agreed to this task, after he made no promises to contact Michael. He glanced furtively at Sonya, but she pretended to be oblivious, focusing on the food on her plate.

"I only have two shirts, some underwear, and two pairs of pants. There is a coat, too, for the colder weather. I had washed everything with insecticide, except the coat, just before the accident. Unless someone else wore them, they should be clean."

"Less work for your brother," chimed Sonya.

"I am sure it will put my brother at ease to know I am alive. And Willie, I do appreciate what you are doing. I haven't forgotten about fixing the cuckoo clock you brought me to repair. I am beginning to understand how it works, and I think I can fix it within a couple of days."

"Good," said Willie. "I miss the cheerful little bird chirping on the hour."

"It drives me crazy sometimes," said Sonya.

41

"Don't be surprised if you hear my mother telling it to 'shut up' once or twice," offered Willie.

They continued eating until Willie announced, "Josef, I talked with the doctor today—the one who amputated your leg. He may stop by tomorrow morning to see how you are healing."

Sonya dropped both of her hands on the table.

"Willie, why do you just spring these things on me? Did you ever, even for a moment, think I might have plans for tomorrow morning?" she protested.

"I am sorry, Mother. Do you have plans?"

"No, but I expect you to discuss things with me ahead of time, if they are going to involve me."

"Please forgive me, Mother."

"If it is an inconvenience for you, Frau Mirz, perhaps the doctor can come another day," offered Josef, as he looked questioningly at Willie.

"No, Josef, tomorrow will be fine," said Sonya as she lifted her glass.

Josef still didn't believe the doctor needed to amputate his leg. He was convinced the doctor had simply done the expedient thing, although he had no evidence to back this feeling.

"Does the doctor speak any Polish at all, Willie?"

"No, but you know enough German to talk to him. You talked with him when you were in the hospital."

Young Josef thought about this for a moment. "Yes, I think I do know enough German to ask him the questions I need answers to."

"Be mindful to respect him," cautioned Sonya.

"Yes, Frau Mirz. I'll be respectful," he said calmly. He wanted to make a pointed, sarcastic remark, but didn't want to spoil the atmosphere. Besides, he was a captive. And a guest.

With the shock of the amputation and its preceding infection in the past, he thought Sonya's good food and the clean environment of her home were helping him recover. He was grateful to her and Willie, though angry about his situation. He was becoming bored and wanted to do something other than read the Bible and attempt to read the town's newspaper, which was in German.

Though he was still weak, he knew he had to strengthen his good leg as well as his left thigh and knee. Exercising his upper body would help, too, he thought.

"I can't stay so inactive. If I am going to fix things, I need to be strong. Do you have anything I could use as weights?"

Willie put down his fork and leaned his head on his right hand, a pensive expression on his face. "We may have some weights you can use. I think they are in the shed. I'll look tomorrow. We have books you can use as weights, too, to help you build up your muscles."

Josef picked up his fork and continued eating. Whether Germany lost or won the war, he would need to get back to Poland at some point, and he would probably have to walk part of the way, whether on crutches or a peg leg.

Yet, he refused to think Germany would actually win the war, and bitterly questioned why Willie and Sonya were so worried about a damned cuckoo clock.

Aerial View of Stockach, Germany

Many of the buildings in Stockach are quite old and were there during World War II.

Photo Credit: Stritti, German Wikipedia.jpg, in the Public Domain

8 - Confronting the Doctor

After supper, Josef returned to his room without anyone's assistance. He felt satisfied he was able to do it on his own, and he also felt a little guilty about the ambivalent feelings he had for Sonya and Willie.

Willie had saved his life. Sonya had been distant, but efficient, and Josef could see she had a good heart. Whenever he saw her grief, he had to swallow hard, realizing his own mother was probably grieving, too.

Josef's emotions swirled. He had been living angrily, enraged, and he had vowed never to show his feelings to the enemy. And although Willie and Sonya were technically "the enemy," they were not treating *him* as an enemy.

Why can't I trust them?

He knew he had to let his feelings for Willie and Sonya mature. He couldn't force a friendship out of the situation, no matter how gentle they'd been with him. If a friendship formed, then it formed. If it didn't, then it didn't. He planned to survive either way.

Survive. I want to do more than survive. I want a life I create for myself.

Josef slowly found his way to the bathroom. He was tired of being considered vermin-infested, even when he wasn't. Before bed, he cleaned himself thoroughly in preparation for Herr Doktor's visit in the morning.

As he settled into bed later in the night, he ran through the list of questions he had for the doctor. Sonya had told him to be respectful, and he planned to be respectful, but he would also make sure his questions were answered.

When he awakened the following morning, he went to the kitchen. Sonya had laid out some bread, jam, and on this morning, some cheese. He ate it, and had a cup of diluted coffee.

It wasn't really coffee, but a concoction known as *ersatzkaffee*, made of acorn and barley seeds. It had become prevalent now, with rationing. Everyone called it *kaffee*, though.[6]

After breakfast he washed again, and waited for the doctor.

When the doorbell rang, Sonya answered it, and she and the doctor exchanged the customary, though clearly tepid, *Heil Hitler* greeting. Josef greeted the doctor in the hallway.

Cheerfully, the doctor said, "It's good to see you are up."

"Yes."

"Let's examine your leg."

They went to Josef's bedroom, and Sonya followed them.

"Herr Doktor, do you need me here?"

"Do you take care of this young man?"

"Sometimes."

"Then stay."

Sonya looked at Josef.

"Josef, would you like me to stay, or do you prefer I leave you alone with the doctor?"

Josef was torn between asking her to stay and having privacy to ask some of the hard questions he had to pose to the doctor, but Sonya's presence was comforting for him.

"It's up to you, Frau Mirz."

"Fine, then I'll stay," she said as she walked to the chair by the table and sat down, idly fingering some of the tools Josef had placed on the table.

The doctor removed the bandage and examined what remained of Josef's leg.

"It is healing well. How are you getting around the house?"

"With crutches." He pointed to the crutches next to the bed.

"Have you been doing any exercises to strengthen your muscles?"

"Not yet."

"You need to exercise. Using and training your muscles will make you stronger so you can be up and about, and return to work."

The doctor opened his case and extricated some fresh bandages to cover Josef's leg at the point of the amputation, just below the knee. Suddenly he stopped and asked Sonya to apply the bandage, instead. She looked at Josef, as though asking silently for permission. Josef nodded his head in agreement. Sonya covered the wound, and Josef watched intently so he could do it himself.

She is so gentle with me.

After the doctor listened to Josef's heart and lungs, he demonstrated several repetitive exercises Josef would need to do to strengthen his thighs, knee, and upper body.

"Do you have any questions, Josef?"

I most certainly do, and you'd better have some good answers.

"Yes, I do."

"Well, go ahead and ask."

"Herr Doktor, why did you remove my leg?"

The question did not surprise the doctor. He frequently thought of Josef since the amputation, asking Willie daily how his patient was faring. He knew he should have come sooner to check Josef's progress, but because the reports from Willie were optimistic, he sensed no urgency. Given his own level of fear, the doctor felt he was giving Josef adequate attention, even if it was through another person—Willie. He was not proud of his cowardice, but he was realistic; he had a family to support and protect. He knew he was not as brave as Willie.

"Your leg was very badly injured and you developed gangrene, a serious and potentially deadly infection. When it is untreated, it spreads to other parts of the body and will kill the patient."

"Could you not just treat the infection?"

"The infection was too advanced, and I wanted to save your knee. You see, if I had tried to treat the infection and then found the bacteria continued to spread, you would have lost your knee also. In an amputation of the leg, I have always thought it is best for the patient to keep the knee, if possible."

The doctor's words seemed logical to Josef, but he had to ask the question that hounded him unremittingly from the very beginning.

"Did you remove my leg because I am Polish?"

Sonya gave a short, audible gasp.

Outwardly, the doctor appeared unruffled by the question. He placed his hand on Josef's left shoulder and looked directly at him.

"I removed it because it had to be removed, medically. It had nothing to do with your nationality. Many people live with just one leg. I am sure you will adapt, too. Willie Mirz did you a big favor by taking you to the hospital. He saved your life."

The doctor did not say this harshly. He said it patiently and quietly. He said it as one would expect it to be said to a young patient, recognizing the patient had to learn how to physically navigate in the world differently from the way he did before the amputation; he had to live, maimed, in a militaristic culture where perfection was worshipped.

"Yes, I am very grateful to Willie. You, too, and Frau Mirz. But I want to walk!"

"Get strong first."

Josef knew he had to build his strength, and didn't respond to the doctor's comment. Instead, he said, "Herr Doktor, why did you discharge me from the hospital just a week after the amputation?"

"I thought it would be best for you to recover in private. Not everyone agrees captive laborers should be treated at all."

Josef wasn't sure the reason given by the doctor was the full story. He was aware Germans who helped slave laborers were punished with a prison term and he suspected the doctor did not want to appear suspicious in any way at all. Radio broadcasts, newspapers, and hearsay made it very clear. Captives were not to be helped.

As he prepared to leave, the doctor said, "I'll come by in a few weeks. I want to see some stronger muscles by then."

Turning to Sonya, he said, "Frau Mirz, your good cooking must be agreeing with Josef. Keep feeding him and please oversee his exercises."

"Certainly, Herr Doctor," she said as she walked him to the small foyer.

She bid him farewell, and as she closed the door, she wondered what the doctor was thinking. Willie had told her how reluctant the doctor was to let Josef stay in the hospital for his full recuperation. Yet he made a house call and was very patient and kind to Josef. "Could he really care about this boy?" she wondered.

She peeked into Josef's room and saw him sitting on the edge of the bed, his shoulders stooped, his head hanging, and his crutches resting across his lap.

Josef's pent up anger evaporated when Herr Doktor touched his shoulder. He knew he could deal with the harshness of the labor camp, and with the terrible conditions in the coal mines of Silesia. He could manage the icy cold and heat, the hunger and lice, the sting of a whip, the fear and homesickness. But after years of neglect and outright cruelty, the kindness of others— gentle words, a soft touch, a smile—shattered his heart.

He understood it wasn't the doctor's fault he lost his leg. It was the war's fault, the damned war.

Josef sensed Sonya's presence in the doorway, and looked at her.

"Well, Josef, you received a good report from the doctor, didn't you?"

"Yes, it was, Frau Mirz. I'd like to do my exercises soon."

"We'll talk it over with Willie tonight."

"Frau Mirz, it is a beautiful day. Warm, too. I would like to go outside in the garden. Before I do, is there anything I can do for you here in the house?"

"No, but if you can, please take a look at the doors on the shed. Don't move anything, though. You will need help for the project."

Josef hobbled on his crutches, navigating his way down the hall and into the backyard. The sky had a few dark clouds in the distance, but some puffy white ones dotted the sky overhead. Birds were singing, and there was a very gentle breeze. It was early summer, a time of promise. All the brown things of winter were green and beginning to attain their full beauty.

He made his way to the post-and-rail fence, to where the dry vine he had seen a few weeks ago was now green and clinging to the rails with fresh tendrils. When he got there, he recognized the familiar sent. It was, as he had hoped, honeysuckle. He leaned against the fence on the side of the shed where he was hidden from the view. He plucked a diminutive honeysuckle flower and brought it to his nose, closed his eyes, and inhaled its perfume over and over again.

He could no longer control himself, and heaved with gulping sobs. This was the scent of Sonya's sheets. It was the scent his own mother loved.

Josef had never cried like this. Ever. The horrors of his slave's life, the grief of not hearing from his parents, his stolen youth, his missing leg, his uncertain future...were there tears enough for all this? And yet, the doctor's kindhearted touch and Sonya's unspoken empathy for his situation moved him most.

As he stood by the fence and out of sight, Sonya headed outside with a basket of wet laundry, ready to hang it on the clothes line. She didn't see Josef, but she heard him weeping, hidden from view.

She walked toward the side of the shed where Josef was. His back was to her, about five meters away. She saw he had some honeysuckle in his hand and was leaning against the fence, his head in his crossed arms.

After watching him for a moment, she turned away, wiped her eyes on the skirt of her white apron, and walked into the house, leaving her laundry outside, still in the basket.

"I can hang it later," she said to herself. "I'll go back outside when Josef comes in the house."

But Josef chose to stay outside on the pleasantly warm day. After he collected himself, wiped his eyes, and took a few deep, honeysuckle-scented breaths of air, he walked to the shed's hinged doors. He touched them. The white paint flaked onto the palms of his hands, and he examined the hinge plates. There was significant wood rot beneath them, and the doorframe couldn't support the weight of the doors much longer. He knew he would need to replace the entire doorframe.

The act of analyzing the work he needed to do had a calming effect. It gave him a purpose. The doors were a project, and he needed a plan—a plan to represent an activity projected into the future, albeit not very far into the future, as though he had a future.

He made a mental checklist of what he would need, and extended the project beyond replacing the doorframe and re-hanging the doors. He wanted to scrape and sand the doors along with the rest of the shed, prime and repaint it all, and reorganize everything inside, building shelves if necessary. He wanted it to be perfect, like it probably once was.

Maybe it could be red, or green, or maybe a deep blue. Maybe a sunny yellow.

When he returned to the house, he went into the kitchen and asked Sonya for some paper and a pencil.

"I've figured out what the shed needs, Frau Mirz."

Acting ignorant of Josef's crying, she cheerfully said, "I was wondering what kept you outside for so long. Would you like a glass of water or some tea?"

"I'll have some water, thank you."

"How bad are the doors?"

"The doorframes need to be replaced, and the doors can then be hung. But the paint is peeling badly. The doors need to be scraped, primed, and repainted."

"If you repair the doors so they look new, then the rest of the shed will look shabby...don't you think so, Josef?"

"You are right, I think. I may have to paint the whole shed."

51

"Josef, it's too big a job for you to do alone. I plan to ask Willie to get your brother to work here for a few days, to help. Do you think Michael will be able to help you?"

Josef smiled, and wanted to hug her. "Yes, I am sure he can."

"Good, but right now I need to go outside and hang my laundry before it gets too late. I want it to dry before the sun goes down."

Sonya returned to the backyard, and Josef peered through the window by the sink. He stared at Sonya. *I thought she hated me, at first. She is certainly stern, forbidding, and the undisputed monarch of the Mirz house. But still, she is kind. And wounded. I wonder if she really believes all that Nazi nonsense about a master race. I doubt it.*

He saw she was struggling with the wet, heavy laundry. He joined her in the fresh air to help her with her chore. When they were almost finished, Willie poked his head from the open kitchen door.

"It is a beautiful day to hang laundry, isn't it?"

"Only someone who doesn't do laundry would say that," teased Sonya. "How come you are home early?"

"I took some time off this afternoon. I saw the doctor and he told me you are doing well, Josef, but you need to start an exercise regimen. I also saw your brother this morning."

Josef's face visibly brightened. "What did he say? How is he?"

"Let's sit down at the table, in the shade."

Josef wasn't even in his seat yet, when he asked, "How is Michael?"

"He is fine and very happy to hear you are well."

"The labor detail leader let him have fifteen minutes off, so he and I could talk. He is getting your clothes and ration stamps from the barracks, and I will be picking them up tomorrow."

"Did you give him the bread I saved for him?"

"Are you referring to all the stale bread?"

"Yes."

"Better—I gave him some fresh bread and cheese my mother prepared for him."

Josef swallowed hard. He thought he would cry again.

"Thank you so much, Willie...I miss Michael."

"He misses you too. I'll get some drinks from the kitchen. Then you can tell me what the doctor said."

As Willie headed for the house, Josef thought of Michael. He wanted to see his brother very badly, but he did not want to pressure Willie. Eventually, he knew Willie would come around and bring Michael to work on the shed doors, and certainly, Sonya would have a hand in making it happen.

He was beginning to appreciate how wise Sonya was, and how much Willie needed to think he was in charge.

Willie returned from the kitchen with two glasses, a pitcher of water and several bottles of ale.

"Would you like some ale, Josef?"

"Sure...my father used to let me taste it when I was a youngster. But I haven't had any in years."

Willie poured a half glass of ale for Josef.

"Drink it slowly; we don't need you drunk. Mother will be furious at us both. Trust me; it's not worth upsetting her."

Josef nodded his head in agreement, "I suspect you are right, Willie."

"So what did the doctor say?"

But Willie knew the answer already, because he had talked to the doctor before he came home.

"He said I am healing well, but I need to build up my muscles. He also said he had to amputate because the wound was too severe to save my leg."

"Have you been questioning the amputation?"

"Yes. I am a slave laborer, remember? I thought he removed the leg because it was the most expedient thing for him to do."

"It was necessary. I saw how infected your leg was at the factory. You would have died if the leg wasn't removed. Do you understand this?"

"After talking to him today, I do understand, but I was very angry at him after he operated."

"He is a good doctor, Josef. He would not amputate your leg unless it was necessary."

Josef gently shook his head up and down in understanding.

"Did he give you some idea as to the exercises you need to do?"

"Yes, they require weights. Do you have any, Willie?"

"There are a few weights in the shed. My brother and I used them when we were younger. I don't remember exactly how heavy they are. Let's finish our drinks and see what we can find in there."

9 - A Growing Friendship

Willie and Josef scoured the shed for the rest of the afternoon, like two kids on a treasure hunt. Josef helped as best as he could, but Willie did most of the work, pulling out old toys, stools, and a stack of old magazines, including some racy ones he and Gunter had hidden from Sonya. Josef and Willie sat next to each other on old wooden crates. They flipped through the pages of the magazines, making comments about the attributes of the ladies and nudging each other with their elbows whenever one of them found a particularly revealing image.

Josef interrupted their daydreams. "Do you have a girlfriend, Willie?"

"No one in particular—I see a lot of girls. I guess there is some advantage to being a young man in a town where most of the men are older or at war. But what about you?"

"Do you mean a girlfriend?"

"Yes, a girlfriend."

"You know it's against the law for me to have a girlfriend — German, Polish, or otherwise. There is a women's barracks for the female laborers, but we are separated by walls and barbed wire. Any contact is forbidden, and as far as German girls are concerned, I could be executed for practically just looking at one, let alone talking to one."

"I mean, did you have a girlfriend in Poland?"

"No, I left when I was almost fifteen. There was no real girlfriend, but a couple of girls I liked. I have no idea if they liked me, though."

Josef turned a few pages in one of the magazines. "But they didn't look like these girls!"

"I don't think any real girl does," laughed Willie.

Eventually they put the magazines aside, and Willie found the weights, which ranged from two to twenty pounds.

Still sitting, Josef immediately lifted the ten-pound weights in a maneuver he knew would strengthen his biceps. But the weights were too heavy for his physical condition, and he put them down, opting to use five-pound weights instead. He even placed a two-pound weight across the front of his right foot, and straight-legged, lifted his leg several times.

Seeing his exercise attempts, Willie suggested Josef use a belt or some other kind of strap to attach the weight to his left, weaker thigh. He removed his own belt and used it to fasten one of the two-pound weights onto Josef. They both laughed when the weight slipped through the belt, fell to the side, and rolled.

The laughter surprised Josef, and somehow, it made him feel just a little bit hopeful.

They would need to take the collection of weights into the house, thoroughly clean all of them, and plan an exercise program the doctor recommended.

As Willie continued to make new discoveries, Josef thought of his current good fortune, despite the loss of his leg.

Nothing Willie is saying or doing justifies my distrusting him. And Sonya has taken care of me from the beginning. She also sent food to Michael. I have a clean, comfortable place to sleep and good food. There is work for me to do. I need to just take a deep breath and not think too much about the future. Take each day as it presents itself.

He looked at Willie, who was now dusty and sweating. He saw a young man about his brother Michael's age, caught in a war he probably didn't want to be part of...a man who lost his father and only brother.

He didn't, and couldn't understand how Willie felt because of Gunter's death.

At least, I still have Michael. Michael...I wish he could live here with me at Willie's.

He rested his right forearm on one of his crutches, as Willie continued emptying the shed's shelves. *No, there is no real reason to distrust him.*

"Willie, would you stop for a minute?"

"What did you say, Josef?" said Willie, as he looked up from his task, when a few old drop cloths slipped from a shelf.

"Would you please stop for a minute? I want to talk about something."

"Sure, let me come over to where you are."

Willie sat down on a crate to Josef's left.

"What is it?"

"Thanks for saving my life, Willie."

"You've already thanked me."

"And thank you for taking the bread to Michael."

"My mother insisted I do it."

"You would not have done it if she hadn't insisted?"

"I probably would have done it, eventually," he smiled.

Josef tightened the lace on his right shoe, and when he finished, he cocked his head to the left, facing Willie.

"I am sorry about your brother, Willie."

"How did you know?"

"Your mother told me. It must have been awfully difficult to lose your brother—your father, too."

Willie paused and took a breath, "It was horrible to lose them both." He paused again and added, "I think it is more difficult to lose a brother, though."

"I am always in fear of losing Michael. Were you and Gunter close?"

"We were good friends, growing up. We especially loved to ride our bicycles in town and in the countryside. We had some great adventures together."

"What kind of adventures?"

"Stealing apples, racing our bicycles side by side, fishing, talking about girls—those kinds of things."

They sat in silence for a few moments until Josef asked, "Do you know how the war is going? I haven't heard any news."

This was a difficult question for Willie. He knew not all the battles were going well, and he was not aware of what Josef knew. He also wanted to avoid saying anything that would

57

cause someone in authority to think he was not supportive of the war, should Josef ever talk about this conversation.

"It went well early on, but Germany had a terrible defeat at Stalingrad during the winter of 1942 to 1943, and the Allies are doing a lot of bombing, especially in the north's big industrial cities.[7] They are in Italy, now. Many people have died, many of them civilians, even children. And the bombing continues."

"I know about many people dying." Josef said, without a shadow of bitterness in his voice.

He continued, "Through hearsay in the barracks, I heard about the camps where thousands are killed outright, or worked to death. I worked building roads to one of them."

"I have heard rumors of these too, but it is difficult for me to think Germany would engage in such awful acts. We are a civilized country."

Josef didn't find it difficult to believe. He had seen the cruelty, the outright murders. But these were done by faceless, nameless Germans in uniform. Willie and Frau Mirz were not committing these crimes. He suspected many other Germans were not committing these crimes, either.

"Funny, isn't it?" Josef continued. "You and I can sit here and have a conversation, without treating each other as enemies, but our countries can't."

"It's not funny, Josef. It's tragic. In the end, it's a lot of death, blood, and sorrow."

Josef slowly and sincerely extended his hand to Willie. Willie took it, and clasped it.

"Willie, I am really sorry about Gunter and your father. Sorry for you and for your mother."

Willie bobbed his head up and down to acknowledge Josef's remark.

God, I can't imagine what it would be like to lose Michael.

When Willie stood up, he moved the family's bicycles to another side of the shed, telling Josef, "I sometimes ride mine to the hospital and home again. My mother uses hers to go to the market. The others belong to my father and brother. They have not been ridden in years. When you are better, you can try one."

Josef had used a bicycle only once in his life, and he wasn't very good at riding. He always thought he would ride one again, but didn't know if he could actually do it with only one leg. Then, he remembered the decision he had made just a few minutes ago—to take each day as it came.

"We'll see, Willie. There is time, I think, to see if I can ride a bicycle. But I don't think I am allowed to use one. I think it is against the rules. Tell me, though, did you ever own an automobile?"

"No, we had hoped to get one, but then the war came. Gasoline is rationed, too. There is no point getting one until after the war."

"How did you learn to drive?"

"I learned using a friend's car."

"Is it hard to learn?"

"Not at all."

"Did you ever have a crash?"

"Not yet. But I've transported some crash victims to the hospital using the ambulance."

"Were they hurt badly?"

"Some of them, yes."

"Did anyone ever die?"

"Yes, a little girl. It was very sad."

They were silent for a few moments, and Josef resumed looking at the magazines. "Do you have any more of these?"

"One or two; Gunter and I didn't keep many; less evidence for my mother to discover," he laughed.

Willie cleaned and arranged items in the shed, providing a verbal history for each one. Josef enjoyed looking at photographs in the magazines. Both young men remained in the shed until very late in the afternoon, until Sonya called them to supper.

At some point that afternoon, in a rundown shed in the middle of a vicious war, Josef forgave Willie for being German.

59

They gathered up the weights in two boxes, and Willie made two trips into the house with them, while Josef followed.

"What are those, Willie?"

"Weights, Mother. I need to wash them."

"Don't wash them in the kitchen! Go outside and use the hose."

Willie took them outside again, and after their evening meal Josef helped him wash and dry them.

Later, over tea at the kitchen table, Willie, Sonya and Josef planned Josef's exercise routines. That evening, when Josef said goodnight to Willie and Sonya, he did so with a small amount of hope—hope in getting stronger. He washed up in the bathroom, and when he returned to his room, he saw a magazine resting on his nightstand. There was a handwritten note accompanying it: *Ich nehme es zurück am Morgen, bevor meine Mutter wacht auf.*

Willie's note said he would pick up the magazine early in the morning, before Sonya was awake. Josef had never seen a magazine like this one until today. It didn't matter if it was in German. The language of seductive photos was universal, and during the night, he experienced a moment of unbridled pleasure.

When Willie knocked on Josef's door early the following morning, Josef was awake.

"I enjoyed the magazine, Willie. Thank you."

"Well, you know where they are in the shed."

Willie took the magazine back to the shed, and then left for work.

Josef followed his prescribed exercise routine that morning, and Willie gave Michael more fresh bread when he picked up Josef's clothing from him. He brought the clothing bundle home around noon, and Sonya opened it in the yard. She was satisfied they were clean, and free of lice, but she laundered them anyway, and hung them out to dry. She could not help noticing the purple-hued "P" patch[8] sewn onto Josef's shirts and coat. Polish laborers were required to wear the patch, just as Jews were required to wear the Star of David patch. Before letting Josef know his own clothing was ready to wear, she fingered the patches on the shirts and jacket, and then put the clothing down, disgusted.

"All these different patches are ridiculous," she said to herself. "Josef may wear Gunter's shirts here at the house."

~~~

As Josef followed his exercise program for the remainder of the spring, the doctor made two more visits and was pleased with his patient's progress. Willie kept on finding things for Josef to fix, and finally, as summer arrived, Michael was given a series of day passes to help Josef fix the shed's doors. He had dutifully washed himself and his clothing before walking from the barracks to Willie's house.

When Josef and Michael saw each other in the garden they embraced and cried. Both Willie and Sonya retreated to the house, and gave them the privacy they needed to just be brothers.

"Josef, how are you?" Michael asked earnestly.

"I am getting better."

"Are Frau Mirz and Willie treating you well?"

"Yes, they are. I am not sure if they know what to make of me. I'm a slave laborer, but also their guest. It is a strange situation."

"What kind of work are you doing?"

"Fixing things. Cuckoo clocks, lamps, doors, some appliances, even some toys. And now, the shed. I think I will have to repaint it in addition to repairing it."

"What are you—their personal slave?" Michael asked, with a hard edge to his voice.

Josef looked askance at his brother, "No, Michael, no! That's not how it is. I am sure there will be other work. I just can't get around too well. Until I get assignments from the barracks, Willie gives me odd jobs."

Hungry for news of home, Josef asked Michael, "Is there any news about Mother or Father? Have you heard anything about Pyotr?"

"Nothing. The rumor is the Russians, since they've overrun even more of Poland, are worse than the Germans."

"Is there any other news about the war?"

"Some new workers came into the barracks with forbidden Polish underground newspapers. The last one I saw was dated a few months ago. The northern German cities are bombed all the time. Dresden is a mess."

"Willie mentioned the bombings."

Michael added, "Here in the south, we are lucky. We do not get bombed as much."

He looked at the void beneath Josef's left knee. "You weren't so lucky, though."

"I am getting stronger. Someday, I would like to have an artificial leg. It probably won't happen at all if Germany wins the war."

"Do you know why Willie saved your life?"

"No, I don't exactly know, Michael. I had fixed a wristwatch for him once."

"I remember that. Do you think that is why he helped you?"

Josef shrugged his shoulders and shook his head from side to side. "No, probably not. He lost his father to this war a few years ago and his younger brother just last year. Maybe he is tired of it. Maybe he sees his brother in me. Maybe the war just doesn't mean much to him any longer."

"And what of his mother?"

"Frau Mirz is a mother first, and a German second. She is kind. I think the loss of her husband and son broke her heart."

Michael put his arm around his younger brother. "I thought I would never see you again. I thought you were dead, until Willie brought me bread and cheese, told me what happened to you, and asked for your clothing. It was the happiest day of my life."

"I told Frau Mirz about you, and she made sure Willie brought you food."

Michael smiled. "I guess she is kind, as you said."

"I was so upset you probably didn't know I was still alive. I am really sorry you had to be so troubled, Michael."

"It wasn't your fault. And none of this war is *our* fault!"

Michael took a deep breath and then asked Josef, "How long do you think you will be staying here?"

"I don't know...I don't know what else I can do yet because of the amputation, and how it will fully affect me. Fixing this doorframe and door will give me some idea as to what I can do. Let's take a look at it."

The two brothers headed to the shed to size up the situation. Michael reached out to help Josef as they walked, but Josef stopped him. "I am pretty good with these crutches."

At the shed they made a list of materials they would need, and found most, if not all of them, were already on the property. Josef had already made the list, but he enjoyed doing it again, with his brother this time. There were some weathered planks of wood for them to use for doorjambs and trim. The door hinges were fine and did not need to be replaced—just cleaned up, polished, and oiled. All the tools they would need were already on the shelves in the shed.

Willie had previously told Josef he was fine not only with the doors and frames being fixed, but also with the whole building being sanded and repainted. This was good news for Josef, because it meant his brother would be visiting a few times.

Before Michael left, everyone enjoyed a light supper of canned fish, cabbage, and bread, as they discussed the plans for the shed. Michael was happy to have a meal in someone's home, something he hadn't enjoyed in years. He didn't question anyone's motives for saving Josef's life and was happily relieved to see his younger brother alive, recuperating, and getting healthy. At least one of them had a warm place to stay, clean clothes, and adequate food.

As he left in time to return to the barracks by curfew, Michael offered Frau Mirz some of his brother's ration stamps, since she was housing and feeding Josef.

She demurely declined them, "No. No. It isn't necessary; I'll let you know if I need them. Right now, we have sufficient rations to take care of the household. Thank you for offering them to me."

Michael left, but not before giving his brother a tight hug while slipping the ration stamps into Josef's right pants pocket.

Josef went to bed happy. Michael went to bed comforted his brother was going to be fine.

The loss of Gunter stung Willie hard that night, and Sonya was very touched Michael would offer ration stamps, when he had so few himself. She knew she would never accept them unless she was desperate.

Before Sonya fell asleep that night, safe in her own bed, she thought of Josef's mother and the two fine boys she had raised.

10 - The Household Routine

Through the summer and fall of 1943, Josef used the weights religiously, and Sonya even made him a band of material he could slip around his thigh. It had sleeves in it to hold the weights and it helped a lot. Willie, and especially Sonya, made sure Josef performed his exercise routines at least twice a day. The doctor had visited again and was pleased with Josef's progress.

By January of 1944, Josef had been with Willie and Sonya over eight months. His reputation as a fix-it man, a carpenter, and someone who could create parts for machinery was growing. Sonya no longer complained to Willie about having a slave laborer in her house. She saw Josef was both courteous and industrious, and she liked having another young man at home.

In the evenings, Willie and Josef often shared some ale. Willie talked cautiously about the war news, and they both talked about their fathers and brothers. Josef told Willie about the many times he helped his father fix things, and Willie talked about the stories his father would read to Gunter and him before bedtime on cold winter nights.

One night when they were talking about their brothers, Willie fingered the signet ring he was wearing.

"My brother gave me this ring," Willie volunteered.

Josef looked at the ring closely. "It looks like silver and has your initials—WM."

"It *is* silver, and he surprised me when he gave it to me, right before he went into the service."

"What a nice gift. It's a handsome ring."

"It was the last thing Gunter gave me. I will cherish it for as long as I live."

Willie stroked his ring, and Josef silently thanked God he still had Michael.

Normally, their discussions were not melancholy. They talked about the vineyards, the weather, pets, food, cars, motorcycles, girls in general, and, in particular, about the winsome, young, dark-haired girl who was both a maid and an apprentice cook in the big house on the other side of the fence. They figured she was about Josef's age.

Willie occasionally reminded Josef about German girls. They were completely off limits to slave laborers. This was one of the rules. Fraternizing with a German girl would be punishable by death for Josef, and the German girl could be imprisoned. But no rule could stop Josef from *thinking* about the girl next door, even though he had seen her only a few times, and from a distance.

Michael worked at Willie's house several times. The shed doors were fixed; the shed was cleaned up, sanded, and painted an appealing pale yellow. Josef even built some window boxes for Sonya and hung them beneath the shed's two windows. He envisioned bright, red geraniums overflowing from them next year, or tulips, or some other flower...hopefully, with the war ended.

Josef was getting stronger all the time. He was busy several hours a day fixing items either at Willie's house or nearby, but no one knew if he could return to his old job at the barrel factory. Based on requests for workers from various businesses, the barracks commander instructed the chief laborer to assign the workers to specific jobs.[9] The chief laborer in Josef's former barracks gave him work he could do, given his handicap. The assignments were relayed via a telephone call to Willie. Since slave laborers were not allowed to use public transportation, Josef had to walk, and the absence of one leg limited the distance he could travel on crutches. And he still had to wear the "P" patch on the outside of his coat to indicate he was a Polish laborer.

He also had to be back at Willie's house by curfew—usually around 8:00 p.m. Violation of curfew was punishable by beating, or death.

One cold and gray February afternoon, when the smell of snow was in the air, Josef was replacing some electrical outlets in a nearby bakery. The tantalizing bouquet of freshly baked bread permeated the building, which was kept warm by the massive ovens. He offered a silent prayer of thanks for the cozy spot. The aromas reminded him of the days his mother baked bread, his fascination with how the dough grew, and his impatience to cut a slice of fresh bread and eat it, smothered with butter and jam.

When he was halfway through his workday at the bakery, he took a break and approached the counter to purchase a loaf of bread with his ration stamps. The shopkeepers made him wait until all the German customers were served, but he eventually was able to acquire a loaf. He ate some of it during the afternoon and decided to bring the rest back to Sonya.

While Josef's two hands were occupied with replacing outlets throughout the afternoon, his thoughts drifted, like the scent of baking bread, first to his mother's kitchen in Poland, then to Willie's house, to an imaginary girlfriend, and to a pet black and white cat he had as a child. He thought of all the Sundays he had spent in church. Finally, his thoughts made it to the barracks, just a few blocks away, where Michael and the other laborers lived behind barbed wire, in the shadow of guard towers. He wanted to go back, to be in a place where he could speak his own language and live with his own kind.

Josef wondered how to tell Willie, Sonya, and Michael.

They will think I'm crazy for wanting to go back. Maybe I am crazy, but I'll be crazy and speaking Polish.

He had turned eighteen in September of 1943, but he felt middle-aged. He was agonizingly mindful of his stolen youth, the past years which should have been the most carefree of his life. His loss was so complete, so deep, that he was unable to cry about it. It left him numb. Numb, and unable to see a future.

Years of cruelty, hard labor and dehumanization had robbed him of any dreams. He had simply stopped imagining *any* life ahead of him. He had not committed a crime, but was serving a life sentence. The German objective was to consume the young enemy men, and even women—use them until they died, and in the process, remove them from any opportunity to create Polish children.[10]

Young Josef didn't have control of what he did with his time, what he worked on, or where he lived. No matter how hard or how well he worked, he would always have a slave laborer's rations. There were no girls he could date or love. He didn't know if his parents were alive.

A phrase had begun to repeat itself in his head. *I am nothing. I am nothing.* Nazi ideology considered Poles and other Slavic peoples *Untermensch,*[11] meaning "subhuman."

Maybe they're right. Maybe I am really not as good as other nationalities, especially Germans. I've been hearing it for so long, maybe it is true.

In his despair, he found solace in his religion.

Josef was a devout Catholic, as were most Poles. He had not been to mass in many years, and sometimes at night, in bed, he would say the Latin mass to himself...as much of it as he remembered. He wanted to take communion, to sing hymns, smell the incense, and leave the church uplifted, as he always had as a boy. This yearning grew deeper the longer he was denied the ritual of his faith, until it became a gnawing hunger.

No one knew Josef said the mass to himself and prayed several times each day. It became his secret salvation, connecting him to the beauty and ceremony of his heritage, for in Poland, the Catholic Church and Polish nationalism were entwined. He did not know it then, but the act of saying the mass to himself kept a pallid flame of hope alive.

When he finished his work and left the bakery, the weather had turned damp and colder, the cloudy sky had darkened, and a few snowflakes flitted from the sky. He was afraid he would fall on the slippery path, but he managed to stay upright. It was late when he returned to Willie's house, but within the curfew for slave laborers.

The house had a warm glow as he approached it. But he couldn't call it "home."

Poland was home.

As he entered the kitchen door, he saw Willie and Sonya were eating supper, and a place was set for him. He took off his coat and hung it on the wall hook, washed his face and hands in the bathroom, then returned to the table. He gave Sonya the brown bag with the rest of the loaf of bread he had purchased. There were still a few snowflakes on the bag.

"It's snowing?" asked Sonya.

"Yes, just a little."

"What is in the bag?"

"I purchased a loaf of bread today. There is some left. It is for the household."

Sonya looked in the bag. "Pumpernickel?"

"Yes."

"Thank you Josef. I'll add it to what I have in the breadbox. But would you like some now?"

"Yes, please."

Sonya took the bread out of the bag and cut a slice, placing it on the plate beneath Josef's soup bowl.

She didn't want to keep it for the household. Josef needed it. But she thought maybe Josef wanted to express his gratitude in ways other than saying "thank you" all the time. Maybe giving her the bread was one of those ways. Even though rations had been reduced for everyone in the past few months, she could not bring herself to ask Josef for his ration stamps.

"Be sure you take some bread to work tomorrow. Now eat."

She ladled some thick cabbage soup into a deep bowl and handed it to Josef. It had some potatoes in it, and a little bit of chicken. It was steaming hot and warmed him from the inside out.

"How was work today?" asked Sonya.

"Good—I had to replace some electrical outlets in the bakery."

"The bakery is very important to the village. Not everyone bakes their own bread."

"It smelled good in there, too."

"There is nothing like the scent of warm bread," she agreed.

The snow outside continued to fall.

The kitchen was inviting and cozy, but Josef thought of his brother, in the cold barracks. *Michael, try to stay warm.*

Sonya saw Josef was wearing one of Gunter's sweaters, and it satisfied her to see he had warm clothing. The sweater was a perfect fit.

Willie was eating his soup, but his mind was not in the kitchen. He hadn't said anything since Josef arrived, which was unusual for him. Neither Sonya nor Josef knew he was thinking about snow. Snow and Josef's one leg.

"Willie, Son, why are you so quiet? Did you have a trying day at work?"

"No, it was not unusually busy. I had only two patients to transport. I have the ambulance outside because I am on alert again. I'll be called if anyone needs to be transported through the night." He did not answer her question about why he was so quiet.

They finished supper and brought their plates to the sink. Josef could now do this without fear of dropping his plate.

"Would anyone like some tea?" asked Sonya.

"Yes, I would like some," said Josef.

"I'll have some too," said Willie.

As Sonya prepared tea, the two young men moved to the parlor.

"Is something wrong, Willie?" Josef asked.

"No, why do you ask?"

"Why are you so quiet?"

"I am wondering how you are going to manage getting to your jobs with the snow."

"I'll be careful, and will allow more time to get to work."

"Still, going to work when the snow is deep is treacherous."

70

Josef knew this was true and saw Willie's comment as a way to open up the discussion about returning to the barracks.

"Would it be easier if I returned to the barracks?"

Willie sat straight up in his chair, astounded, "Are you mad?"

"No, just homesick, and I miss Michael."

"Is that a good reason to return to the barracks? You can see Michael from time to time. Does he even know you want to go back?"

"No, I haven't talked to him about it. Willie, I miss being with other Poles and speaking my own language. I don't know if you can understand that, but it is true."

"How will you be able to work? What makes you think you are going to be assigned jobs that take your amputation into account?"

"I don't know."

Willie was riled. Life had settled into a routine these past few months, and he desperately needed consistency in his life since taking on responsibility for Josef, since losing his father and brother.

"Let's think this through before you make your decision. May we talk about this in a few days, rather than tonight?"

"I can wait a few days."

Josef had introduced the subject, and it was enough for this particular night. He didn't need to push it. More significantly, he appreciated Willie's choice of words—*your decision*. He hadn't had the luxury of making decisions about his life for a long time.

Willie returned to his newspaper article. Josef was getting better with German, and Willie shared the paper with him. When Sonya came into the parlor with tea, Willie got up to help her with the tray. With the snow falling outside, they settled down for the evening, and the house became encased, flake by flake, in an insulating blanket of white.

Sonya worked on some mending, but Willie was distracted. He pretended to read, but was focused on what Josef had said about returning to the barracks. He didn't want Josef to leave.

He enjoyed having him in the house, and was certain his mother did, too. Furthermore, his concern for the kinds of assignments Josef would have was legitimate. Josef didn't have the mobility of the other workers.

It wasn't long before all three of them turned in for the night.

While preparing for bed, Willie was thinking of snow and Josef's missing leg. He imagined Josef trying to live in the barracks with crutches. Tomorrow, or the next day, when he went to work, he would ask the doctor about an artificial leg.

"It is Josef's choice to return to the barracks," he said to himself, silently. As he rested in bed that night, he realized what he had really said—Josef's choice—an highly unusual phrase concerning a conscripted laborer. Legally, Josef did not have a choice. All he had was the work assigned to him. Willie had surprised himself, thinking of Josef as a man with choices. The thought had come naturally, as though he had been thinking about one of his friends, or Gunter.

And with this revelation, something deep inside Willie had unquestionably shifted.

11 - Missing the Barracks

The following day, no one went anywhere. Schools were closed, public transportation was sporadic, and many shops hadn't opened. As it was with almost any large snowstorm, routines were suspended, and almost everyone enjoyed a welcome break before the tasks of their daily lives resumed.

The snow had fallen heavily throughout the night, and it accumulated to over thirty-eight centimeters by early morning. Roofs bore sheets of snow, sounds were muffled, and the entire world appeared water colored in shades of white and gray. Sky and earth were indistinguishable, and the snow still fell.

Even the slave laborers were excused from leaving the barracks to go to their jobs. It was a rare day off for them, but Josef wondered if they were allowed to rest. He ruefully thought the barracks commander might concoct a diabolical scheme to put the laborers to work on a task that did not need to be done.

And here I am, enjoying a warm house and good food, while Michael is probably cold and hungry.

Around 10:00 a.m., Josef went to the kitchen and asked Sonya, "Is there anything you need me to take care of in the house since I am not working today?"

Sonya thought for a few seconds and responded, "One of the three burners on the stove doesn't seem to work well. It probably just needs to be cleaned. Will you take a look at it?"

"Which one is it?"

"The front, right side."

"Let me take a look."

Josef turned all the burners on and saw the flames were uneven. He decided to clean all of them.

"I can fix this, Frau Mirz."

Sonya thought Josef felt uneasy when he wasn't doing something. She usually cleaned the burners herself. Having Josef clean them was like giving a child a task to do, to keep him busy and out of trouble.

As Josef worked on the stove, he decided to give it a thorough tune-up, check the gas connections, and be sure everything was in tip top shape, including the oven and broiler.

Why fix only one burner? I have the whole afternoon. When he immersed himself in a job, he forgot the world around him. It was always that way for him.

Sonya noticed he was looking at more than just the problem burner. "What is wrong with the rest of the stove, Josef? I think it is working fine."

"I thought I'd just examine everything and see if anything needed to be adjusted."

"That's not necessary."

"It doesn't hurt to be sure."

Sonya sighed and threw up her hands in exasperation. "Go ahead, if you want to, but all I need is for you to fix one burner. I need the stove to cook supper, though, so please be finished by three this afternoon."

"I'll be finished in an hour, Frau Mirz. Don't worry."

As Josef was working on the stove, Willie thought he might phone the doctor and talk about an artificial leg. But after some consideration, he decided not to use the telephone. He didn't want Josef to hear what he was planning to do, or raise his hopes, and then have to possibly disappoint him. He thought it best to have this discussion face-to-face with the doctor. It could wait until he got to the hospital.

Willie also thought that he should visit the barracks to understand how Josef would live. He was certain Josef would be making a mistake returning to them, but he knew, first-hand, how it felt to miss a brother, and couldn't fault Josef for wanting to be with Michael. The irony of it, though, was either Michael or Josef could be reassigned anywhere within the Reich at any time, and face separation. But Willie needed to understand how Josef would be treated if he returned. He made a mental list of who he needed to talk to and what he was going to say, but used the cold and snowy weather to settle down into an easy chair and read a book, hoping there would be no emergency that required an ambulance.

He was still reading when Josef finished working on the stove and entered the parlor. He sat on the sofa, across from Willie.

Willie wanted to wait a few days before talking about Josef's request to be with his brother, but decided this day was as good as any other to discuss it.

"Josef, do you really want to return to the barracks?"

"Yes, I want to be with Michael."

"But tell me, how are you going to walk to your work assignments? You can't travel far on crutches, and it's winter."

"I don't know...I'll manage, just as I do now."

"This makes no sense!" Willie said harshly, provoked by an idea he thought was foolish.

"This whole war makes no sense," retorted Josef.

"Let's not talk about the war. Let's talk about how you can possibly manage."

"Willie, I go around the town now to assignments."

"Yes, but right now you are not in a situation where you are expected to do really hard labor. That could happen, you know."

"I know. I mined coal, remember? I built roads, dug ditches."

"Yes, but you had two legs then. You are proving my point, Josef. You can't do that kind of work now. Suppose you are given an assignment like that, some really hard labor where it would be difficult for you to stand up all day?"

"That could happen, Willie. I know."

"Then why do it?"

"I want to be with Michael and with people who speak Polish."

"Suppose you and Michael are separated?"

Josef swallowed hard, "Michael could be sent anywhere right now, while I am staying with you and your mother. I want to be with him."

There was an awkward silence in the room. The discord between them filled the space.

"Willie, I so much appreciate what you and your mother have done for me. I wouldn't be here today if you didn't take me to the hospital. But it's time to go back."

Sharply, Willie asked, "What would you accomplish by going back?"

This question silenced Josef. He didn't know the answer at all.

Then piercingly, Willie asked, "What are you trying to prove?"

Josef did not think he was trying to prove anything. He thoughtfully and quietly said, "I just want to go back."

Michael slammed the book shut, stormed out of the room, and marched into the kitchen, where Sonya was preparing the evening meal.

"Mother, do you need any help?"

She looked at Willie, and wondered what was going on. Normally, Willie didn't like to do any kitchen work.

"Here, clean and cut these potatoes. Slice them thin. Willie, what's troubling you?"

"Nothing!"

His tone warned Sonya not to continue questioning him.

He cleaned and sliced the potatoes, throwing them in a large pot, and then asked, "Is there anything else you need done?"

By the way he dumped the potatoes in the pot, Sonya could tell something was bothering him.

She gave him some carrots to clean and slice. He, too, needed something to do. After he prepared the carrots and dropped them in the pot with the potatoes, he returned to the parlor.

Josef had already gone to his room, and Sonya was left standing in the kitchen, wondering what was going on. For the second time that day, Sonya had given a young man a task to do, just to keep him busy. She knew she would eventually find out what caused Willie's bad mood, and hoped there was no disharmony growing between her son and Josef.

The snow stopped in the middle of the afternoon, and the temperature plummeted. The sky was a steely gray when Josef, through the kitchen window, saw the girl who lived in the house behind Willie's come outside in the snow. She was not shoveling snow or playing in it. She seemed to be drinking in the cold, fresh air, bundled up to her nose in a blue coat and thick black scarf and hat. He had seen this girl before, and he remembered Willie told him she was both a maid and cook-in-training at his neighbor's household.

Josef looked intently at the girl for a while. She was slight, though bundled up. There was something about her that unsettled him.

Transfixed by the girl, Josef remained at the window, and Willie went outside to wipe the snow off the ambulance. Josef broke his reverie and joined Willie outside, to help him. He also wanted some fresh air, however cold it might be. When the body of the vehicle was cleared, Willie then focused on shoveling snow away from the wheels and tires, so the ambulance could move. They worked together in silence, and despite the disturbing conversation they had about the barracks, Willie couldn't resist forming a snowball and lobbing it at Josef. Startled and amused, Josef returned the favor, but not before nearly slipping onto the ground when he tried to pick up some snow. They tossed a few more at each other, but Willie stopped the snowball fight. The last thing he needed was for Josef to get injured.

When Josef brushed away the final wisps of snow from the windshield, he was thinking of the girl he saw earlier. He thought a lot about her. He had been thinking about all girls, lately.

The two young men leaned against the driver's side of the ambulance, admiring their snow removal work, and Josef turned to Willie.

"Willie, what do you know about the girl who lives in the house behind yours?"

Amused, and yet a little alarmed at Josef's question, he said, "Not too much. She is a servant who does cooking and cleaning."

"She's German, isn't she?"

"Yes. Why do you ask?"

"I saw her outside in the snow today."

Willie's eyes bulged. "Did you talk to her?"

"No!" Josef snapped, as though the question was an absurd one. "It looked like she was just enjoying the fresh air, seeing how pretty everything looked all covered in white."

As an older brother might warn a younger sibling, Willie admonished Josef, "Good, keep very far away from her. Very far. Very, very far. An SS officer lives in that house, although he is rarely at home. Keep away from any other German girl...any girl, of any nationality, for that matter. You know it's not allowed!"

Josef folded his arms across his chest, disgusted.

"I'm just asking! How old do you think she is?"

"We discussed this once, remember? I think she's about your age. Maybe a little younger; sixteen or seventeen, I would estimate."

"Is she from this town?"

"No, I think she is from Heidelberg. That's not too far away from here. It's a pretty town, too."

"How do *you* know she is from Heidelberg?"

"My mother talks with the other ladies in town. They know everything."

"She seemed sad," Josef said, pensively.

"Who, my mother?"

"No, Willie, the girl!"

"What makes you think she's sad? She has a roof over her head and a job."

"I don't know. I just think she is."

"I don't know if she is sad, or lonely, or very happy. I don't care. And you shouldn't care, either. Josef, absolutely do not talk

78

to her. Pretend you never saw her. Pretend she doesn't exist. I don't like ordering you around, but don't do anything to get yourself into trouble. It's not good for anyone—you, me, my mother, or the girl. She doesn't exist for you, so get her out of your mind."

Josef folded his arms across this chest. "You said an SS officer lives in the house. Does he know I am here with you and your mother?"

"Yes, he does. I am not going to hide that fact; besides I have all the necessary papers. There is no deception going on."

Josef teased his friend, "Are you sure *you* aren't interested in her, Willie?"

"No, I am not interested! I've never met her."

"Why not?"

"I am dating Helga, one of the nurses at the hospital. We have been going out together for about two months now."

"Are you going to bring Helga home sometime to meet your mother?"

"Only if she is the special one. You know what I mean—the girl I plan to marry. I am not sure yet, but I certainly do like her."

"How can you tell if she is 'the one'...that special girl, Willie?"

"I am not sure. I've never been in love before. If I find myself thinking of her all the time, and missing her when I'm not with her, or seeing her in my daydreams about the future, maybe that will be a sign I'm in love and ready to have her meet my mother."

In a sudden burst, Josef blurted, "It's not fair that I can't have a girlfriend!"

"Those are the rules of the world we live in." As though to soften his words, Willie added, "Who knows what will change in the future?"

Willie surmised Josef was thinking of girls often, and in particular, he was thinking about the girl in the adjoining backyard. "Keep away from her. I mean it, Josef."

"Do you know her name, Willie?"

"I think her name is Ella." He looked directly at Josef, staring straight into his eyes. "Josef, I mean it. Drop this now. It's not worth it."

"I was just curious, Willie."

"It's a perilous thing for you to be curious about. Now, let's go inside."

The two young men returned to the house. Josef went to his room to rest and Willie returned to the parlor.

Willie didn't know which scenario was worse: Josef getting into trouble for becoming involved with a girl; or the authorities expecting Josef to work at a job he couldn't possibly perform. Either way, Josef could be executed.

Willie settled into his chair again and picked up the book he was reading earlier in the day. He couldn't concentrate, though, and closed the book, resting his head on the back of the chair. He just didn't understand how Josef would want to go back to the barracks. Why, why would he return to meager food, cold, lice, diarrhea, and disease? Typhus and tuberculosis outbreaks were not uncommon in worker barracks.[12]

He headed to the kitchen for ale. Sonya was preparing a casserole of potatoes, carrots, cheese, and some diced ham, mixed with milk and a little butter. She had just removed two loaves of bread from the oven and the kitchen aromas were tempting.

Sonya looked at her son as he opened the bottle of ale. "Willie, just one bottle? Doesn't Josef want one?"

"Josef went to his room."

"Is he not feeling well?"

"I think he is tired from helping me remove snow from the ambulance. He had a hard time balancing with his crutches."

"Son, you were in a bad mood earlier today. That's out of character for you. You are usually pleasant. Has something happened?"

"No."

"Weren't you in the parlor with Josef right before you came into the kitchen earlier today, when you cleaned the potatoes and carrots?"

"Yes."

"And nothing happened?"

Willie exhaled a deep sigh, "Mother, we were just talking. He misses his brother, and wants to return to the barracks."

With her lips tightened, Sonya sat down and stared at Willie.

Willie added, "He wants to be with Michael. He wants to be with his own people and speak Polish, or so he says."

"How can he do this? He can't walk far. He can't be given just any kind of work!" Sonya responded, agitated.

"I am worried about it too."

"How can he just leave us? I don't want him to leave."

"Mother, since he is assigned to me, I could keep him here. But I don't want to do that. He may be a prisoner, but he is not *my* prisoner, and I won't treat him like one."

"Of course you won't, Willie. But he just can't leave us!"

Willie took a gulp of his ale and looked at Sonya.

"It's what he wants. But I will try to convince him to stay with us until spring. In the meantime, maybe the doctor can find an artificial leg and Josef can learn to use it while he spends the rest of the winter with us."

Sonya relaxed into her chair, somewhat relieved. "Willie, can you believe it is already 1944? The war has been going on for almost five years, and Josef has been a slave laborer for a good portion of it. It's already almost a year since he came to live with us. I can't believe he wants to return to the barracks."

She took a deep breath, "I guess I knew this day would come," she said wistfully. "He needs to be with his brother and we cannot pretend he is Gunter."

"Mother, I don't think we've pretended he is Gunter. I know I haven't. I just see him as a young man, still a teenager, caught on the wrong side of the war."

"I am not convinced, Son."

Willie raised his eyebrows in skepticism, "No, Mother? Aren't *you* pretending he is Gunter?"

"No, not at all. He is just a young man with a mother who misses him. It doesn't matter whether or not he is German...his mother still misses him."

"That's the problem. We no longer see much of a difference between us and the rest of the world." Willie took another sip of ale. "I didn't even question it that he thought he had a choice to go back to the barracks. I was back in my room when I realized he has no right, officially, to ask for permission to return to the barracks."

"That is true, Willie, I know he does not have any rights."

They each sat, lost in their thoughts, until Willie announced, "Mother, tomorrow I am going to talk to the doctor about getting Josef a leg."

"Did Josef ask you to do this?"

"No...no."

"He never asked the doctor, either," said Sonya, "not in my presence. Did you tell him you were going to talk to the doctor?"

"No. I don't want to tell him until I know he can have one. Why get him excited about it, if it wouldn't be possible?"

"I see what you mean, and I won't say anything either, Willie. But I might mention to him that I know he wants to return to those awful laborer barracks."

"I plan to talk to Michael about life in the barracks, and what it will be like for Josef...what it would be like for him to navigate around the camp."

"If you are going, let me know ahead of time. I'd like you to bring some food to Michael."

Willie got up and returned to the parlor. He felt better, having talked to his mother. That was usually the case; it was almost as though she had the ability to read his mind, knowing when he was upset about something.

Sonya was troubled, though, and this disturbing news was on her mind through supper.

She eyed Josef as he ate. He was enjoying a warm casserole, sitting in a cozy, clean kitchen, safe from the weather and from the war. She quietly wished he would stay. But just as Josef was willing to abandon the warmth of her home to be with his brother, Sonya was certain that she, too, would leave her comfortable home if she could see Hans and Gunter again.

The conversation at the table was about the heavy snowfall in town, memories of large snowfalls in the past, sleeping spring bulbs that relied on snow for warmth and moisture, and hungry birds looking for food. But the light conversation was merely a strained, thin veneer of civility. Deep down, Willie disagreed with Josef's decision and wanted to avoid the pending disruption of the comfortable routine that had been established in the household.

Josef, however, was relieved he had planted the seed about returning to the barracks, and was wondering how he would tell Michael, and what Michael would say.

VERORDNUNG

betreffend die Verpflichtung zum landwirtschaftlichen Ernte- und Felddienst.

§ 1.

Jedermann ist verpflichtet auf Aufforderung der zuständigen deutschen Behörden landwirtschaftliche Ernte- und Feldarbeiten zu verrichten. Das eigenmächtige Verlassen landwirtschaftlicher Arbeitsstellen ist verboten.

§ 2.

Wer der in § 1 genannten Aufforderung nicht Folge leistet, oder dem in § 1 ausgesprochenen Verbot zuwiderhandelt, wird als Saboteur erachtet und dementsprechend mit Zuchthaus oder mit dem Tode bestraft.

§ 3.

Die erforderlichen Durchführungsbestimmungen erlassen die deutschen Land- und Stadtkommissäre.

§ 4.

Die Verordnung tritt sofort in Kraft.

O. U., den 30. September 1939.

Für den Oberbefehlshaber:
Der Chef der Zivilverwaltung.

ROZPORZĄDZENIE

dotyczące obowiązku służby rolnej, robót żniwnych i polnych.

§ 1.

Każdy jest zobowiązany na żądanie przynależnej władzy niemieckiej, roboty rolne wykonywać. Samowolne opuszczenie miejsc robót rolnych jest wzbronione.

§ 2.

Kto w § 1 wspomnianego żądania nie posłucha, albo działa wbrew zakazowi wspomnianemu w § 1, będzie winnym sabotażu i odpowiednio ukarany ciężkim więzieniem albo karą śmierci.

§ 3.

Potrzebne zarządzenia do przeprowadzenia tego, wydadzą niemieccy komisarze wiejscy i miejscy.

§ 4.

Powyższe rozporządzenie nabywa natychmiast prawo mocy.

M. P. dnia 30. września 1939.

Za Naczelnego Wodza:
Szef Zarządu Cywilnego

Death Penalty Notice

This document is a death penalty notice stating any Pole who refused to work in the harvest was subject to execution. It was printed in German as well as Polish.

Image is in the Public Domain

12 - News about a Leg

The three of them retired for the night, earlier than normal. They drifted to sleep with the house enveloped in a soft cocoon of snow, nestled snugly into a world where harsh edges and steep, slate-shingled roofs were softened by a deep, insulating mantle of white.

The sun was blazing the next morning, and it transformed the town as bright light bounced off the snow. After a quick breakfast, Josef left to finish his assignment at the bakery. He allowed double the amount of time, given the snowy streets. Willie gave his mother a quick kiss on her cheek, and left for work.

When he got to the hospital, he asked to see the doctor who operated on Josef. Herr Doktor was in surgery for the morning, so Willie made an appointment to see him at 3:00 p.m. Willie's morning was routine, with just two transports of patients, and he decided to have lunch with his friend at the factory where Josef used to work, and where Michael still worked. He needed some information.

He parked the ambulance and headed for the office with his lunch. He caught a glimpse of Michael working on the factory floor, and, after lunch with his friend, went to see him.

"Michael, how are you?"

"Ah, Willie, fine, and how are you?"

"I am well, thank you, and Mother is also well."

They did not shake hands. Michael was aware that his were soiled from the work he was doing, and Willie did not extend his hand. But their words were cordial.

"And how is my brother, if you don't mind my inquiring?"

"He has been doing odd jobs around the town. For the past few days he has been doing some electrical work in a bakery. He is developing a reputation for being talented at fixing things."

"He can fix things, for sure," replied Michael, "and he can also build machinery, if he has the necessary parts and equipment. Josef is very capable in this way. He has a natural gift, I think, one he inherited from my father. Can you tell me, Willie, how is he is walking? I haven't seen him in over a month, so I don't know."

"He is doing well on his crutches, but with the snow, I think he has to leave the house earlier in the morning than usual, and take his time."

"I am glad he is staying with you and Frau Mirz. It is better for him than staying in the barracks."

"I have no doubt it is," Willie said. "Since you haven't seen Josef in a few weeks, would you like me to arrange for you and Josef to meet again?"

"I would very much appreciate that."

"Would you tell me, Michael, how is work assigned in the barracks?"

Willie had a fairly solid grasp of how work was meted out, but he wanted to hear Michael's explanation.

Michael interlocked his arms in front of his chest. "The local employers—stores, factories, and farms—request workers from a central agency. The agency then informs the commander at the camp about the labor requirements. He lets the lead laborer know what kinds of skills and talents are needed for a particular job, and then the lead laborer makes the assignments. Don't you receive a phone call about where Josef is to report to work?"

"Yes, I would have no idea otherwise where he would be working." With hopeful curiosity he added, "You don't have any choice as to assignment, do you?"

"Choice?" Michael asked, incredulously, his eyebrows raised. "No, no choice. If someone has a specialized talent or skill it is taken into account when work is assigned, but there is no choice."

"How about if someone is not able to physically perform a job?"

"That's harder. Some lead laborers take it into account."

Willie knew better than to ask if anyone in authority at the barracks was bribed for specific assignments. He assumed some corruption was common, and suspected Michael would not admit to it, anyway.

"I am glad they take special talents under consideration when assigning work." Willie said, and added, "Special circumstances, too...sometimes. It was good to see you again, Michael."

"Please send my regards to your mother, and let Josef know I will see him before too long."

"I will do that," Willie replied, with a smile.

They nodded their heads in farewell, and Michael returned to his work. Willie returned to the hospital and proceeded to the doctor's office to meet with him. He sat in the waiting room with other patients, and when he was finally called to see the doctor, he was greeted with a firm handshake.

"Willie, are you ill?"

"No, Herr Doktor. I am here to talk about getting a leg for Josef."

"Sit, please," said the doctor, as he pointed to a chair in his office. "Tell me how the boy is doing. But first, how is your mother?"

"She is well, Herr Doktor, thank you."

"And Josef?"

"It is remarkable, I think. He is doing very well, walking and maneuvering on crutches, but with the snow it is more difficult. And he wants to return to the barracks."

"That is unwise, but it's understandable that he would want to be with his countrymen. He is a stubborn young man and knows what he wants. It may annoy us, but I think that stubborn streak helps him survive."

"Herr Doktor, do you think it would be possible to get him an artificial leg?"

"I know I can get him what is called a peg leg, which has a cup that fits over the stump of his amputated leg, and a broomhandle type of post that reaches the ground. But that is not what you are asking for, am I correct?"

"I was hoping he could have a device that looks more like a real leg, with a calf, ankle and foot."

"Those are harder to acquire, but if you can give me a few weeks, perhaps I can locate one."

"How can we pay for this, Herr Doktor?"

"Let's worry about that after Josef is fitted with a prosthesis, regardless of whether it is a peg leg or a more natural looking one."

"In the meantime," Willie asked, "would it be helpful for Josef to have the peg leg you mentioned while you are trying to find an artificial leg?"

"Using either one—the peg leg or the more natural one—is going to take quite a bit of practice on Josef's part. He may develop some sores on his stump, even with the padding that will be required. I'd rather he do this only once and would prefer he wait until I can locate a more realistic leg than a peg leg. If we can't acquire one in a few weeks, I can give him the peg leg. Does he know about this, Willie?"

"No, I don't want to give him any false expectations. Nor has he ever asked if it is possible to have a leg. I think he may assume it is not available to him."

"He will remain disabled. How will his work be assigned?"

"Already, he is disabled, with just a single leg. Probably his work will be doled out as it is today, by the head laborer, and based on the requirements of the businesses and farms. Since he returned to work, his jobs have taken his limited mobility into account. But I don't know if that is done by design, luck, or outright bribery by his brother. I have no idea what will happen when he returns to the labor camp."

"What kind of work is he doing now?"

"No hard labor. He can't balance himself too well on crutches. He has done some electrical work, some machine repair, simple building repair, jobs like that."

The doctor stood from his chair and moved to Willie's side of the desk, a signal for Willie to leave.

"Let's get Josef on two feet, and let's hope the war is over soon."

"Thank you, Herr Doktor. *Heil Hitler.*"

Willie worked the rest of his shift. When he returned home Sonya was not there yet. He wanted to tell her about his conversation with the doctor. Instead, he settled into his chair in the parlor and read the newspaper. He built a fire in the fireplace, took his shoes off, and warmed his feet, enjoying the inferno as it unhurriedly dwindled to a slow, comforting crackle.

The house was too quiet, too empty, and he could hear the wall clock ticking. He was relieved when he heard the door open and saw his mother walk in, carrying a satchel of groceries. Without his shoes, he got up, greeted her, took the satchel, and placed it on the kitchen table.

"It's cold out today!" Sonya exclaimed.

"Would you care for some hot tea, Mother? I'll get it ready."

"That would be nice, thank you, Willie. How was your day?"

"Work was normal, nothing unusual, but I did talk with Herr Doktor about getting Josef a leg. It seems hopeful, I think."

"I am surprised to hear that. Isn't it difficult to get artificial legs with so many of our soldiers wounded in the war?"

"The doctor didn't give any indication that it would be impossible. At the very least, Josef can get a peg leg. Do you know what that is?"

"Yes, I do," Sonya replied. "I guess it would be better than nothing, but it would be nice if Josef could have a leg that looked more normal."

"That is true, of course, but let's not assume it will be a leg that looks realistic."

"I suppose that would be wise," responded Sonya, "but I am going to put my hopes in a leg that looks like a real leg."

Willie continued, "I also saw Michael at the barrel factory today. He verified my understanding about how laborers are assigned work. And, Mother, may he visit for a meal sometime in the next couple of weeks? Maybe Josef will listen to him."

"Yes, Michael may come for supper, as long as he is clean."

Willie smiled at his mother, and shook his head from side to side, "I know, I know, as long as he is free of lice."

"And clean. Don't think badly of me, Willie. I just can't have bugs and dirt in my home!"

"I understand, Mother."

Willie prepared tea as Sonya continued to put away her groceries, leaving out some vegetables she would be using for supper. She peeled some potatoes and sliced red cabbage while Willie poured her tea into a white porcelain cup and placed it on a matching saucer. Both pieces of china were delicately painted with gold, red, and pink roses. He handed them to Sonya and poured his own tea into a white mug.

She took the cup and saucer and slid into a chair at the kitchen table, absentmindedly smoothing the white tablecloth that had wrinkled where she placed the grocery sack. Willie sat across from her. Sonya gently blew across the steam rising from the tea.

"Willie, did the doctor give you any idea of how long it will take for Josef to get a leg?"

"He can have a peg leg right away. The doctor indicated it would take time to acquire the more lifelike leg. Weeks, months, maybe never. He never knows when one will become available, and Germans get them first."

"Are you going to let Josef know about this?"

"I'd rather wait until Herr Doktor lets me know which one he can get. He does not recommend that Josef get accustomed to a peg leg, and then have to readjust to another type of leg."

As Willie was telling Sonya the doctor sent her his regards, Josef entered through the kitchen door.

"Good evening, Frau Mirz, Willie. It is freezing today!"

Willie nodded.

"Some tea, Josef?" asked Sonya. "It will help warm you."

"No, thank you. I am going to wash before supper, and rest. Is there anything you need me to do in the house before I go to my room, Frau Mirz?"

"No, supper is cooking. Go wash up."

Josef headed for his room. As soon as he got there, he sat on the bed and removed his right shoe. It had taken extra effort to navigate in the snow with crutches, and he was more weary than normal. He rested on his bed and quickly fell into a dreamless sleep.

An hour later Willie knocked on Josef's door, calling him to supper. Josef washed his face and hands and then joined Sonya and Willie at the table. Sonya had made a winter stew of potatoes, carrots, onions, and red cabbage cooked with some ox tail. It was a rich and meaty meal.

No one spoke of a new leg that night at the kitchen table.

After supper, Josef offered to help with the dishes. Sonya declined, saying there was very little to do.

Willie gave Josef his work assignment for the next three days, which was to perform some carpentry projects at a factory. It was a longer walk to the factory than to the bakery, where he had just finished the electrical job. Despite the meal he had just enjoyed, Josef was tired and went straight to bed. He needed his rest for his longer walks in the snow.

It was dark and ruthlessly cold outside, and the rest of the household retired early that night.

Within three days, the doctor sought Willie at the hospital. He had good news. Very good news.

"Willie, we had an unfortunate death last night. A veteran of World War I died of natural causes. He had received a new artificial leg just a year ago, and I think it might work for Josef."

"That's fantastic!" He felt just a little too enthusiastic and immediately added, "I am sorry about the gentleman who died, but I am so glad you think the leg might work for Josef. Are you under any kind of legal obligation to report to the authorities that a leg is available?"

"No, I am going to keep it here in my office."

"Herr Doktor, it seems as though Josef has a guardian angel looking after him."

The doctor smiled and raised his eyebrows. "It does seem that way. Please let me know when I can visit him to fit the leg."

"I will talk with Mother. Is it possible for you to come on a weekend when Josef does not have to work?"

"I can arrange that. Just call me tomorrow and let me know. Do you plan to tell Josef about the leg or would you like me to do it?"

"I want to do it," responded Willie, "and will tell him tonight."

They parted with a flaccid Nazi salute.

Willie finished his work for the day, and when he got home he found Sonya in the kitchen, ironing some of his shirts on the old ironing board she had set up. The heavy iron smoothed the wrinkles, and the scented linen water she sprinkled on the shirts gently wafted through the room like a gentle puff of summer blossoms. She smiled as Willie greeted her.

"How was your day, Son?"

"It was a normal day, Mother, with one exception."

"Oh? Was someone seriously hurt?"

"No. Herr Doktor has a leg for Josef. It's a leg that has a foot, not just a peg."

"That is wonderful news! When can he be fitted with it? The sooner the better, don't you think?"

"The doctor can come this weekend. Do you have a preference for Saturday or Sunday?"

Sonya paused with her finger on her lip, "Saturday would be best. It will give Josef some time to practice with it before Monday. But how is it that Josef gets a leg when there are so many soldiers who may need one?"

Willie raised his eyebrows and pursed his lips. "I think it is because he is so good with his hands. The work he does seems to be well regarded and really necessary." Willie paused a moment and added, "Or maybe he is just lucky. Besides, he has pride in his work, even as a conscripted laborer. Josef is unique in that respect, and all the businesses and shops he's worked in give him high praise, even if it is offered reluctantly. This isn't a very big community, and word gets around."

"But with his new leg, Willie, won't he need some time to learn how to use it properly?"

"He will need a lot of practice with it, and he will need some padding for the remaining part of his leg—the stump beneath his knee."

"I can make some padding for him, Willie. Have you told him about the leg yet?"

"No. I just found out this afternoon. I'll tell him tonight, during supper."

Sonya stood still at her ironing board, frozen for a few seconds. With several of Willie's shirts still in the ironing basket, she turned unexpectedly, went to the cupboard, and opened the sugar canister.

"This calls for a real dessert, Willie. I'm finished ironing for today."

"What are you going to make?"

"I was thinking of making some fresh apple cake, the one with the apples on top. It only takes a cup of sugar. I know you love it. Do you think Josef will, too?"

"I am sure he will."

"Willie, with Josef getting an artificial leg, won't he be leaving soon?"

"He agreed to stay until spring, don't you remember? He also has to learn how to walk on the leg. That doesn't happen overnight."

"I wish he would not return to the barracks," Sonya said quietly, almost imperceptibly shaking her head from side to side in a gentle and melancholy "No" movement. "His being here reminds me of when I had two sons."

"Mother, we can't bring Gunter back. Or Father, either."

"I know, but the house is just a little bit livelier with Josef here."

Willie studied Sonya and saw a woman whose face bore lines placed there prematurely by the war. He saw a woman who suffered quietly, a woman whose hair was turning gray at the temples, a woman whose face was no longer as radiant as it had been. Sonya had agreed, although reluctantly, to house the enemy, in the guise of a Polish teenager, regardless of what any of the neighbors would think. Willie realized his mother was not only a strong woman, but a woman of character. He loved her dearly.

"Mother, let me put the iron and ironing board away for you."

"Thank you, Willie. I need to peel and core the fresh apples."

"Do you need help?"

"No, go relax in the parlor."

As late afternoon turned to evening, Josef was not yet home from his work. Willie and Sonya sat at the kitchen table and were already eating their supper of a small pork roast, supplemented by a plate of potatoes and carrots. Everyone's rations had been reduced again since more food was needed for the armed services. Bombings had destroyed the railroad tracks used by trains to bring food to the town, and all across Germany. Josef offered some of his own ration stamps and Sonya reluctantly accepted them. It was an offer that made the pork roast easier to attain, and she enjoyed preparing it. And everyone was tired of carrots, potatoes, and cabbage. Especially cabbage.

Josef returned to the house a half hour later than normal. He greeted Willie and Sonya and quickly washed before taking his seat at the supper table.

His eyes grew wide at the meal before him.

"A roast?"

My God, what is Michael eating tonight?

"Yes, a roast, thanks to your ration stamp offering."

Sonya placed two pieces of meat on his plate, along with some vegetables and a slice of bread. Josef ate his supper silently as Sonya and Willie finished theirs. Willie even ate another slice of bread so Josef would not have to eat alone. When they were done, Josef offered to help with the dishes, but Sonya told him to remain seated.

She got up and returned to the table with the apple cake she had made.

Willie and Josef were like two little boys caught stealing some pastry from a bakery. Their eyes and smiles said it all. This was a treat, for sure.

"Cake, Frau Mirz? Is to someone's birthday?"

"No, Josef, we are having a celebration tonight." She looked at her son. "Isn't that right, Willie?"

"Yes, that's right; we have some very, very good news, Josef."

"Is the war over?" Josef asked hopefully.

"No, the war is not over," replied Willie, deflated. "Josef, Herr Doktor has found an artificial leg for you. It has a foot, ankle, and calf. It is not just a peg."

"An artificial leg? Do you mean I won't have to use crutches any longer?" Josef gasped as his face turned red, and he fought tears.

"It will take some time for you to get used to it. I wouldn't put those crutches aside just yet."

"When? When will I get the leg?"

"This weekend. Herr Doktor will come to fit you with it on Saturday."

"How will I ever pay for it?"

"The doctor told me not to think of payment just yet."

A second ago, Josef was worried about paying for the leg, but a scene was emerging in his mind, a scene over which he had no control, a scene he did not want to control. He saw himself standing in the garden without crutches, walking to the wood fence, his pants legs fully extended. The snow had melted, and the ground was soft and smelled of spring promise. He saw himself raising his hand and waving to the girl in the adjacent yard. Ella was her name. And he saw her wave back.

Yes, he was very happy to be getting a leg.

Josef blurted, "But how did Herr Doktor get a leg?"

"A veteran of the previous war was an amputee, and he died last night. The doctor said the leg he wore will probably fit you. Not perfectly, but close enough."

Josef was speechless. In an instant, he could see himself walking. He could see a future.

Sonya broke the silence. "Let's have some cake and tea."

They ate their dessert, and afterwards, Josef and Willie placed their plates in the sink.

"Do you need some help, Frau Mirz?"

"No, Josef, go enjoy the fire in the parlor."

Josef and Willie went to the sitting room and shared the newspaper. They didn't talk of the war, and when Sonya joined them she brought a basket of sewing with her. There were buttons to reattach and socks to darn. Each member of the household was lost in private thought for almost an hour when Josef got up to say goodnight.

"Willie, thank you for the wonderful news. I can't wait to tell Michael."

"Oh, I forgot to tell you. I saw your brother. Mother has invited him to supper in a couple of weeks. He mentioned to me how happy he is that you are staying here, rather than at the barracks at the camp. I didn't say anything to him about your decision to return...nothing at all; I would surmise he would think it is not a very good idea for you to return to that situation."

"I'm sure he doesn't think it would be a good idea. Maybe he'll feel better about it when he sees I have a leg."

"I guess we will find out, won't we?"

"Yes, we will," replied Josef.

Then, extending his hand to Willie, Josef said, "Thank you, Willie." Willie grasped Josef's hand firmly and warmly.

"Sleep well, Josef."

Josef turned and approached Sonya who was sitting in a corner of the divan. He stood before her.

"Frau Mirz, thank you for the wonderful meal tonight and for the cake. I love apple cake. It is my favorite. My mother made it often, back in Poland. Sometimes she used plums, instead."

Sonya smiled broadly at him. "Maybe I will try it with plums sometime."

Before she could say anything else, Josef reached out to touch her hair and bent forward awkwardly. He gently kissed the top of her head, right above her forehead.

"Good night, Frau Mirz."

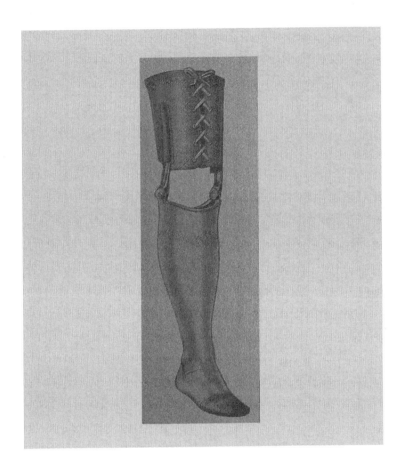

A Prosthesis Similar to Josef's

This artificial leg is American-made and of the same era as the leg Josef received in Germany during the war. Josef's leg had leather straps with buckles that were fastened around the thigh, while this one has a cuff and laces. Notice the hinged metal bars on the sides, at the knee.

Image is in the Public Domain

13 - A Leg

The next morning Willie called the doctor and they decided on Saturday afternoon for Josef to receive his leg. The physician cautioned Willie against getting rid of the crutches, because Josef would surely need them for a while longer.

Happy expectation permeated the household for the remainder of the week. Josef had visions of walking as he did prior to the amputation. He saw himself striding confidently to his work assignments, climbing stairs, with no one aware he had only one leg. He pictured himself standing without crutches in Sonya's garden, and waving to the girl next door.

Willie was happy for Josef, but as an ambulance driver who spent a lot of time at the hospital, he had seen the struggle amputees face when learning to walk with an artificial leg. He saw their frustration, their disappointment, and ultimately, their triumph. Willie decided he would not say anything about this difficult process to Josef, and instead, let the young man grow into the realization at his own pace. And he'd be there to help him through it. Josef seemed genuinely happy, almost content, and Willie did not want to dampen his joy.

When Saturday afternoon finally arrived, the doctor entered the house with the leg under his right arm. It was cold from being in his automobile.

He greeted everyone and had some tea, making small talk about the weather. As he lifted the teacup to take a sip, he addressed Josef.

"I am waiting for the leg to warm up a bit."

"That's fine, Herr Doktor."

"You are looking much better, and I can see from your muscles that you have been doing your exercises."

"Frau Mirz makes sure I do them! And I do feel better. Thank you for finding a leg for me. I did not expect it."

"Don't thank me yet. It is going to take some time and practice for you to become comfortable with it. You will be sore, too, and you should continue to use your crutches, especially outside."

Josef nodded his head.

The doctor finished his tea, and stood up. "Are you ready to try it on?"

"I think so."

"Fine. Let's go to your room. Do you mind if Willie comes along? I would like him to understand what you will need to do to get used to the leg."

"Certainly, that would be fine."

The three men walked to Josef's room where the doctor directed Josef to sit in the chair by the table. He examined Josef's stump.

"It has healed very well," he said to Josef and Willie while he gently lifted Josef's left leg and inserted it into the prosthesis.

The doctor smiled at Josef.

"It will be easier to get accustomed to the new leg with an amputation below the knee, like yours."

There was a knock at the door.

"Come," commanded Willie.

It was Frau Mirz.

"I think I need to know how to help you, Josef. Do you mind if I watch?

Josef did mind. He was a little embarrassed by the whole thing, but he knew Frau Mirz was right. "Please, come in Frau Mirz," he said cheerfully.

The doctor removed Josef's leg from the prosthesis, and then carefully wrapped washable bandages around Josef's stump. They would cushion it as Josef stood and exerted pressure, and also help fit the prosthesis snugly.

The doctor looked at Josef, then at Sonya. "You can also use soft socks as padding, just as long as they do not slip. You can get blisters if they move around too much."

"I can provide socks," Sonya offered.

The doctor unwrapped the bandages and handed them to Josef.

"Now you try it. Try wrapping your leg for the prosthesis," suggested the doctor.

All of them watched Josef apply the bandages.

"That's quite good for a first try," the doctor smiled.

Sonya offered a thick ointment to soothe the remains of Josef's leg and assured Josef she could provide at least four socks to use as bandaging.

When the doctor was satisfied Josef was wrapping the end of his leg adequately, he explained the various parts of the prosthesis and pointed out the hinges that would flank Josef's own knee; they would help Josef with flexing the artificial limb.

He asked for Josef's left shoe. When he saw it, it seemed much less worn than the right shoe Josef had been using for months. He asked Josef to place a sock over the artificial leg's foot. Willie got a dark sock from the dresser drawer and handed it to Josef.

As Josef held his new leg across his lap, he felt silly putting a sock on a piece of wood. Instead, he examined the leg both with his eyes and his hands. He ran his fingers along the leg's wooden calf, shaped just like a human calf. He noticed the calf tapered into a shin, and found the light-toned wood smooth, with no splinters, and varnished to a soft sheen. He saw the ankle was not hinged, and wondered how that would affect his gait. The foot was fashioned with slight grooves at the tip that made it appear as though it actually had toes. Shallow indentations simulated toenails. Running his hands back up the leg, he examined every inch. There was a metal rod on each side of the leg. They were attached to a supple, yet thick leather wrapping that would be worn around the thigh, then tightened by straps attached to the leather wrap. A leather cup was hidden in the top of the wooden leg, to cradle his stump.

"Josef, are you going to put the sock on the foot?" Willie prodded.

"Dress the leg just as you would your real leg," advised the doctor, as he pointed to Josef's real leg.

Josef slipped the dark sock on the foot.

That went on smoothly. He then turned down the cuff on the shin, just as he did on his real leg. It all seemed silly to him—dressing a wooden leg. Then he slipped the shoe onto the foot and tied it. It seemed to be almost a perfect fit.

With the leg dressed in its sock and a shoe, Josef stood it up on the floor, right in front of him. It looked like a comical bodiless form getting ready for a stroll in the park. He stared at it for a long time. Willie opened his mouth to say something, but the doctor touched Willie's sleeve and shook his head "No." The doctor knew his patient needed to digest what was happening, to accept the fact the prosthesis was not a flesh and blood leg.

Josef was both fascinated and repulsed by the leg. It reminded him of times when, as a boy, he would closely examine a bug that was both glorious and hideous all at once.

A heaviness was rising in his chest. *I don't want this. I want my own leg!*

As though he knew what Josef was thinking, the doctor touched Josef's right shoulder to reassure him. "Let's try it on," he quietly and firmly said, as he lifted the leg and handed it to Josef. "Go ahead and slip it on."

Josef inserted his stump into the device's leather cup and adjusted the leather straps around his left thigh. His trouser leg was still rolled up, as though there was no leg to cover.

"You will need to make adjustments to the straps and bandaging as you walk and gain or lose weight, Josef. The leg is not exactly the same length as your right leg, but it is the best we can do for now."

"I can see that, Herr Doktor," replied Josef.

"Do you want to try to stand?"

"Yes!" he replied with enthusiasm, his anger and resentment in check for the moment.

"But will I limp?"

"You may have a slight limp; first let's get you up on your feet. Try to balance your weight evenly between your wooden leg and your real leg. Willie will stand on one side and I will stand on the other to support you."

The two men positioned themselves at Josef's sides.

This is it. I am going to walk on my own even if I hate this log of a leg.

Josef stood up, grasped securely under his arms by Willie and the doctor.

Immediately, he felt the pressure on his stump. He was standing, but there was no feeling of solid ground beneath his new leg. It was disquieting, standing up and not being able to feel the floor. He sat down again. The doctor, Willie, and Sonya waited for him to say something. But he was silent, looking at the leg attached now to his left thigh.

"I'd like to try standing up again."

They repeated the exercise several times with the doctor and Willie continuing to supporting him.

"I'd like to try it on my own, if you don't mind."

With Willie and the doctor hovering a few inches from him, Josef stood up and supported himself by grasping the table. He straightened his back and rotated his left thigh back and forth, with his new foot on the floor, and the prosthesis bearing no weight. *Lead. I hate it.*

"I think the strap needs to be tightened."

The doctor tightened the strap a notch. "But we have to be sure the strap does not cut off your circulation."

"That's better, Herr Doctor."

"Josef, can you lift the leg?"

He froze, afraid to lose his balance. Willie noticed his hesitation.

"I'm right here, Josef. Go ahead and try to lift your new leg. I'll hold on to you," offered Willie.

Supported by Willie, Josef lifted his new leg. *Thank heavens I did all those exercises.*

"How does it feel?" asked Frau Mirz.

"Heavy, very heavy. Like cement...like lead."

The doctor cautioned Josef. "Remember, you've had no leg, no weight on your left side for many months. You will adapt to it."

"How am I supposed to lift this thing and walk?" Josef asked, almost panicked, his voice slightly quivering. "How? If feels like I am dragging around a dead body!"

The doctor had seen this initial reaction many times—the shock of a new leg, weighty and awkward, after the loss of a real one. Josef's reaction was normal, and the doctor wanted to encourage his patient.

"Learning to use your new leg is a process. It does not happen all at once. You just can't get up and walk across the room. You have to learn how to walk with it. Thousands of people have learned to walk with an artificial leg, and I am certain you will be successful."

Josef knew learning to walk would take time, but he was young and impatient. And very anxious. He wanted to walk immediately.

The leg represented so much more to him than being able to walk without crutches. It meant restoration, a re-establishment of some semblance of the state he had been in before the barrel accident, before the war. It also would be there forever, reminding him of what the war had done to him.

Still standing, Josef reached for the chair and sat down. He was tapping the fingers of his right hand on the table, and shaking his right leg in short, rapid, up and down movements, anxious and impatient.

"I know I have to work with it, Herr Doktor, but I thought it would be easier, that I could walk right away." His obvious disappointment was palpable. Sonya cleared her throat lightly and left the room hurriedly.

Willie asked, "Herr Doctor, do we have a regimen for getting Josef walking?"

"Yes, I've written it for you."

The doctor searched his case and pulled out a set of typed instructions, several pages long. Willie quickly scanned them.

"I am not sure I know how to help Josef with all of these instructions. Although I have come in contact with amputees of all kinds—legs, arms, hand—at work, I have never been involved in helping them with their rehabilitation."

"We have to do the best we can. There are so few expert medical people around, with the war. Call me for guidance, and I can come back to help if you need me."

"I can only help him in the morning and in the evening. Mother can help, too. There are only so many hours in a day."

"I don't need anyone to help me." Josef protested, a little angrily.

The doctor looked at his patient who was sitting dejectedly on the chair.

"Josef, it is important to continue practicing sitting down, standing up, and balancing your weight, followed by lifting your left leg, and then putting your weight back down on it. We practiced these movements today. Once you feel confident with standing, lifting, and sitting down again, then you may begin to take a few steps. Willie or Frau Mirz will need to support you until you feel secure. Wear the leg every day, even while you are still using crutches."

"What's the point of wearing the leg to work if I can't walk with it yet?" Josef spit out.

"Wearing it helps you get accustomed to its presence—its weight, the space it occupies. It also gives you the opportunity during the day to work on standing, lifting, and balancing. And please, use your crutches. They are like having Willie and me to support you." Softly, the doctor added, "And you can roll your trouser legs down and wear a shoe."

Josef hadn't thought of that. He hadn't thought that would help make him appear normal, and his mood brightened.

It all made sense, but Josef just wanted to be left alone for a while, alone with his new leg, with his anger, with his hopes.

"Herr Doktor, thank you again, and I'll follow your plan."

"I will check on you in a few weeks."

Josef stood up, using the table for support.

"Thank you, Herr Doktor," Josef said again and shook the doctor's hand.

The doctor and Willie left Josef in his room, and Josef sat down, stupefied, his leg still attached. *Lead, I am going to have drag around a bucket of lead the rest of my life.*

It did not turn out to be the type of day he thought it would be. He still could not walk. He reviled the heavy leg. He wanted his real leg back.

He glanced around the room and judged the distance from the chair he was sitting in to his bed at about three meters.

Just three meters.

14 - A Step at a Time

As this waning winter afternoon in early 1944 melted into evening, Josef sat at the table in his room. He repeatedly examined his leg with his hands as well as his eyes, and periodically glanced at the space between him and the bed, wondering if he could get there on his own.

Three meters; it is only about three meters.

He practiced standing up and sitting down as the doctor had shown him. He practiced lifting and moving his newly-attached prosthesis, using either his crutches or the table for support.

In the kitchen, meanwhile, Sonya and Willie reviewed the doctor's notes on how to help Josef walk.

"Willie, will you have time to help Josef?" asked Sonya. "You already work all day and he will need help."

"Mother, if you can help him in the morning by making sure the leg is on securely and he can walk, even with his crutches, then I can help in the evening. I expect he will be sore and I can encourage him to apply the salve you have."

"That might work. I am too busy in the early evening preparing supper. You can help him then."

She cocked her head. "Willie, would you see if Michael can come for supper next Sunday? I think many of the laborers do not work on Sunday."

"I'll ask him, and don't even say it—I'll be sure he cleans up and is treated with insecticide. What time would you like him to be here?"

"By 1:30 p.m. would work. That way he can visit with his brother, have a late afternoon Sunday supper with us, and be back at the barracks before curfew."

"Fine, Mother, I'll contact him this week."

Willie left the kitchen and headed for the parlor. He paused in the hallway, debating whether to knock on Josef's door, but decided against it. He thought it would be best to leave Josef alone with his new leg.

Sonya turned her attention to preparing a supper of potatoes, eggs, green onions, and bread. She tried to make her meals as filling and nourishing as her provisions would allow.

Her mind raced, posing question after question: Surely, it is not a good sign for Germany that our rations have been reduced, is it? What is really happening out there on the battlefields? How bad are things for people in Cologne, bombed to rubble by the British? Hitler can't fool anyone about that! What became of Cologne's beautiful cathedral? Is it now just a crumpled, skeletal phantom? And what of the port of Wilhemshaven, pounded by the Americans? How are people faring in Hamburg, also bombed? What is the death toll among citizens and soldiers because of the bombings? How are the young children of Germany bearing all of this? How much of the news is the truth about the war? How much is nothing more than national propaganda?

With the media controlled by the state, she did not know the answers to these questions. She only knew what she saw in the newspapers or listened to on the radio. She heard rumors from neighbors, though, including the one about the Soviets marching deeper into Poland from the east, preparing to capture the parts of Poland currently held by Germany. She now put more credit in their whisperings than in the official reports. Everyone was becoming concerned about the outcome of the war. And Sonya was beginning to more fully understand what the people of Britain may have felt when London was so heavily bombed. What of her lost son and husband? And what about Josef, the young man so affected by the war that he would never walk normally? Would he ever see is parents again? What would the war do to him next?

But Josef was not immediately concerned about the outcome of the war at this moment. The gaping space below his left knee had been an unfamiliar, empty abyss when his leg was first amputated, and now his new leg felt like an alien entity. His new leg was his only concern, and what could he do other than try to use it?

Although he had spent the afternoon practicing standing up and sitting down, he now stared for a long time at the four things he had to focus on: his leg, his crutches, his bed, and three meters of floor. He wondered what he could accomplish before supper.

Maybe I should just practice standing up and sitting down again. Maybe I should stick to moving my left leg up and down, and side to side. I can lean on the table. Or, maybe, just maybe, I can walk a step or two with the crutches to support me.

Josef did not think of falling. All he could envision was walking.

He stood up, placing almost all of his weight on his real leg, while clutching the table. Then he balanced his weight between both legs, letting go of the table, yet supported by his crutches. Unaccustomed to the odd sensation of no pressure on his artificial left foot and no sensation of floor beneath it, he did sense the very real weight of his body bearing down on his truncated left leg inside the leather cup of the prosthesis.

I am going to have to learn to walk all over again.

He sat down again in the chair by the table, deciding what to do next. When he stood up again, he gripped both arms of the chair and stood on both legs, trying to balance his weight while standing up.

As he stood, his weight was not evenly balanced, and he used his crutches for security; but he thought he had stood with more weight on his left leg than previously.

Encouraged by this small success, he supported himself with his crutches, and took a step forward, leading with his right leg—the one that was still, well, human. He then slowly drew his left leg next to his right leg, and put his weight as evenly as he could on both legs.

He had taken a step.

Looking down at his legs, he talked to them as though they were sentient beings with minds of their own.

Good! Do you think you two can do this again?

He wasn't overjoyed to have taken his first step; he realized he had a major task ahead of him, learning to walk. He wanted to make sure his legs understood what they had to do.

He took his next step.

Good again, legs. That's progress. Let's try another step. Do you think you can do it?

He continued his journey to the bed taking his next step the same way as the first. Between each step he gave his legs a pep talk. He and his two legs were a team.

Learning to walk is going to take forever. Forever! I'm counting on you, legs.

As he reached the side of the bed, he looked back and saw the distance he had traveled. He did not feel any satisfaction or joy. He did not allow himself that pleasure. There was just too much work to do.

Josef's right leg had done most of that work. It was not a normal way of walking, and he was impatient to look normal. But he planned to walk down the hall to the kitchen for supper, even if his right leg had to bear most of the load. He would not worry right now about initiating a step with his artificial leg.

He sat on the bed and lifted his left leg on it, shoe and all, followed by his right leg. Those few steps and the events of the afternoon had drained him, and he reclined on the bed to rest.

I want my own leg, he whispered to himself.

I want my mother.

He remembered some things about his mother, Magdalena — her high cheekbones, her blue eyes, and her dark blonde hair. Yet he had no immutable, distinct image of her. He wondered if he would recognize her if he ever saw her again. She had become a vague image in his mind.

But the images of standing on his own, walking to the garden fence, and waving to Ella were piercingly distinct.

Willie rapped at the bedroom door, instantly ending Josef's reverie. Josef bolted to a sitting position.

"Yes?"

"May I come in?" asked Willie.

"Just a moment."

Josef smoothed his hair with his hands and slid his right leg off the bed and onto the floor, while his still-dressed, wooden leg remained on the bed.

"Come in."

As Willie entered the room he saw Josef on the bed and noticed he was wearing his leg. He wasn't sure whether he had just put it on or if he had actually walked from the table to the bed.

"How did you get to the bed?"

"I walked."

"By yourself?"

"I used the crutches, but tried to put some weight on both legs."

"Let me see."

Josef sat on the bed with both legs dangling over the side, his crutches at hand. He clutched the side of the nightstand to his right, supported his left side with a crutch, and stood up. He placed most of his weight on his right leg, but then quickly balanced the weight more equally. He straightened up as tall as he could and looked at Willie, despite the pressure on his stump.

"Well, what do you think, Willie?"

"My, my, I am impressed! Can you walk to me?"

Willie was standing at the room's door. "Would you prefer I help you, Josef?"

"I would prefer to walk on my own, someday without a crutch...but not today."

Josef moved as he did earlier, beginning each step with his right foot, and then lifting his left one to meet it. When he reached Willie, he smiled.

"I did it!"

111

"That is remarkable, even with crutches!"

Josef replied, "It may be remarkable, but it is going to take a long time for me to walk normally."

"Would you like to try walking back to the bed without a crutch? I can stand on your left side to help. I'll be your crutch."

Josef took a deep breath. He did not want to fall. With the safety of his crutches, he turned to the right with his good leg, brought his left leg up to it, and said "Let's try it."

Willie positioned himself on Josef's left side, and extended his right arm around Josef's back, to steady him. He then threw the crutches on the bed. Josef took a step with his right leg, and then took a step with his left leg, this time putting weight on it and not just placing it next to his right one. He tottered, and Willie held him up.

It was his first weight-bearing step on his artificial leg.

Josef took a deep breath, "What's strange is that there is no feeling in the foot. It's all beneath my knee, as though my knee is my foot. It is disconcerting."

Willie nodded his head, but he really did not know what to say. He empathized with what Josef was saying, but he really couldn't understand it because he had never experienced it, and hoped never to have to, either.

"Don't you think that in time you will become more proficient with walking?"

"Yes, but I thought it would happen more quickly."

"More quickly? You just got the leg a few hours ago and I think you are doing incredibly well. Would you like to try another step?"

"I'll try again. But this time, let me put my left arm through your right one, as though we are walking arm in arm."

They took this stance, and Josef once again took a step—right leg first, followed by his left leg. This time, he knew what to expect, and because he was unsteady, Willie still held him firmly. Then he did it again. Right leg first, followed by bringing his left leg to meet his right leg.

"It's a good thing I did all those exercises. The strength I have in my thighs really helps me support my weight."

They continued taking steps until they returned to the bed, where Josef was relieved to sit again. Willie sat in the chair at the table.

"Let's not overdo it, Josef. Why don't you take the leg off for the rest of tonight?"

"No, I want to walk to the kitchen for supper, to surprise your mother."

"Well, I know she will be happy if you can do it, but she also understands that you might be sore, and learning to walk will take time."

"I'll worry about the soreness later tonight. The salve your mother gave me should help, and tomorrow I will practice again. Maybe you can help me walk outside a bit?"

"Only if the weather is good. Now why don't you wash up for supper and then I will help you to the kitchen. I'll keep my mother distracted. I don't want her to see you walking to the bathroom and ruin the surprise when you walk to the kitchen. Do you need my help getting to the bathroom?"

"No, just help me to the bedroom door, the way we just did, with my putting weight on the left leg. Then I'll take the crutches and walk to the bathroom the way I did before, by placing my left leg next to the right one after each step.

Josef walked to the bedroom door, with Willie supporting him. Willie left the room and went to the kitchen where he engaged his mother in conversation. Josef fought his way to the bathroom and freshened up for supper.

I can't wait for Frau Mirz to see me walk.

Willie met him at the bathroom and they walked slowly down the hall, reaching the entrance to the kitchen arm in arm. Sonya's back was to the two young men as she stirred supper in a pot on the stove. There was silence for a few seconds until Josef cleared his throat loudly.

"Good evening, Frau Mirz. It smells delicious."

She whirled around. With her mouth wide open at the sight of Josef standing on his leg, she let the contents of the stirring spoon drip to the floor. Sonya stared at Josef's left leg with its trousers rolled down to the ankle and a shoe on the foot. She was speechless.

"Well, Mother, what do you think?" asked Willie.

"I can't believe it! *Mein Gott!*"

"Let me see you walk," she ordered Josef.

Willie stood next to Josef, and arm in arm, they walked to the table, with Josef gingerly putting his weight on his left leg, and Willie supporting him.

Josef sat down.

"I can't believe it, Josef. You only got your leg earlier today!"

Josef was pleased that *she* was so pleased.

"I have been practicing in my room."

Sonya shook her head from side to side in happy disbelief. Her hands on her hips, she grinned at Willie and then at Josef. She was delighted for Josef.

"Stay here—I'll have supper ready in a few minutes, and I don't want you to have to walk back to your room."

They had a simple meal of eggs, potatoes, onions, and green peppers, accompanied by rye bread and sliced apples.

After supper Josef returned to his room, with Willie's help.

"Don't you think you've made enough progress today?" asked Willie. "If you overdo it, you might be much too sore to walk tomorrow."

"Perhaps you are right. I'll remove the leg soon and put some salve on."

"Do you need some help?"

"No, I don't think so, but I remember you said that you were going to invite Michael for supper sometime. Will he be coming soon?"

"Are you excited about showing him your new leg?"

"No, I'm excited about showing him I am going to be able to walk."

114

"I'll try to see him this coming week and ask permission for him to come to the house soon, possibly this coming Sunday."

"Thank you. I want him to see I can return to the barracks."

"Oh, that again," Willie said, almost under his breath. "Just rest tonight. We can practice walking again tomorrow."

Willie left the room, closing the door softly.

Josef changed into his nightshirt, sat on the bed, and removed his left leg. He placed it near the nightstand. *It looks like a faithful dog watching over me.* He looked at the end of his amputated leg, and saw that it was red and felt a little hot. He applied the cool, thick salve Sonya provided and covered his stump in a sock to keep it warm. As he settled into a comfortable position in bed, he felt more hopeful than he had earlier in the day. It had been a trying, though exciting day, and he was exhausted from the physical and emotional effort.

He stretched and did his thigh exercises, and when he was finished, he said his nightly prayer:

Hail Mary, full of grace, blessed art thou among women, and please help me learn to walk well. Holy Mary, Mother of God, help me learn to walk quickly, too. Pray for us sinners, pray for my family, for Willie and Frau Mirz, and for the war to end. Pray the Allies win. And pray for Herr Doktor. Even now I don't think he really had to amputate my leg, but he has found me a new one. Amen.

He was asleep.

But Sonya and Willie were awake, talking together in the parlor.

"I am amazed he can already walk a little, Willie!"

"He is motivated. He wants to return to the barracks, remember?"

"Yes, I know. Will you talk to Michael this week? I think next Sunday will work for him to come here. I think I mentioned that to you already."

"Yes, you did, Mother. I'll ask the camp commander if he can come over."

"Thank you, Son."

115

Sonya reached into the basket on the floor next to the chair she sat in, beside a bright floor lamp. She removed some socks from the basket, to darn them, but before she got fully engaged in her project, she looked up at Willie.

"What do you think is going to happen with the war? We are being bombed frequently in the ports and major cities."

"No one knows, Mother. Many of us are weary of this war by now. I know I am."

"What do you think will happen to Germany if we lose?"

Willie shook his head from side to side, "I do not know, but I know Josef will be happy if Germany loses."

"He doesn't seem to bear us any hatred, Willie."

"Face to face we aren't enemies."

Sonya smiled gently, and looked lovingly at her son.

"Sometimes, Willie, you are so wise."

"Just sometimes?" Willie teased.

"Yes—a young man your age shouldn't be wise in all things. You've borne a burden being both head of the house and son to me. This war has taken some of your youth. Don't you know that?"

"Yes, I do," he said, his head nodding.

Sonya and Willie were lost in their thoughts the rest of the evening, and then they retired for the night.

Early the next morning, with the sun barely up, Sonya and Willie were awakened by the sound of the teakettle whistling on the stove.

15 - Ella

Standing on two legs with his crutches nearby, Josef heated the water in the kettle and then poured it into the teapot where he had deposited two small scoops of strong black tea. Tea was also rationed, and those two scoops would have to steep for a while to make the tea strong.

When Willie and Sonya came into the kitchen, they were greeted by a proud Josef, standing on his own. Sonya brought the tea and cups to the table.

After a simple breakfast of bread and cheese, Willie offered to take Josef outside into the garden to walk. Willie went to the kitchen peg to get Josef's jacket, but Josef stopped him. Using the table for support, Josef stood up and walked with his crutches to the peg, where he pulled down his jacket. He stood on his own, and put it on.

"Let's go," he said to Willie.

Willie grabbed his sweater and walked arm in arm with Josef into the garden. Josef had left his crutches in the kitchen, relying on Willie for support.

The shrubs and trees were at that moment in very late winter when they redden and swell, preparing for the feast of green soon to come. The honeysuckle vine on the rustic fence was readying itself for its spring glory, too. It was becoming supple, and scratching the still-brown vine would reveal a light green, ripening pulp. There were tiny patches of snow on the ground here and there, but the air was no longer crisp and wintery. It had softened.

They walked the length of the yard once, and Josef had to rest. They did it again, and talked about Willie's job and his latest dates with Helga. Willie even expressed his concern about the outcome of the war, and Josef repeatedly glanced at the adjoining yard to see if Ella was outside. He had to be sure

Willie wasn't looking at him when he did that, because both Willie and Sonya had warned him several times about making friends with a German girl.

Willie was all business, not having a clue about what Josef was actually thinking.

"Josef, how do you plan to get to work this week?"

"Probably, I will get up an hour earlier in the morning to be there on time. I am working on some framing for new windows at the fire station."

"But you are definitely taking your crutches, aren't you?"

"Yes, of course. I wouldn't think of *not* taking them. I am going to try to take a few steps at a time without them. I do plan to have them with me all the time."

Josef was unsure of himself on his new leg and couldn't initiate a step forward on it without holding on to Willie or supporting himself with his crutches. He wanted to get over that hurdle, but he just was not ready.

"Later this week I would like to try walking unassisted across my bedroom."

"Unassisted?"

"Yes, without your support and without crutches."

"Are you sure? I can understand you want to do this, but why set a date yet for doing it when you don't know how long it will take you to be steady?"

"I need to have a goal. Then next time I see Michael, I want him to see me walking on my own. Having a goal motivates me to push myself."

"Don't you think he will be happy just to see you with an artificial leg?"

"He will be happy, I am sure. But I want him to see me walking on my own, being independent. It will not only make me feel better, but I think it will make him feel better, also. Will you help me?"

Willie knew that he could not refuse Josef. "I'll help you. Mother will too, if you ask her."

"Your mother has been more than kind to me. She is a wonderful lady. The only problem I have with her is that she makes me realize I miss mine so much. I don't want to confuse her with my own mother."

"Do you realize how hard it is for me not to confuse you with Gunter, my younger brother?"

Josef stopped walking. He hadn't thought of that.

"Willie, we are in the same boat, aren't we?"

"It seems so, but let's get back to your goal. I will be asking your brother to come for supper next Sunday. Let's see what we can accomplish on your walking by then."

"That sounds good. I hope Michael can come."

For the remainder of the week, Willie and Josef practiced together and Josef grew gradually more confident. By the weekend, he could walk cautiously and slowly across his bedroom, unassisted by either Willie or crutches, although he held the crutches in his right hand. Josef practiced the walk from his bed to the door, and back again, time after time, until he thought he would wear a groove in the wood floor. He was getting better at initiating a step with his left leg, but he felt more secure using his natural, right leg, first.

When Michael arrived for Sunday afternoon dinner, Josef greeted him at the front door of the house, his crutches hidden to the side.

"Michael!"

"Josef!"

The brothers hugged and Michael held on to his younger brother. He then held him at arm's length, looking at his left leg.

"So, what do you think, Michael?"

"You are standing on your own. And walking! Willie told me the doctor was able to secure an artificial leg for you, but I didn't realize you had made so much progress using it. Show me."

119

As the two brothers walked away from the front door, Josef walked to the hallway that led to the kitchen.

Willie greeted them, took Michael's jacket and placed it over a bench in the hall. The three of them went to the kitchen.

Sonya greeted Michael. "Michael, how are you?"

"I am well Frau Mirz, and I hope you are, too."

He handed her a brown paper package of rye bread he had purchased at a bakery.

"Thank you, Michael, but that was unnecessary."

She tried very hard not to overly scrutinize him for the level of cleanliness she found acceptable. Nonetheless, Sonya noticed that his clothes were worn and thin, but they looked and smelled cleaned.

"Please, sit down. We will be eating soon. Would you care for a cup of tea before supper?"

"No thank you, Frau Mirz. I will wait for supper. Thank you for inviting me."

"What do you think of your little brother? He has made good progress, don't you agree?"

"Yes, I am dumbfounded, Frau Mirz."

Josef stood there, a little uncomfortable being the subject of conversation, as though he was not standing right there in the room.

He asked Sonya, "Frau Mirz, do you need any help?"

"No, Josef. The table is set and we are ready to eat. Willie, will you please fill the glasses with water or beer?"

Willie did as he was asked, and within a few minutes, they all sat down to eat. Though the feelings among them were cordial, it was a supper shared among enemies. The conversation was light, and no one talked about the war, despite the fact the war was the only reason why the Mirzs and the Walkows knew each other.

They heartily ate the cabbage and potato soup, seasoned with a little bacon. They enjoyed ersatzkaffee accompanied by a small coffeecake for dessert.

Fully understanding the two brothers probably wanted to talk, Sonya dismissed them and suggested they walk in the garden.

"It is light outside and you can see how well Josef is mastering his new leg," Sonya suggested. Josef knew that a suggestion from Sonya was really more of a command, so he and Michael put their jackets on and went outside.

"Do you want me to support you in any way, Josef? The ground is a little uneven," Michael asked.

"Just stay close by. I'll hold onto you if I need to."

They walked about seven or eight steps. Walking continued to feel unnatural to Josef, and each time he took the first step with his left leg, he wondered if he would fall.

"Michael, what do you hear about the war? And is there any news from home?"

"The war is easier to talk about. Rumors say Germany is being pounded by the Allies. There is heavy bombing, especially in the north. I guess we are lucky to be in the south. And I've heard talk around the barracks about an Allied invasion that might occur in the coming months."

"But how does anyone really know this? I see the newspapers Willie reads, and the reports of German victory seem to be everywhere. I suspect some of it is just propaganda to keep spirits high for the Germans, but I don't really know. How much faith do you have in the rumors you hear at the camp?"

"Some. People hear things where they work, and sometimes people report what they've heard on illegal radio transmissions. And the Germans have had their rations reduced, as we all have. That should mean something."

"Yes, that's true. I surmise that is not a good sign for Germany, then—supplies can't get through."

"I agree," Michael said. "Maybe the war will be over sooner than we think."

"If it's over soon, Germany *must* lose. I can't imagine what our lives will be like if Germany wins, can you, Michael?"

Michael shook his head "No," and didn't need to speak.

"I am ready to return to the barracks," Josef blurted.

Michael tried to say something, but Josef silenced him. "Just hear me out, Michael. I've thought about this for a long time, and prayed about it, too. I want to be with you and with other Poles. I am lonely and want to use my own language. My brain is tired of trying to talk and read German all the time. Frau Mirz and Willie have been wonderful and made me realize that even in war, individuals considered enemies share their humanity. That is a valuable lesson. But I have had enough. I know the only reason why I have a choice is because Willie is allowing me to have a choice. In reality, he could force me not to return to the barracks. But he won't do that. He has always treated me with respect, and it has made the past year bearable. But my mind is made up; I am returning to the barracks."

Michael smiled, surprised his brother was so adamant, and delighted he had become so articulate. He also knew there was no point in talking him out of his decision. Josef had always been stubborn. That hadn't changed, but he thought he'd give it one last try.

"Do you know you could be given an assignment you couldn't possibly do?"

"Don't you think they'll take my amputation into account, Michael? Why would they assign me something I can't do? That doesn't make sense."

"Sense? You think anything actually makes *sense*, Josef?"

Josef could hear the frustration and sarcasm in Michael's voice, and his own heart started to race.

"Michael, I believe people will be reasonable. They know what I can do and what I cannot do, and what I am good at doing."

Michael answered ruefully, "I think you have been away from the barracks for too long. You think people are reasonable." He sighed and continued, "When are you coming back?"

"Within a month, I hope. It depends on how well I walk."

"There is nothing I can do to talk you into staying here with the Mirz family?"

"Michael, suppose the war doesn't end soon? Suppose the Germans win? Do you really think I can stay with Willie and Frau Mirz forever?"

Michael let out a long sigh this time. "No, I suppose not."

"Then it's settled. I will be back at the barracks as soon as I can walk steadily on my own."

The two young men walked to the far side of the yard and leaned on the wooden fence.

"You know, this is a honeysuckle vine, Michael, like Mother has." Josef paused a moment and added, "I am forgetting the details of her face, and Father's too. I wonder what Pyotr looks like. He was just a kid when you joined the Army and I was captured."

Michael was quiet, resting his elbow on the top of the fence. "I've forgotten what they look like, too," he said. "They're hazy."

"Do you think Mother and Father are alive, Michael?"

"Maybe. I hope so." The both were quiet.

After a few minutes, Michael and Josef pushed away from the fence and returned to the house. It was late afternoon and Michael wanted to return to the barracks well within curfew. Besides, he wanted to think about what he could do to help Josef get assignments that would be appropriate for his condition.

He thanked Frau Mirz for supper and bid farewell to Willie. Tired from the walk in the garden, Josef grabbed his crutches and walked his brother to the front door, where they once again embraced.

"We'll be together, soon, Michael," Josef called out as Michael buttoned his jacket while walking rapidly down the front walk.

I wonder if I will ever be able to walk that fast again.

Josef returned to the garden after his brother left, hoping to catch a glimpse of Ella. He slowly and carefully walked around as he ostensibly examined the vines and bushes, all the while trying to appear nonchalant and steady on his feet. He made sure he left his crutches inside. *God, don't let me fall. Don't let Ella see me if I fall.*

He was rewarded for his persistence. Ella had come into her employer's garden via the house's back door. She had a book in her hand, as usual, and wore a white apron, the kind that covered her from the hem of her skirt to the top of her blouse. He wondered what she was reading, what she had cooked that day, and if she liked learning to be a cook, in addition to tending to her duties as a maid.

He stood there, gazing at her. She looked back, clutching her book to her chest.

This German girl fascinated him. He had no idea why. Maybe there was something special about her and maybe there wasn't. Maybe just her being female was the fascination.

What he was about to do was in flagrant disobedience of all the rules in all of Germany. It was a punishable offense. But he did not care.

Josef raised his right arm ever so slightly and waved to her.

She waved back.

16 - Ella and Josef

After their initial, timid waves to each other, Josef decided to meet Ella the following evening, a Monday night, along the fence section on the far side of the shed. There they would be concealed from the line of sight to Sonya's kitchen door.

Ella had similar thoughts. If she walked to the end of the garden that belonged to her employer and then continued toward the fence that separated her yard from the Mirz yard, she would be hidden by a stand of evergreen trees. Thickets of old blueberry bushes shielded her from the houses on either side of her employer's house.

Until that first wave, Josef and Ella had not communicated with each other in any way. Whether through hope or curiosity, serendipity or fate, they both knew they would meet in the garden again.

Ella didn't know much about Josef except that he was a Polish laborer and had lost a leg. Sometimes the other help in the household would talk about the Mirz Family and gossip about Sonya and Willie, thinking they were somehow given special permission to keep their own laborer. Often they expressed surprise Josef had been allowed to live, given his injury. Ella didn't know what the master and mistress of the household thought about the prisoner next door. She rarely saw them, being confined mostly to the kitchen and her culinary chores, when she wasn't in her room in the attic. When she had some free time, she spent it reading, or walking in the garden. On occasion, she would visit her mother and half siblings, when the trains were running.

Josef's knew a few things about Ella. Willie had told him she was German, about his own age, and from Heidelberg. Since she usually had a book with her, Josef assumed she liked to read. Her hair was dark and she had a slight frame, but he didn't know anything about the details of her face or the color of her eyes.

On the pretense of practicing his walking on uneven ground, he decided he would walk in the garden every evening after supper, without depending on his crutches. Spring was just a few days away and daylight was lingering later. He had never seen Ella up close, and was grateful the increasing evening light would let him see her face, even though any meeting would have to occur at twilight or nighttime.

He felt neither fear nor passion. Fear would have come from a possible death sentence if the authorities discovered he had fraternized with a German girl. Passion, he hoped, would be more likely in the future. He had no idea how or where he could exercise his passion. Instead, he knowingly allowed his youthful recklessness, rather than his premature wisdom, rule him.

The Monday after Michael's visit, Josef went to his assignment as usual. When he returned home, he rested his left leg and put some salve on the stump, as well as more padding. After supper he announced he was going outside to practice his walking. Willie offered to accompany him, but Josef suggested Willie just relax and read his newspaper. He wouldn't be long outside.

Willie didn't resist Josef's suggestion and retreated into the parlor.

Josef entered the garden and rested his crutches against the house. He did not intend to take them to the far side of the shed. As he took a step forward, then two, he changed his mind. He turned back to the house and retrieved his crutches. With the stability they offered, he walked around the garden to a spot where he could see Ella if she came out of her house.

He did not have to stand there long.

She emerged from the back door and was bundled in a sweater and scarf. Perhaps they read each other's minds, because they didn't wave to each other, but simply looked across the gardens at one another.

They had both been thinking the same thing, it seemed.

Josef made a deliberate turn to the right, and walked slowly to the other side of the shed, where he would not be seen. He hoped Ella understood what he was doing so she would come to the fence to meet him.

Their silent language worked.

Ella strode along the fence, looking behind her, to the left and the right, verifying she could not be seen. Josef, too, walked along the fence. He was thankful Willie's backyard had a high hedge along one side of the garden and a stone wall on the other side. They offered privacy from the houses on each side of the yard, and the hedges in the front garden hid the rear yard from the street. Night's darkness also sheltered them from view.

The stopped along the fence, facing each other. Ella extended her right hand while introducing herself.

"Hallo, ich bin Ella Stichler."

Josef felt her hand. It was small and surprisingly soft. He had expected it to be large and rough from kitchen work.

"Hallo, ich bin Josef Walkow."

They dropped their hands, and Ella folded her sweater more tightly around her as she crisscrossed her arms over her chest. Josef pulled up his jacket collar. Neither of them was truly cold. They just needed something to do to break the awkwardness of the moment.

"So you are Ella, the girl I see sometimes, always with a book in her hand."

She laughed lightly, "You describe me well. I love books."

Her voice enchanted him. It was light and playful, very much as he had imagined it in his mind when he thought of her.

"Willie Mirz tells me you are the cook for the people who live in that house." Josef pointed to the house behind Ella.

"I am not the chief cook. I am an apprentice, learning to cook all the dishes the family likes. I also am a maid."

"Do you enjoy being an apprentice cook and maid?"

"I guess the job is fine, especially the cook part. My work here provides me a living."

127

Maybe she doesn't really like working at the house.

"What are you reading?"

"Oh," she laughed, "it is just a romance story. Do you like to read?"

"Yes, but I don't read German too well. I prefer Polish. I can't get any Polish books here."

"I know, only German literature is available. But what about you, Josef? How long have you been in Stockach?"

Josef sighed. He didn't want to scare this girl away or say anything that would make her not want to meet with him again. Yet he also wanted her to know the truth about his presence in Germany.

"Do you know Germany invaded Poland in 1939?"

"Yes, I know that," and she nodded as she spoke. "Everyone knows that."

"About a year after the invasion, I was taken as a slave laborer, along with many other boys—some young women, too. I worked in Poland for a while, in mining and construction, but then was transferred to the barrel factory here in town. There was an accident, and my leg was injured. Willie was visiting a friend at the factory and he saw my leg was badly infected. He took me to the hospital—he *insisted* I go to the hospital—and the leg had to be amputated or I would have died. He was kind enough to let me live with him to recover."

Despite the soft, non-accusing tone she sensed from Josef, Ella looked down at the dark, brown earth. It was almost black now in the evening light.

"I'm sorry."

Josef did not acknowledge her apology.

"I hope you don't think all Germans agree with the slave labor idea, or...or...that all of us are cruel," she added.

Is she now going to say she isn't a Nazi, that she doesn't believe Hitler is the savor of the world, and that he did some good things for Germany before the war? Is she going to admit there is no such thing as a master race? I'll give her the Nazi thing, though. I know not all

Germans are Nazis. Frau Mirz and Willie proved that to me. Herr Doctor, too.

But Ella said none of these things. She said nothing at all.

Josef replied, "No, I do not think all Germans are cruel. Certainly, Willie and Frau Mirz are not, and some of the shopkeepers and business owners I've worked for have been decent."

Ella didn't know what to say. She had never met an actual enemy of Germany and, so far, she found all the stereotypes she had seen and heard to be false. Josef hardly looked subhuman or sounded stupid like Nazi propaganda described Poles. Nothing seemed Untermensch about him. No, nothing at all.

"Well, I think I'd better get back into the kitchen. I have some food the chief cook said I have to prepare for tomorrow morning. It was very nice to meet you. I've seen you in the garden from time to time, either alone or with Willie. I hope I see you again."

"I'd better be getting inside too," Josef responded. They'll wonder what I'm doing out here."

Don't let it end here...convince her to meet with me again.

"Ella, I will be out here in the garden again tomorrow night, assuming it is not raining."

"I'll try to come out, too."

Josef extended his hand and Ella shook it. He noticed she had drawn closer to the fence, and he held onto her hand for perhaps a moment too long. She looked at him and retrieved it, hiding both her hands in her skirt pockets.

"Good night, Josef."

"Good night, Ella. Sleep well."

They returned to their respective houses, though neither home belonged to either of them.

Josef re-entered the Mirz house, and placed his jacket on a wall peg in the empty kitchen. He walked to the parlor, largely unassisted by his crutches, though he carried them with him all the time.

There was a fire burning in the fireplace, just to take the chill out of the air.

"You were out there a while. Is it a nice evening outside?"

"Yes, Willie, it is very pleasant tonight."

It is more than pleasant. It is delightful. Ella's hands are soft, her voice is pleasing, and she did not run away when I told her my story. I discovered her eyes are brown, and her curled brown hair brushes the bottom of her neck. Yes, it is pleasant outside tonight.

"It is a little too cold me for to go out at night," offered Frau Mirz, who was in her customary place, with her hands busy, as always. Tonight she was repairing a hem on one of her dresses.

"How is your walking coming along?" she asked Josef.

"It is improving, but I still feel more comfortable using the crutches for any distance other than a dozen meters. And my leg is always sore at the end of the day."

"Perhaps you might consider staying on with us until you manage your walking better. Isn't that right, Willie?" She looked at her son to confirm the suggestion, but Willie did not respond. His head was buried in his newspaper.

"I would like to return to the barracks in about a month, assuming I can handle the walking."

She looked up from her mending. "Please be certain you can walk safely before you go."

"I will," he smiled, "and I am going to bed now. Good night Frau Mirz, Willie."

"Good night," they said simultaneously.

As Josef walked toward his bedroom, he shook his head. *I'm an idiot! What a time to want to return to the barracks. How am I going to see Ella if I return? Where will we meet? Will we meet at all?*

As he changed for bed, he couldn't stop thinking about Ella and what a relationship with her would mean. He worried if she really did want to be with him.

Suppose she doesn't want to see me? Suppose anyone suspects we are seeing each other...as boyfriend and girlfriend. What will happen to us? Us? There is no "us" yet. What will happen to Willie and Frau

Mirz if the authorities think Ella and I are seeing each other? What will happen to her family in Heidelberg? To Michael? To her? Hell, what will happen to me?

He was dizzy from the questions and their unknown answers. But he knew he had to see her again, he had to return to the barracks, and if he had to take a risk like this one, he would not have it reflect on Willie and Sonya. He just would have to figure it out.

Ella, meanwhile, returned to her employer's kitchen and prepared some fresh vegetables for the following day. As she peeled carrots, she thought of the young man she had just met. His hand was warm, and she liked that. He did not express any sorrow for himself, and she liked that, too. His answers were factual and not accusatory. He didn't complain. She wondered why she was drawn to a Polish prisoner, rather than to the German young man next door. She had no answer, figuring that when it came to attraction to someone of the opposite sex, maybe logic did not apply.

She thought about the few words she and Josef had just exchanged, fully aware any relationship, whether fleeting or intimate, would be dangerous.

And the Nazis were wrong. There was definitely nothing Untermensch about him. Not one thing.

During the next month, Josef and Ella met at the far side of the fence several times a week, weather permitting. No matter how challenging the task he was given to do, Josef's days flew by in anticipation of evening. He hoped Ella felt the same way.

Their signal to each other was always the same. Near or just after dusk, one of them exited their house, walked in their respective gardens, and waited for the other one to see them. They would then proceed to the fence on the far side of the shed, well-hidden from the street and the neighbors.

The days were getting longer with the arrival of spring, so they met later and later. It was late April of 1944, and rumors about an Allied invasion kept circulating, though no one knew for sure when it would happen, or where it would happen, or if it was even true. Like most Germans, the residents of Stockach were war-weary and looked forward to peace. For Germans, that peace preferably came with a German victory.

But every evening in the garden, the war was not the topic of conversation. Ella and Josef had graduated from shaking hands, to small pecks on the cheek, and then to more lingering kisses.

He was almost nineteen and she was seventeen. He was giddy with passion, and she felt special with this gentle and sensitive young man. The young couple kissed and held hands more than they spoke, and his desire for Ella left him yearning for more physical contact.

They talked about anything and everything, as though they were old friends and had no language barrier between them. Josef's German was improving, but he still wondered if Ella truly understood a word he was saying. Ella came to understand how angry Josef was because of his amputation. The treatment he received from Willie and Frau Mirz raised Ella's opinion of her neighbors. And Josef learned more about Ella.

One evening he asked her about her work as a cook and how she came to be in that particular household.

"Ella, what made you decide to become a cook?"

"I didn't decide. My mother needed more money, and my wages help her. She also thought it would be a good idea to learn some kind of trade. Then she took me out of school when she learned of the job here." Ella tilted her head toward her employer's house.

"And what does your father think?"

Oh God, maybe her father is dead...why did I just say that?

"My father had no say in it. He left my mother when I was just a little girl, and I don't know him. My mother remarried and now I have two half sisters and a half brother."

She paused, and then added, "I feel like I've been thrown out of my own home."

Josef knew how it felt to be taken away from home, and he nodded in agreement.

"Doesn't your stepfather provide for the family?"

"I don't know if he does or not. All I know is that my mother insists I keep this job."

"Do you really want to be a cook? There is nothing wrong with that, but is it what you *want*?"

"You know I love to read. Books can take me anywhere I want to go. Once you open the pages of a book, you can be a villain or a princess, a nurse or a missionary, a world traveler or a recluse."

"Yes, but what is it that *you* want to do?"

"I was getting to that. I dream of being a librarian and spending my days among books, helping people find what they are looking for, perhaps even sparking a love of reading in children."

"Why don't you do that—become a librarian?"

Ella gave him a patronizing smile, as though he was a child who just didn't understand how the world works.

"It is not possible...not at all, with the war going on. Maybe someday I can do that, when the war is over and life returns to normal."

"The war can't last forever. You have plenty of time to make your dream come true. When the war is over I would like to study engineering."

"Suppose Germany wins the war? What will you do then?"

"I will run away and take my chances. I refuse to spend my whole life as a captive."

Feeling his anguish, she gently stretched her arm across the fence to touch the hair just above his left ear. In the light of a half moon, he reached across the fence, drew her to him, and kissed her. Hard.

And she returned the kiss.

The fence was between them, and he knew it wouldn't separate them for much longer in the coming nights.

And so did she.

Ella also knew his arms felt right, and she belonged in them.

When he released her, he coughed slightly.

"I need to tell you something."

"What is it?"

"I am returning to the laborers' barracks. I want to be with my brother and people of my own nationality."

She stepped back, stung.

"Really? Why? You have it good here with Willie and Frau Mirz. I don't understand!" She felt a spreading dread.

"I just need to go back. I can't completely explain it."

After an awkward silence and a penetrating glare at Josef, Ella asked, "When are you going back?"

"Probably within the next week or two. I am getting much better walking with my artificial leg, and that is what really determines when I will go back to the camp."

Her voice quivering, she asked, "Does this mean we will not see each other again?"

"We will continue to see each other!"

"But how?"

"I have no idea yet. I have to figure it out."

"Maybe you are being a little reckless, Josef," she said coldly.

"No, I am not. I am taking charge of my own life to the extent that I can during the war."

Ella sighed, "I see."

"I'll find a way for us to continue seeing each other. I promise," Josef said earnestly.

She couldn't bear to lose him. Having never been in love, she didn't know if what she felt for him was love, but she knew that right now, there was pain and near panic in her chest. Why would he go back to the barracks? What would happen to *them*?

They kissed goodnight, and when they parted there was a little lover's rift between them. Josef realized he should have figured out how they would meet before he told Ella he was leaving the Mirz home. He hadn't handled it well, yet they agreed to meet again the following night at the fence on the far side of the shed—their usual spot.

Ella Stichler

Teenage Ella Stichler with classmates

Ella Stichler is in the front row, first girl on the left. She is wearing a light-colored skirt, and a sweater with white buttons. She has long braids. She was approximately fourteen years old in the photograph. The year would be late 1940, when the war was in progress.

Courtesy Monica Walkow Dudzinski

17 - Josef Returns to the Barracks

Josef wondered if Willie was suspicious of his nightly forays into the garden, yet Willie never mentioned them.

Willie had already contacted the barracks commander who drew up the papers to transfer Josef from Willie's oversight to his. Michael had talked with the commander about the kind of work Josef could do, and was told there were plenty of assignments for him. It helped that Michael offered special gifts of some of his rations to the labor detail leader, who was a fellow Pole.

Josef's timetable for leaving Willie's house in a month had been pushed out to six weeks, and now, with his departure date drawing closer, Ella and Josef met in earnest. Ella climbed over the fence to Josef's side. One thing led to another, and the little blanket Ella usually brought with her into the yard every night was put to use as they spent their pent-up, youthful passion on each other.

The two lovers could not get enough of each other, and Josef vowed to see her every night until he returned to the camp. His plan for how he was going to accomplish their meetings after he returned to the barracks was to stay out until the last possible moment before curfew. Ella thought she could save him some food from suppertime. Eating was important of course, but not as important as the passion they shared and the growing love between them.

Sonya mended some clothing for Josef and provided more of Gunter's old clothes. She laundered and repaired a set of old sheets for his bunk at the barracks. Willie was absent often, dating Helga. Josef suspected he knew about Ella.

If it was true, Josef admired Willie for his discretion.

Finally, the day came for Josef to return to the barracks. It was a Sunday, when most of the laborers were not working. Josef placed his meager belongings in the hall—a bundle of clothing and sheets, crutches, and some food Sonya had given him—and then went into the kitchen to bid farewell to Frau Mirz. She was sitting at the kitchen table, drinking tea. Her face looked drawn, and Josef thought she had been crying. He knew he would miss her and sat on a chair across the table from her.

"Frau Mirz, I have come to say farewell and to thank you for everything you have done for me. You have made my life bearable and provided me with a clean and safe place to recuperate. I will always remember your kindness."

Sonya sighed, "I know you feel you must be with your brother. But I will miss you, and whatever happens with the war, I wish you well. I made some bread for you and Michael."

"I packed it already, Frau Mirz, and will share it with Michael. It looks delicious, as it always does. Thank you."

He paused for a moment.

"We've shared a lot of bread and tea together this past year, haven't we? It seems we got to know each other over bread and tea, doesn't it?"

Sonya gently nodded in agreement, and quickly added, "Yes, and cabbage, too. We've eaten a lot of it," she smiled, reaching across the table to take Josef's left hand in hers.

"Take care of yourself, and you are welcome to come by if you can. Maybe I can even find an excuse for you and Michael to do some work here and you can come together. Maybe."

"Frau Mirz, *Danke. Vielen dank für alles*—thank you so much for everything."

Josef got up and so did Sonya. She walked to him, and hugged the boy who had been through so much, the boy who reminded her of Gunter, the boy who lost a leg in a war that was not his doing, the boy who was now a young man.

His voice cracked, "Goodbye, Frau Mirz." He headed for the front door, where Willie helped him with his gear.

"I'll be home later, Mother," Willie called.

"Yes, Willie," she called back.

As Willie and Josef headed outside, Sonya slowly stood up, placed her teacup in the sink, and looked out her kitchen window. It was a sunny afternoon, and although the spring air was warm enough to enjoy the outdoors, she wrapped a large scarf around her neck and buttoned her sweater right up to it. As she stepped in the backyard, she felt the earth give a little under her feet. Everything smelled fresh, and the sun warmed her face as she walked around the garden, beyond the small vegetable patch. There was a granite rock alongside it, a rock her husband suggested he remove when they cleared some of the yard for a garden. Their sons were both under seven years old at that time, and she told him she preferred to keep it since it was just large enough to accommodate the bottoms of two little boys. At about their knee-height, Willie and Gunter liked to sit on the rock together. She could see them, even now. In the warm weather they would sit on it back to back, and read. She pictured them in their shorts, long stockings, and white shirts—talking, eating apples, making designs in the dirt, and tossing small pebbles, trying to outdistance each other.

"Where has it all gone?" she wondered, wiping tears from the corners of her eyes with the tips of her two index fingers.

"How many times did I look out the kitchen window and see my two boys together on that rock? And what will become of Josef now? Willie, Gunter, Josef—what does it matter who is German or Polish? They are all just boys, and each is someone's son, some dead, some alive."

She understood Josef unwittingly filled a void left by Gunter's death. Yet she also knew Josef wasn't Gunter and had another path in life to follow. A flurry of concerns raced through her mind. "Would he break some rule and get in trouble? Would he too, be killed? Would he get sick? Would he ever be free?"

Most of all, she wanted him to be free. "Isn't that the greatest demonstration of a mother's love, even a surrogate mother, to want her child to be free, to have choices in life? How will Josef survive?"

She approached the granite rock and gently touched it, as though she could caress her two young sons again. And as she looked to the right toward the stone wall separating her yard from her neighbor's garden, she saw a cluster of wispy, spring-green clover pushing its way through a fissure in the heavy gray stone, softening the hard edges of the wall. Below it, on the ground, a cluster of crocuses she had planted years ago was beginning to bloom, their heads barely above the soil. She was always amazed to see delicate young plants punch their way through soil or light snow, reach for the sun, and then grow bright and strong, despite their inhospitable environment, despite their seeming fragility.

"Is this not Josef?" she laughed.

Her amazement gave way to relief, and then to conviction. Josef, like the clover in the wall and the crocus in the ground, was stronger and more resilient than anyone suspected, and she believed he, eventually, would thrive.

"If his freedom means he has to escape, or that Germany loses the war, so be it."

Sonya continued her walk in the garden, greatly relieved by the good omens she believed she saw in the rock and in the soil, surprised at how nonchalantly she could even think of Germany's defeat.

She was unaware Willie and Josef were still in the ambulance in front of the house, saying their goodbyes. Willie insisted on driving Josef to the camp. Expecting him to walk with a bundle of his belongings, some food, and crutches, was not realistic. Driving a laborer was against the rules, but so was taking him to the hospital, feeding him, clothing him, and giving him a place to recuperate from surgery.

Willie absentmindedly twirled his signet ring, and looked at Josef in the front passenger's seat.

"Are you a ready to go?"

"Yes...and thank you, Willie. Thank you. You saved my life. You, the doctor, and your mother."

"I was glad to help and I enjoyed having you in the house. I hope all goes well for you and Michael. And I hope the war is over soon."

They clasped hands firmly and held them longer than one would normally hold hands in a handshake.

"Willie, take care of your mother. She is a gentle lady who has been hurt by the war. And you have been a good friend."

"If you ever have a chance, stop by the house. And please don't do anything that will get you into trouble. We've all worked too hard to save you and get you well."

I think he knows about Ella and me!

"I'll be careful, Willie," he lied, "and I'll attempt to obey the rules."

They drove to the barracks in silence, just ten minutes by automobile. When they arrived, the guardsman opened the gates to let the ambulance on the grounds, past the barbed wire fence.

At the barracks office, all the necessary paperwork was signed and stamped, transferring oversight of Josef to the commander. It was late afternoon, and the soft glow of a waning sun bathed the whitewashed buildings in a golden tone. They almost looked inviting, in a rustic way. Weeds in various shades of green and yellow were sprouting at the bases of the buildings, and low bushes were beginning to show buds and a fuzz of lime green, softening the hard edges of each cabin.

Although Josef hated his life as a prisoner, returning to the barracks to be with his brother and other Poles gave him a feeling of coming home.

As they parted, Willie and Josef nodded to each other and simply said "Goodbye." They did not shake hands or show any other sign of familiarity. No action between them indicated one had saved the other's life, or cleaned out a shed together, or talked of girls, the war, and their families, or shared a fire on cold nights, or drank ale together. To an outsider, Willie was just

Josef's ride to the barracks. To an outsider, there was no friendship.

And so they parted silently, not knowing when, or if, they would ever see each other again.

~∾∾~

Josef was assigned to the same cabin as his brother, and he promptly went there. As he stepped over the wooden threshold, all eyes turned to him.

Michael jumped off his bunk and embraced his younger brother. Of the nine men in the room, Josef knew six of them, who greeted him with smiles and waves, handshakes, and warm hellos. The others were quickly introduced.

The first thing Josef noticed was their old, overused clothing. Most of their shirts and slacks were faded and all the boots were worn, some even sporting holes on their soles.[13] However, they looked clean. The German bureaucracy had a process for repairing clothing or getting replacement clothing for laborers, but compared to the clothing Frau Mirz had provided him, they wore rags.

He also saw how gaunt they were, compared to him. He had been like them too, but a year in the Mirz home had allowed him to fill out to a weight approaching normal.

He refused to dwell on the shabbiness of the place or to rue his decision to leave the comparative luxury and genuine cleanliness of Frau Mirz's house. This barracks camp is where he belonged. He had rarely spoken Polish in the last year, and now, the conversation would be easy, and his brain wouldn't have to work so hard, thinking in Polish and speaking in German. It wore him out.

Michael directed him to a lower bunk. There was a straw palette, and Josef suspected it was teeming with bugs of some kind. He stood before it, hesitant, wondering if he had made the right choice, after all. Slowly and deliberately, forcing the thought of vermin out of his mind, he unfolded the old white sheet Sonya had given him and laid it on the palette, gently tucking in the corners, as though he had the finest bed in Germany. His blanket would be a quilt she insisted he take. Laborers who worked on farms were usually provided with a palette and blanket by the farmers, so he did not feel he had overly luxurious bedding compared to everyone else. The difference was his were crisp and scrupulously clean. Coming from Frau Mirz's house, he knew there wouldn't be a germ on them for a while.

Everyone was interested in his story about the accident and amputation, and, of course, he showed off his new leg.

Michael took him aside and cautioned him.

"You'd better make sure no one steals your leg when you are asleep. It could be sold for some good money. It would be best if you sleep with it."

"I am not going to sleep with the leg on! It's too heavy."

"Then take it to bed with you. Put it next to you in bed. What do you think will happen to you if you don't have it?"

Josef was speechless. "They are Poles, just like us! Who would steal it?"

"Someone who is desperate."

"Who?"

"I don't know. It could be anyone, either today, tomorrow, or a month from now. Please don't chance it, Josef. Sleep with the leg."

After he prepared his bunk, he walked around the room, familiarizing himself with it again. He had never paid much attention to the printed rules posted on the walls. Most of them were official sets of instructions about how slave laborers must behave; others outlined for the prisoners what Germans were not allowed to do in their interactions with slave laborers or other captives, such as prisoners of war.

They were written in German, and in some places, there were Polish translations handwritten next to them. As Josef read them, he realized the extent to which Frau Mirz and Willie had taken chances by helping him.

Germans were not allowed to eat with the laborers; Germans were prohibited from offering them transportation or providing them with clothing; Germans were to consider the laborers and prisoners of war as enemies at all times; Germans could not provide medical assistance; Germans were not to offer or share newspapers with captives, or make radio broadcasts available to them.[14]

Maybe they were tired of the war, or maybe they had just seen enough suffering, because Sonya and Willie had broken all the rules. Every one of them. He pictured the authorities sending a list of rules to each household in Germany, outlining what they could and could not do, regarding slave laborers. Josef said a silent prayer for Willie and Sonya, asking God to relieve their grief over the loss of Herr Mirz and Gunter.

The most obvious regulation regarding forbidden activities concerned contact with the opposite sex. Bold, large letters screamed at the reader, stating that any prisoner involved in a romantic or sexual liaison with a German would receive severe punishment—usually death.

But Josef knew this rule already. He had ignored it and planned to continue ignoring it.

Michael and Josef ate a simple meal of bread and some cheese that night. Josef was told about the different jobs the workers were doing. Since it was late spring, many of them spent long days on nearby farms tending to ground preparation, planting, and animal care. All the workers arose before dawn, and farm workers were on the road by 6:00 a.m., walking to their assignments. Farm laborers were usually fed a simple breakfast by the farmers, as well as lunch, and sometimes supper. The farmers and their families usually ate at the same table with their workers, ignoring the rules and finding it too much of an inconvenience to create a separate table, as they were required to do.[15] As the war droned on, workers believed many Germans were not as eager to follow the rules, and some farmers seemed to have good relationships with their laborers.

Josef had been working on carpentry jobs throughout the village, and he had been told he would continue to do that kind of work. The walk from the barracks to the job site was a little longer than from Willie's house, so he would have to get up a little earlier. He was unable to stand on his feet all day and do farm work even though, in the warmer weather, he would have preferred to be outdoors.

He and Michael talked a lot that night, before lights out at 10:00 p.m., sharp. Michael mentioned that there had been a big push for more sanitary conditions in the barracks and as a result, the workers could shower more frequently, although with cold water, and wash their clothing more often, too. Insecticidal soap was also readily available for them now to keep the lice at bay, and sleeping palettes were treated monthly. Josef wondered if Frau Mirz had marched to the commander's door, banged hard on it, and demanded more cleanliness. He smiled warmly as he envisioned her lecturing the tall man in his crisp uniform.

Michael talked about the war and what he had heard. He was working on a farm, and people talked—Germans, Poles, and anyone else.

1944, so far, had not been a good year for the German war effort, and the year wasn't even half over. It was only late May.

The Allies had landed in Anzio, Italy in January, and the German Army had retreated from its stronghold there. The Allies also bombed the monastery at Monte Cassino, while the British had dropped over three thousand tons of bombs on Hamburg, and the Germans had surrendered in the Crimea.[16]

The laborers, though, did not know with certainty if any of these events had actually transpired. All they knew is what they overheard when the Germans talked among themselves, as though the prisoners were not in their businesses, factories or farms, working right alongside them. Sometimes, a worker had an opportunity to glance at a newspaper. But newspapers, being highly censored and full of pro-German propaganda, were not to be trusted, either. If a German newspaper reported a German defeat, the prisoner who saw the headline hoped it was being understated.

As the hopeful buzz about a massive invasion persisted, it seemed logical to some of the slave laborers that it might come from the south, through Italy, since the Allies were already making headway there—if they could believe the rumors. But since Switzerland was a neutral country positioned between Italy and Germany, some laborers thought it would be more logical for an invasion to come via France. Others thought that if it came, it would come from both the west and the east, with the Russians spearheading it from the east, and the rest of the Allies heading toward Germany from the west.

Among all this speculation, the daily lives of the captives remained unchanged. They got up, worked until they were bone tired, ate meager rations, and received their pittance of a salary. Laborers usually earned considerably less than one *Reichsmark* for a day's work, actually closer to about half a mark, which was barely enough to offer them subsistence foodstuffs and supplies. Laborers were not allowed to keep German currency; it had to be exchanged for a kind of prisoner scrip which they could use to buy what they needed from some of the local merchants who agreed to sell goods to the laborers, all within the boundaries of the rations allotted to them.[17]

Brought up-to-date with what the prisoners believed was going on with the war, Josef lay in his simple, crude bed that night, sorry he had not made plans to meet Ella after work and before curfew on the next night, a Monday. Their meeting would have to wait until Wednesday, even if it was raining, as they had agreed when they last saw each other. They worked out a plan where Josef would meet her in a park, after dark, near her house. She would provide some supper. That would give him time to get back to the barracks by curfew; but neither of them knew if they would be able to carry out their plan.

146

Josef turned on his right side and glanced at the rules on the wall. They were faintly visible in the moonlight illuminating the room through the high windows. As though to taunt him, the most visible rule from his bed was the boldfaced edict about fraternization with Germans of the opposite sex.

Ella. Is she thinking of me?

He removed his prosthesis and placed in next to him in the bed. Beneath Frau Mirz's quilt, he held it against his chest and clasped his arms around it as though it was his lover. Knowing he had no future without it, he covered it completely with the quilt, hiding it from view, although everyone in the room knew it was there.

Hail Mary, full of grace, the Lord is with thee. Blessed art thou among women and blessed is the fruit of thy womb, Jesus. Holy Mary, Mother of God, pray for us sinners now, and at the hour of our death. Give me strength to face whatever comes next; please eliminate all lice and fleas from the planet, and give peace to Frau Mirz and Willie. Help my family in Poland, and keep Michael safe. Watch over Ella. Amen.

Within a few minutes he fell asleep to the gentle snoring, in Polish, of his older brother.

The Walkow Brothers

Left: Michael, the eldest; Middle: Pyotr, the youngest; Right: Josef
Estimated date of each photo is approximately late 1940s.

Courtesy Monica Walkow Dudzinski

18 - Living Dangerously

In the weeks following his return to the barracks, Josef continued to work at carpentry and machinery assignments throughout Stockach. Everywhere, there was a stir in the air, and the laborers heard snippets of information gleaned from whispers among the Germans about an impending Allied invasion somewhere on the French coast.

"Could it be true?" all the laborers wondered.

At the barracks each night, rumors about an invasion were always the main topic of conversation. Each laborer shared anything he may have heard during the day.

It gave the Poles a cautious hope; it was a hope they wanted to believe in, a hope they inhaled with shallow breaths, fearing it would dissipate when they exhaled. Their hopes seemed to be vested in the Americans who, of all the fighting Allies, seemed to the laborers most likely to succeed. They had officially been in the war since late 1941, and were considered the freshest forces, although they had been fighting for almost three years.

But life in Stockach was still quiet compared to the rest of Germany, and Ella and Josef took every opportunity they could to see each other.

They met in a nearby park a few times and discovered they were not the only mixed nationality couple to take advantage of the night. They would sometimes spot other young couples also engaged in forbidden relationships, furtively hiding among tall, full bushes, trees, and granite rock outcroppings. They checked their surroundings often, to be sure they were undetected. Ella was particularly upset to be considered a criminal simply for loving someone, and Josef consoled her by kissing her tears. The more they met, the more they feared the authorities would raid their venue, and they found other places to meet—on the side of her employer's house or in the backyard. Ella usually brought him something to eat. Though he was so close to Willie's, he didn't make an effort to visit, focusing only on Ella. He would find a way to visit them when an assignment took him past their house—again, he would be breaking a rule. He did not want to compromise them and even more, he rebuked himself for putting Ella in grave danger, yet he couldn't keep away from her.

What am I doing to her? Suppose she gets caught? Her head would be shaved. She'd lose her job; she'd go to prison. I am going to stop seeing her! I have to see her! She is a spot of warmth in my life, a spot of softness and caring. What am I doing to her?

He was also embarrassed by the possibility of lice. Since he returned to the barracks, he was continually cleaning both his bed and himself with insecticidal soap to the point where his skin was raw, but he had Ella to consider. Some of his paltry pay went to purchasing the harsh products and he wondered if all the poisons were accumulating in him somehow, and if someday they might make him sick. But "someday" was something Josef thought about only in terms of being with Ella—not of living to old age, or becoming ill.

He decided they needed to talk about their future, or even if there was a future. It was a heavy burden for the young lovers to contemplate. This should have been the most carefree time of their lives, but it was fraught with intrigue and anxiety. They were certain of two things: they wanted to be together whatever happened with the war; and one of them would never again live in his or her homeland.

One night they identified various situations that might play out:

> Germany would win the war and Josef would remain a slave laborer.

> Germany would win the war and Josef would become a free man living in Germany,

although he would be considered a second-class member of society. They did not know if this specific scenario was even possible, but they made it one they should consider.

Germany would win the war and Josef would return to Poland.

Germany would lose the war and Josef would remain in Germany.

Germany would lose the war and Josef would return to Poland.

The war would never end. They didn't think this could happen, but they included it, nonetheless.

After they identified the options, Ella added, "I wish I could tell my mother about you."

"Do you think that would be wise?"

"No, it would be completely foolish for me to tell her. But being in love with you, I want to tell everyone how wonderful you are."

Josef smiled. *She doesn't know how stubborn I am. Maybe this is what "love is blind" means, after all. And, as kind and as pretty as she is, I am sure there are some things I won't like about her either, but right now, she is perfect.*

"Why are you smiling, Josef?"

"Oh, I am just thinking about how wonderful love is."

He kissed her and they held their embrace, drinking in each other's scent so they could hold on to it until their next meeting.

"Josef, have you told your brother about us?"

"Not exactly. But I think he knows. He keeps reminding me of the rules posted on the barracks walls. Besides, there is a

Polish girl he likes in the women's barracks, but that's forbidden, too. So I think he understands how I feel."

Ella sighed. Since any public acknowledgement of their love was forbidden, they spoke of dreams, what-ifs, and maybes.

"When the war is over, Ella, I think we should get married."

"Married? You are asking me to marry you? Do you suppose we would be allowed to get married?"

"I don't know."

"Maybe we would need to get out of Germany, maybe go to Poland, to be with your family."

"Ella, as much as I love my family, as much as I miss them, returning to Poland is trading this life of slavery for another one where I would have no right to make my own decisions about my life—what education I could pursue, what job I would have, where I would live. Have you exposed yourself to what happened in Russia during and after the Bolshevik Revolution? Did you study it in school?"

"Yes, of course we studied it. And it was not presented in a favorable light. We learned private property was confiscated, food shortages were common, and people were not free to select their own jobs or even move from place to place. I wouldn't want to live like that, either, at least not forever."

"My country—Poland—has been overrun from both the east and from the west many times in the past. This war is another set of invasions, from both of those directions. Poland is invaded by tanks and aircraft, and we fight back with horses and swords. It's impossible! And now, with all the reports we hear of Russian advancement into Poland, the country seems to be headed for an existence under Russian control and will, I think, probably turn Communist. Poland does not possess the ability to repel the Russians or anyone else."

"I'm curious. Do we call them Russians or Soviets?"

"Who cares, Ella. They're invaders. It does not matter at all what they are called."

"Isn't German control better, then, than Soviet control?"

Josef had been looking down at the ground and his head shot up at Ella's comment.

"Not for me, Ella," he snapped.

She stared at him. "I'm so sorry, Josef. I should not have said that. I think the only way you would want Poland governed is by fellow Poles."

Before he responded, he carelessly grasped Ella's shoulders with an earnestness that made her wince. He saw her response and weakened his grip.

"I'm sorry, Ella. I didn't mean to hurt you."

She withdrew from him, and annoyed, she tightened her lips and did not respond.

Josef explained his sudden intensity. "Communism is not for someone with his own ideas. I want to direct my own life, with you by my side. I will not go back to Poland it if turns Communist."

She had never seen him quite this intense about politics.

"But if you don't return, you may never see your parents or friends again."

Josef didn't have any real response. He looked at her, nodded, and replied softly, "I know...I know."

"Josef, I don't want to be the reason you may never see your family again."

Taking her hand, he responded, "I will see my family again, Ella, but it may not be for a few years." He paused, and took a deep breath—a breath of resignation, as though he knew the next few seconds would change his life.

"I love you. Will you marry me?"

"Yes, I think so," she nodded and looked into his eyes.

"You *think* so? You aren't sure, Ella?"

"I am sure about you. I'm just not sure about the world. Yes, I'll marry you, if we can."

So their plans had begun. Somehow, someday, they'd marry. What came after that, they didn't know. And that night they agreed to see each other less frequently, limiting themselves to about once a week. They wanted to decrease the odds of getting caught, separated, and punished.

~~~~

The long-rumored Allied invasion happened at Normandy, France on June 6th 1944. The Germans had been fooled into thinking it would have occurred elsewhere along the French coast,[18] so the element of surprise the Allies counted on was effective. They made progress liberating French towns and villages.

As spring warmed into summer, news came about Cherbourg, France. The Americans had liberated the town and the British liberated Caen, France, while the Soviets liberated Vilnius in Lithuania. Florence, Italy was liberated, too. It seemed the Allied invasion from the west and south, and the Soviet invasion from the east were freeing city after city, and town after town from Nazi rule.[19] All of the prisoners considered this good news, and the quest for information by any means became an obsession with the laborers in the barracks. There had been another plot to kill Hitler, and the perpetrators were hanged or shot.[20] The war in the Pacific was still raging. The Americans freed Guam and the Marianas Islands, expecting to use them as naval bases for the eventual attack on the Japanese mainland. But the war in the Pacific seemed remote to the prisoners, as though it existed in another dimension.[21]

Josef sometimes thought of Willie and Frau Mirz, and how they were handling all the news. Late one afternoon, as he was repairing some windows in a shop, Willie saw him and stopped to talk.

"Hello, Josef."

"Hello, Willie! It's nice to see you. How is your mother?"

"She is busy, as usual." Willie started to say "She misses you," but checked himself. They were out in public.

It was awkward. They wanted to shake hands, but avoided showing any signs of friendship. Again, the rules, always the rules....

"You know, the shed needs some work again. Would you like for me to arrange for you to come by and fix it?"

"What needs to be fixed, Willie?"

Willie leaned in closer to Josef. "Nothing," he whispered. I just thought it would be nice. I can ask the camp commander, if you would like."

"That would be fine. How about Michael?"

Lately, Josef noticed Michael was uncharacteristically moody, vacillating between bouts of verbal irritability and uncommunicativeness. He worried his brother might collapse emotionally someday, and try to escape.

Unlike Michael's experience, and despite the loss of his leg, Josef had enjoyed a respite from the war's harshness by spending a little over a year with the Mirz family. Michael, on the other hand, had been unrelentingly deprived of cleanliness, adequate nutrition, and warmth far longer. Having a day out at the Mirz house might improve his spirits, so Josef did not hesitate to ask Willie to include Michael in the visit.

"I'll ask about him too," Willie offered. "If anyone wants to know, I need to mend the shed's roof. It leaks a little, and I store some ambulance supplies in the shed. We can't let them get wet."

"I don't think I can climb on the roof."

Willie leaned in to talk in a whisper again, "Josef, I said there is nothing that needs to be fixed. I can climb on the roof, or Michael can, and we can *pretend* to fix it."

Josef smiled, "I understand."

"How is your leg, Josef?"

"I am doing well, and getting more accustomed to it every day. Please let your mother know I use the socks she gave me as padding."

"I will let her know."

Within a month, Willie arranged for the two brothers to make a Sunday visit, with a meal, of course. After they played at fixing the shed's roof, they all ate supper outside in the garden. It was simple fare: potato pancakes, applesauce, some bacon, cabbage, rye bread, and a few pears. They did not talk of the war, although it was the topic on everyone's mind. Ella saw them, but did not wave. She and Josef had planned their strategy ahead.

Sonya noticed Josef was thinner and Michael was restless. She prepared a package of potato pancakes for them to take back to the barracks.

"They are good warm or cold," she advised.

As they parted, Michael extended his hand to Willie and then to Frau Mirz. "Thank you for supper. I enjoyed the food and the company, and will always appreciate the compassion and generosity you've shown to my brother and me." He said it as though he did not expect to see them again, as though the war would soon end. He then added, "If the time comes to make it known, I will be sure to mention your kindness to the Allies, if they liberate us."

Sonya drew in a short breath. Willie's jaw clenched. Josef was dumbstruck, stunned Michael would say what he did. He looked at his brother through fierce eyes, as though telling Michael to "Shut up."

"I suppose it is possible the war will end soon and Germany might lose," offered Willie, stiffly. "I have just never heard it mentioned before."

"Willie, Frau Mirz, I do not mean to offend you, I merely wish to acknowledge you."

Willie walked them to the door. The brothers left the house with enough time to return to the barracks by curfew.

As they walked back to the camp, Josef angrily upbraided Michael, "How could you be so rude?"

"It is a very real possibility the war will end soon, and not end well for Germany. Thank God!"

"But these people have been wonderful to me—and you, too."

"That may be so, Josef, but they are still Germans, still the enemy, just as we are their adversaries. I can't imagine they want their country to lose the war. I know you've lived with them and trust them. I do too, to some extent, but not as completely as you do."

"Didn't you see how shocked Frau Mirz was when you implied Germany might lose the war?"

"Do you have any idea how shocked *I* was to be a prisoner of war, and then a slave laborer? Don't you remember how shocked *you* were to be captured and sent away from home? Don't you remember *that*?" Michael hissed back, his voice escalating.

"Michael, don't hate them. In some ways they are victims of Hitler's war, too. Heart to heart, they aren't our enemies."

They walked to the barracks in silence, at Josef's pace. Josef despondently realized his brother's heart had been broken and his spirit scarred, and nothing could ever fully restore them. As he walked beside Michael, he understood the wounds of his brother's long captivity might be deeper and more searing than the irreversible loss of his own leg.

Michael silently kept an unhurried pace walking alongside Josef. Josef did not interrupt his brother's silence. He was too angry at him, and too heartbroken for him.

Once or twice Michael looked over at Josef, who did not know his words, "Heart to heart, they aren't our enemies," had greatly impressed his older brother.

In September and October of 1944, the war news was gloomy for Germany, although the official media always tried to put a positive spin on battles, retreats, and defeats.

But much had happened.

Paris had been liberated and De Gaulle paraded the length of the Champs Élysée in triumph, courtesy of the Allies. An uprising against the Nazi regime was still in progress in Warsaw, Poland, and Allied troops had entered Belgium. Finland made peace with the Russians. On September 22nd, the Germans fighting in France, at Boulogne, surrendered. Romania was liberated from Nazi rule by the Russian and Romanian troops. The U.S. First Army arrived in Germany and occupied the German border city of Aachen after much Allied bombing.[22]

The laborers in the barracks were smiling more now. With news, however fleeting or scant, of every German defeat, they felt the chains of their bondage grow weaker. They also noticed a change in attitude among their German employers. Some seemed more talkative. Others offered more food, if they had it. It was subtle, it was small, but the change was real to the prisoners. They cautiously dared to hope the end of the war and Germany's defeat were imminent.

Ella and Josef continued to meet whenever they could, and they always talked about all the permutations of what might transpire in the future.

On one of those nights, Josef lost track of time. In a panic, he realized he would not make it back to the barracks, despite the new, later curfew—9:00 p.m., rather than 8:00 p.m. He needed to return immediately. He was grateful that lately, the gates had not been closed at 9:00 p.m., but closer to 10:00 p.m., when the prisoners were locked in the barracks.

Ella wanted him to stay in the town, in a park somewhere, or feign illness and collapse on the street. But Josef told her he couldn't do that and was concerned about what might happen to Michael if the guards discovered his absence.

They parted quickly that night, terrified they would not see each other again.

As he slowly walked away, Ella stood in place, staring at him until he was out of sight.

Fortunately, the night was moonless. Josef walked a dozen steps at a time, then stopped to hide in bushes or behind buildings. He wore his jacket inside-out, to hide the "P" patch.

When he neared the camp, he concealed himself behind some fully leafed bushes. Stealthily, he studied the guard on duty, and noticed the guard's back was toward the gate for about two minutes at a time on his route. Normally, it wouldn't be a security risk because the gate would have been closed. But the guards had become sloppy lately, and their laxity offered an opportunity that would work to Josef's advantage.

Although he knew the guard on duty, he had to assume he might nonetheless be reported to the commander for returning after curfew. Nothing could be taken for granted.

Josef made his move. He entered the compound while the guard's back was toward him. He made it to one of the buildings, where he had to hide again, sheltered by shadows and more dense shrubbery. Finally, he made it to his building.

He opened the door, entered the building quickly, and sighed with relief. But his panicked, furious brother pushed him hard against the wall. Sobbing and terrified, Michael grabbed him by the collar and shook him hard.

"What are you doing, you fool? Are you crazy? Don't do this Josef! Don't get yourself killed when the war is almost over."

"I'm sorry, Michael. I lost track of time," Josef protested.

"It's not worth it. Who is she?"

Josef didn't answer him, and wrenched himself away from Michael's grasp. It seemed so much harder for Michael now, with the end possibly in sight. *Maybe he can smell freedom, and is terrified it will never come.*

Josef would not betray Ella, but promised his brother he would never miss curfew again.

He kept that promise.

Remains of WWII German Gunnery Turret

This photograph shows the interior of a German gunnery turret on the bluffs of Pointe du Hoc, Normandy. It is one of many the Germans used to defend the French coast and try to repel the Allied D-Day assault on Normandy.

Photo credit: Patricia Walkow

19 - Speculation and Hope

The winter of 1944-1945 seemed very cold to Josef and Ella. They could not meet outside for very long, nor could they be seen together. With each passing week, the war news sounded more dismal for Germany. Ella was not overly upset at her country's possible defeat, since it meant it would all be over and she and Josef could be together. She was angry, though — angry at the news trickling out about concentration camps, and horrified at how her country could do such things to people. Mortified, actually, and unsure if it was completely accurate. The rawness of the news made her wonder if it wasn't mostly Allied propaganda. How on earth could her country do what it was accused of doing? And was it true so many roads and railways had been bombed to rubble? Transportation of goods had become difficult, and she felt threatened by the resulting food shortages, clothing shortages, fuel shortages, and dozens of tragic newspaper images of bombed cities all over Europe.

She turned to books to quell her anxiety. Sometimes she read passages she thought were beautiful or inspiring to Josef. She helped him read German better, and he introduced her to some Polish words and phrases. Near Christmas Day they exchanged small presents. She crocheted him a scarf from some old wool she had scavenged in town, and he whittled a small wooden bird for her.

She knew two other young women who were seeing Polish captives. While they didn't talk about it together, they would acknowledge each other in the street or in a shop, with a simple nod. They knew each other from glimpses they caught of one another in previous months, warmer months, when they spent evenings in the nearby park.

Ella was a little surprised no one raided the park, but she was also grateful.

161

Josef did see Willie and Sonya again, presumably to repair something relating to the ambulance. Josef expressed his regret for his brother's behavior when they were all together in the garden the previous summer.

"I want to apologize for what my brother said the last time he was here. It was rude of him. He is tired of the war and he should not have said what he did."

"He spoke his mind," Sonya replied.

"No one ever openly mentioned to us the war effort might be lost for Germany. Hearing it was a shock, even if sometimes I think it to myself," Willie said. "Your brother's saying it made it seem so very possible. That is what troubled us."

"I think it is going to end soon," Sonya said "and I am glad of that, but I fear what will happen to we Germans if we lose."

Josef was quiet at Sonya's comment. He could only think about what he had seen during the course of his assignments before he came to Stockach. He thought of the many reports being made now, accompanied by disturbing photographs of concentration camps with emaciated, nearly mad survivors, and piles of bodies.

He suspected liberating forces made sure these images were made public in any media possible: descriptions in Allied radio broadcasts, flyers, newspapers, and film. Although the Nazis still controlled the media within Germany, the free world had access to newly discovered horrors. His mind raced.

Certainly, the entire world will be incredulous and vengeful. Certainly they will hate the Germans and not believe them if they deny knowledge of the concentration camps. Certainly ordinary Germans might be blamed for not stopping the cruelty and slaughter. How could they not have known? Are they so detached? Are they wearing blinders? Why haven't any of the attempts on Hitler's life been successful? Germans in high places have wanted him dead, probably dreading what he has done to Germany. Will today's German children and children not yet born have to bear both shame and responsibility for their nation's actions...actions they had nothing to do with? What would be the burden for any children he and Ella may have—half German, half Polish?

He expected Willie and Sonya had read and heard the same stories he had, but didn't know if, during the war, they suspected or even knew the concentration camps existed. He, however, was acquainted with them from his time in Gliwice, a work camp associated with the Auschwitz network of camps. If Poland had committed the crimes Germany had, he surely would have been ashamed. No doubt Willie and Frau Mirz were appalled. They were good people and he didn't need to rub salt into their wounds.

So, after a long silence, he just nodded at Sonya's comment expressing her concerns about what would happen to Germans if Germany lost the war. He also noted how drawn she looked.

"I don't think any of us knows what it is going to be like when the war ends, Frau Mirz," he responded.

Perhaps Michael was right to say he'd put a good word in for them with the Allies.

As they parted that night, Josef, Sonya, and Willie were still on good terms. He could not imagine how Sonya felt—losing a husband and a son to a cause that might be lost.

The men in the barracks went about their jobs that winter anticipating relief in the hopefully, not too distant future. As February of 1945 turned to March, and the March air turned warmer, even Michael brightened. It seemed each report or rumor of Allied victory buoyed him.

Late one night as they rested in their bunks, the brothers speculated about the end of the war.

Josef asked, "What do you think the end of the war will be like, Michael?"

"Wonderful."

"Be more specific. What do you mean?"

"Wonderful—that's all it has to be, for me."

"Come on, Michael. I'm serious. Of course it will be great when the war ends. Do we just pack up our gear, exit the gate, and walk east? Just like that? Like the years 1939 to 1945 never happened?"

"I don't know what it will be like. I hope to get to know Stephania better."

Stephania was the girl Michael seemed to be interested in. She, too, was a Polish captive and their relationship thus far had just been smiles and nods.

"Won't we need papers, or something? Don't we have to be released from our jobs, Michael?"

"We aren't here voluntarily, remember? We shouldn't have to wait for anyone to release us from anything, right?"

"I'm not sure. Maybe we have to wait for official transports to take us somewhere."

Michael leaned over the side of the top bunk, looking down at Josef on the bottom bunk. "I don't trust the Germans to send us anywhere!"

"You're right about that. But, it would be the Allies, not the Germans who would be directing things. Don't you think?"

"That's true."

Josef mused, "I wonder what our little brother looks like. And mother and father, too. Their faces are less and less clear to me, Michael."

"I know what you mean," replied Michael. "I'm also happy Pyotr has not been forced into captivity, too, although I don't know why."

They had recently received a letter from their younger brother. Based on the postmark date, it had taken over four months to get to them. Their parents were alive and living in the eastern lands, part of Ukraine. For Josef and Michael, the letter's arrival was a relief from the abyss of unknowns about their family. They quickly wrote back to Pyotr, but did not mention Josef's lost leg. They realized it might take months for the letter to reach Pyotr, if at all. In the earlier days of their captivity, letters arrived fairly quickly. With Germany's physical and service infrastructure impacted by the war, they didn't know if their letter would ever get to Poland. And they realized they probably wouldn't recognize their little brother if they ever saw him again. After all, he was just a little boy when they left.

"So, Josef, what will you do when the war ends?"

That was a difficult question for Josef. He didn't think his brother would understand he could not live without Ella, even if it meant he would never return to Poland, or see his parents or little brother again. His greater fear was being trapped in a country turning Communist. Both rumor and news reported the Soviets had installed a pro-Communist government in Warsaw when they freed it from German occupation in January of 1945. The effect, though, was a Poland that remained unable to chart its own course in the world. German occupation had been replaced by Soviet occupation.

"Why don't you answer me?" Michael prodded.

"I am not sure what I am going to do. I'm really not. I don't want to leave Ella, and now I can walk on my own and don't need crutches. Maybe I'll get a better leg from the Allies. I think I can stay here and find work."

Josef had just recently told Michael about Ella. Surprised at his selection of a German girl, Michael perpetually worried that Josef might get caught, while Josef frequently reminded him he was old enough to make his own decisions.

Ella, meanwhile, had visited her family in Heidelberg. Her mother, now Frau Zimmerman rather than Frau Stichler, since she had remarried after Ella's father abandoned them, remarked at how well her daughter looked, though thin. Many times Ella stopped herself from telling her mother about Josef. It was always on the tip of her tongue, and during her visit she feared she would blurt it out. She was relieved to return to Stockach.

The unfairness of having to hide her love stung her deeply. Secretive meetings, images of dead bodies, destroyed cities, and battle maps were not the backdrop she ever dreamed of during courtship with the man she loved. Courtship should have included romantic walks in manicured public gardens, trekking in the hills, boat rides on Lake Constance, picnics in the sun, and lunch in cafés.

She felt unduly denied an experience she always thought would exist in her life. And she blamed Hitler, Germans who supported him, and the entire Nazi party.

She once thought of keeping a diary, writing about her life and feelings. But she couldn't. It was not because she didn't know how, but rather because she didn't wish to be found out. Instead, she substituted baking the perfect apple cake for journaling her thoughts, and stewing the most tender herb-crusted roast, when it was available, for chronicling the injustices she saw and suffered.

20 - It's Over

It was as though all Europe was holding its breath.

In the spring of 1945, the Allies continued to push into Germany from all directions. In March, the Americans crossed the Rhine using the Remagen railroad bridge, and the British troops crossed the Rhine at Wesel. The Allies built pontoon bridges to move heavy equipment across the Rhine at several locations, allowing them to forge deeper and deeper into Germany. American General George Patton's troops captured the city of Mainz. Berlin continued to be bombed. Frankfurt was taken. By the end of April, the Americans liberated Buchenwald and Dachau concentration camps, while the British freed the Bergen-Belsen concentration camp. The Russians were victorious at the battle of Königsberg, less than 370 kilometers from Stockach.

In Germany, the captive laborers still toiled at their assignments. Ella still cooked, and now also prepared the fire in the fireplaces long before anyone rose in the morning. Willie continued to drive an ambulance, and Sonya endured. The guards at the barracks did their daily rounds. The laborers' employers seemed to show more respect.

Report after report of Allied progress proliferated quickly. Regardless of whether the end of the war would liberate them or occupy their homeland, people of all nationalities were anxious about what would come next.

Amid a country besieged on all sides by the Allies, Hitler celebrated his fifty-sixth birthday, secure inside his bunker in Berlin. But Berlin had been invaded by the Russians, or as some called them, the Soviets, and, on the 27th of April, the city was encircled by the Red Army. On April 30th, Hitler committed suicide, a day after he married his long-term partner, Eva Braun, who also took her own life.[23]

Fighting for a now hopeless cause, many German troops surrendered to Allied forces throughout Europe.

On May 2nd, the Battle of Berlin ended. German General Helmuth Weidling surrendered the city—unconditionally—to Soviet General Vasily Chuikov. It was the surrender scenario most feared by the German populace, as the Soviet treatment of conquered peoples was known to be brutal.

On May 8th, the cease-fire took effect at 12:01 a.m., and the day became known as V-E (Victory in Europe) Day.

The war in Europe was officially over.

Whether conquered or triumphant, the people of Europe finally and slowly exhaled.

On day one of the rest of their lives, Josef, Michael, and their barracks mates awakened naturally at around 5:30 a.m. There was no banging of chains as the doors were being unlocked. No command to hurry, *schnell, schnell,* from the guards.

Some men pushed the doors of their buildings open with little resistance. The chains gave way, since they had been quietly unlocked in the early morning hours, immediately after the cease fire took effect.

There were no guards at all, anywhere in sight. The gates to the compound were also wide open.

The men recognized what this meant, and they shouted to the air and hugged each other. Their jubilance ran out into the streets, which were devoid of any Germans.

But what now?

Unlike most of the Allied world—The U.S., Soviet Union, France, England, Netherlands, Norway, and many other countries—the euphoria of May 8th did not last all day for the men in the barracks. They didn't know what to do.

Always relying on the traditions of their Catholic faith, the men from the barracks formed a group and said simple prayers.

As usual, Josef privately amended his Hail Mary prayer:

Hail Mary, full of grace, The Lord is with thee. Thank God it's over and help me figure out what on earth to do next. Holy Mary, Mother of God, pray for us sinners, now, at the hour of our freedom, and forever. Amen.

Some of the men ran to the administrative office to see what they could take. But there was little there, except for some paper and pencils, chairs, and a desk. Within a few minutes the office was bare and anything in it was finding its way back to a cabin. Other men ran out of the complex and into the streets toward some shops. Many were just stunned and stayed in place, not sure of what to do. A few left and were never seen again.

Michael and Josef, with most of the other men in their cabin, returned inside and had a breakfast of whatever food was on hand, mostly bread, some cheese, and some onions. They were strangely quiet, and their joy dissipated rapidly as they faced reality. In the coming days, how would they cope with not knowing what they should do, where they should go, or where their next meal was coming from?

One of the men asked, "Who is going to pay us for the work we have all been doing? All the camp staff is gone, and they are the ones who exchange payment from the employers into prisoner scrip."

No one answered at first. Finally, Josef said, "Since we are no longer prisoners, we don't need scrip. We have to get hold of some cash." The men nodded in agreement. Josef added, "Why don't we each go to our employers and ask them to pay us? Besides, if they still need us to do any other work, we will have some money coming to us. Only this time, we'll tell *them* how much the work will cost."

"Why would I want to spend another minute working for *them*?" one of the men said, angrily.

"Because you might be able to make some money to make it easier to travel home," Michael responded in support of his brother's idea.

169

"I'm afraid they'll shoot us if we ask them for the money they owe us," replied another worker.

"They should be more afraid we will shoot them," replied yet another man.

"Too bad we don't have any rifles," Michael said.

"I'd like to go home," someone said.

"We probably can't just go out and head toward Poland," responded Michael. "At the Polish border—and we do not even know where that is now—the guards will demand proof we are Poles who worked involuntarily in Germany."

A few men nodded in agreement.

Thinking aloud, Michael added, "We have our booklets of work assignments. They may or may not be enough verification of our nationality. The books were issued by the Germans, which might add some credence to their authenticity. And Poland is hundreds of kilometers away. Do any of you have the strength to make that journey on foot right now? I know I don't."

Most of them did not have that strength. All of them were undernourished, poorly clothed, and tired. Thankfully, none had contracted typhus or tuberculosis.

Josef added quietly, "And we must think about what it means to return home to a Poland being pushed toward Communism by the Soviet Union. It was already happening before the war. I can't imagine Russia will withdraw from Poland."

No one responded to his comment. He wondered if he was the only one thinking about it. He was also thinking about Ella.

As yet, there was still no official announcement to confirm the war was over. It left them in an uncomfortable, expectant state.

After they finished breakfast, they took stock of what they needed to do, as a group: they would alternate staying behind for part of the day to guard their belongings; most would go to their jobs and demand payment of some kind; everyone would try to obtain food; all would pool their food and plan their meals for the next few days; they would discuss how to let the Allies know they existed, and find out what would happen next.

Uncomfortable with the absence of their daily routines, the men went about the day as they had planned. Josef decided to finish the job he had been doing, if his employer agreed to pay him, and then visit Willie and Ella. He had been repairing and replacing plumbing pipes in the local hospital's kitchen. It was the same hospital where his leg had been amputated. He would, however, require immediate payment.

~~~

When Josef returned to the hospital, members of the kitchen staff stopped whatever they were doing and tentatively greeted him.

What a difference. I'm suddenly not invisible.

It was a strange new feeling for him, and an empowering one.

"I am here to finish my work, but I need to make sure I am paid. Who should I talk to?"

The workers looked at each other, not sure of what they should do. But one of the women volunteered to fetch her boss for advice, and she left the room.

Another worker offered Josef a cup of coffee and a slice of bread, which he readily accepted. He couldn't remember the last time he turned down any form of food.

Are they being nice to me because they are afraid of me? Or are they really good people who were too afraid of the Nazis?

The woman washing trays returned with her boss, the man who had sought slave labor to help with the plumbing. He and Josef walked into an alcove to talk.

Josef was direct, but not harsh.

"I want to be paid for the work I've already completed. And I want to be paid at the regular rate, not the captive rate. I also want some payment in food. Today. I will complete the work, but I insist on being paid beforehand."

The man swallowed.

The tables have certainly turned.

The man unemotionally and quietly told Josef to meet him in his office, three doors down the hall to the left.

The man left, and as the kitchen workers returned to their routine, Josef extracted the plumbing repair tools stored under the kitchen sink and arranged them on a table. Someone turned the radio on and there were announcements about the end of the war, complete Nazi defeat, and Allied victory. It had not yet been twelve hours since the war officially ended. Not knowing any other way to behave, everyone in the kitchen simply went about their chores as though nothing had changed.

Josef exited the kitchen and turned left, to the third door, as instructed. He knocked crisply, waited for a response to "Enter," and walked into the room. There was a white envelope on the desk.

"I wrote this for you," the man said, as he handed the envelope to Josef.

Written in beautiful script was a simple sentence: *"Den Arbeitnehmer, die mit diesem Hinweis genug zu essen für drei Tage zu geben."* It said, "Give the worker bearing this note enough food for three days."

"I already paid your guard for this week's work—he has the money."

Josef replied, "The guards are gone, and there is nothing in the office—no money, no supplies, nothing."

"There is nothing I can do about that."

"I am not going to work for free. I am not a volunteer," he said coldly.

The man was quiet for a moment, before he exhaled a sigh, a deep one, a sigh of resignation.

He opened his wallet, and handed Josef some money. *"Hier sind fünfzehn Marken. Es ist, was wir einen regulären Arbeitnehmer dafür zahlen würden, was Sie tun."*

"Here are fifteen marks, what I would pay a regular worker."

Josef thought a regular worker would have been paid more, but he saw it was almost all of the money in the man's wallet.

He did not insist on more money. *Better to have a job tomorrow, than be greedy today.*

"If you need any more work done at the hospital, you can find me at the barracks and we can talk about a price."

"I will keep that in mind," the man answered.

"Thank you," Josef said, as he slid the money in his pants pocket along with the hand-written note.

It took him three hours to finish the plumbing job. As he was making the repairs, no one asked him why he was continuing to work. The war had ended, but Josef had pride in his work and would not leave any of his assignments unfinished. But there was a more fundamental reason for completing the work — cash.

When he was finished, Josef washed his hands and face, and presented his note to the woman who headed the kitchen. He reproached himself for not asking what was included in a day's worth of food. But he soon found out.

She read it and went to the cupboards and icebox to get the necessary supplies: one large cabbage, four potatoes, a cup of ersatskaffe to brew, two large onions, a slab of bacon, some cereal, a loaf of dark bread, a chunk of cheese, two cups of dried apples, and a bundle of twelve cigarettes. *What am I going to do with cigarettes? Maybe I can trade them for something.*

It had been a long time since Josef saw so much food at once, the last time being in Frau Mirz's house. Yet, they were inadequate rations by any account, and he would still need to find more food. The provisions were wrapped together in newspaper, except the two cups of apples. Josef asked for them to be wrapped separately.

He left with no work assignments to do from then on. The freedom was real. It was also frightening. How would he obtain money for food or clothing?

The rest of the afternoon he could do as he pleased. It was a strange feeling for him, and he stopped himself several times from looking over his shoulder all afternoon, as though a guard would want to know what he was doing wandering around. He made his way to the Mirz house, and on his way there, he realized he wanted to see Frau Mirz even more than he wanted to see Willie or Ella.

~~∽◦∾~~

Josef knocked on Frau Mirz's front door, hoping someone was at home. Sonya answered the knock, and smiled.

"Welcome, Josef. How are you?"

"I am fine Frau Mirz. And you?"

"Good," she replied.

"And Willie?"

"Willie is working right now; he isn't home, but he is fine. Why don't you stay for a while?"

Josef was glad she asked, and he agreed to visit. But he could see she wasn't good at all. She was gaunt and pale.

"I have something for you," Josef offered.

"Me?"

"Yes, hold out your hands."

She cupped her hands, one slightly overlapping the other. Josef opened his small package of dried apples, and poured about half of them into her waiting palms.

"Thank you, Josef! But are you sure you don't need them yourself?"

"No, I have a few more. I want you to have them."

"Walk around the house. Meet me in the garden," she cajoled as she gently placed the dried apples in her apron pocket.

They sat on wooden benches facing each other across the old, weathered table. It brought back memories. Much had happened since the day she brought him some of Gunter's clothes and placed them on this same table.

"Frau Mirz, I'm certain I do not have lice," he said, and pulled a pinch of his hair straight up, exposing his scalp.

Frau Mirz looked down, more than a little embarrassed Josef could so easily read her mind. She reached for his hand.

"It's good to see you, Josef. The war. It's over, you know," she quietly and rather sadly said. "All over, just like that," and she snapped her thumb and middle finger together.

"Yes, I know," he said softly.

"Over...just like that," she said again. "Like some magician performed a magic trick and no one died."

Josef was silent. After all the bloodshed and bombings, after all the rationing and propaganda, it was over. And no one knew what would happen tomorrow or next week.

For her, the war will never really be over. How do you get over losing a husband and son?

"I don't know what happens next, what to expect, Josef," she complained.

"None of us knows what comes next, Frau Mirz."

"Do you know when you will be going home?"

Josef wasn't planning on returning to Poland if he had to leave Ella. But he didn't want to talk about all that right now.

"No, I don't know when any of us may go home, but I did hear from my younger brother recently. My parents are alive and live in what the Soviets now call Ukraine."

"I am so glad to hear that!"

"But how is Willie?"

"He is fine, still working, driving the ambulance. I am sorry he is not home right now, but I will tell him you stopped by."

"Please do that, Frau Mirz. I am looking forward to seeing him and will stop in again."

"Would you like some tea, Josef?"

He and Frau Mirz had shared so much tea together. He came to love her has a surrogate mother over tea. Now, whenever he thought of his own mother, Frau Mirz's face intruded on his memory.

"No thank you. I have someone else to see today."

He noticed she responded with an ever-so-slight smile as her eyes barely moved in the direction of the house adjoining her yard.

She knows! She knows about Ella and me.

Fear didn't seize him. It was relief, instead. But he did not acknowledge her smile.

"Where are you staying from now on?" she asked.

"I'll be returning to the barracks tonight."

"You're returning to *that* place?" she asked, incredulously.

"We are going to pool our food, make plans for the coming days, and figure out how to let the Allies know who we are."

"That sounds like a plan for you. But I have no idea what I should do, or shouldn't do."

She looked at him questioningly, as though he suddenly, being liberated, had all the answers. But he had none.

"I am sure we will all find out soon, once the Allies run things."

"The Allies," Sonya echoed. "Yes, I suppose they will tell us what we can and cannot do. I hope it won't be the Russians...the Soviets. I am afraid of them. The reports of how they are raping women all over Germany terrify me. They've been doing it ever since they were on the march towards Berlin."

Josef blushed when Sonya talked about the Russians. He hadn't thought about the Allies taking out their rage on the women, treating them like spoils of war.

He tried to comfort her, "I would be surprised if this part of Germany will be run by the Soviets. I think it might be the Americans or the French."

"We will find out soon, but I don't know if any of them will be any better than the Russians."

Josef nodded. "Let's hope whichever occupying force governs this part of Germany will be more reasonable."

Sonya nodded and Josef added, "I had better be on my way, Frau Mirz."

They both stood up, and Sonya continued to hold his hand.

As they walked together to the front of the house, Sonya asked, "Why do you still wear your jacket with the "P" patch showing? Don't you want to get rid of the patch now?"

"I had to wear it in the past to identify myself as a Pole. Now I still wear it to let everyone know I am a Pole. It should help with the Allies, I think. Funny about the patch. Nothing about it has changed, yet yesterday it identified me as the enemy, and now it lets everyone know I am not the enemy."

She gave him a sad, silent smile. "And your brother. How is he?"

That is just like Frau Mirz, to ask about Michael even if he said some upsetting words to her the last time they saw each other.

"Fine, Frau Mirz. Michael is doing well, considering how long he has been a captive. Thank you for asking. Please send my warm regards to Willie. Let him know I am thinking of him and hope to see him soon."

"I will."

They parted at the front of the house. Sonya returned inside. Standing alone in her kitchen, in front of sparsely provisioned cupboards, she searched her apron pocket for a dried apple slice. She removed one from its hiding place, and devoured it.

Josef walked around the corner to see if he could steal a glimpse of Ella. He didn't see her outside in the garden, and thought of throwing pebbles at the kitchen window or ringing the front doorbell.

Too early for that. The war ended not even twenty-four hours ago. I might frighten them.

He walked past the house a few times, trying to see if Ella was there, and if she was looking out a window. After a few tries, he headed back to the camp.

I'll visit on another afternoon.

The war was over now, and he didn't expect to hide in the shadows with Ella.

But he was wrong.

Celebrating the End of the War

Churchill, with his signature cigar, waves to a happy crowd in England on the day he broadcast the war with Germany had been won. May 8, 1945 has been known as VE (Victory in Europe) Day since then. Yet the war in the Pacific continued into August of the same year.

Courtesy The United Kingdom Government, in the Public Domain

21 - Limbo

Ella had seen him.

As Josef was trying to get her attention earlier in the afternoon, she stole a surreptitious glance at him through the kitchen window. Staring at him, she felt strangely dispassionate about the Polish young man she loved, as though he was an ant walking along a railing, undeserving of acknowledgement. She was disquieted by her vague and unfounded annoyance with him. He had done nothing to irritate or anger her. Yet she resented him.

As she washed the dishes from lunch, she realized the entire landscape of their relationship had changed since yesterday. It wasn't his fault, she knew, but his freedom disarmed her. She was unsure if she loved him only because he was available, because it was forbidden, or because she felt sorry for him.

She wondered if the end of the war would also be the end of their relationship. She asked herself if he still would want to be with her, and would she want to be with him. Because of her closeness to Josef, she was afraid she might be punished by whoever would be in charge.

The entire household had been listening to radio broadcasts that blared about how the Russians controlled eastern Germany. Stockach was in the southwest corner of the country, far away from Soviet forces. Even before peace was officially declared, conquering troops looted and humiliated the vanquished Germans. Radio and word of mouth reported how the Russians set upon any woman, of any age, and raped her, often as a gang rape, and frequently in front of any remaining male family members.[24] Such savage, ruthless acts were rampant and initially encouraged by Red Army leadership. It was as though someone in command had said "Our boys suffered; let them do what they want to Germans, including the women and girls. Debase and ravage them as much as you want, and your behavior will emasculate any remaining German men, too."

It had been a horrible day for Ella, and it was barely half over. The events of the day and the previous week, when all seemed lost for Germany, plunged her into confusion, fear, and hope, all at once. She didn't know what to think, and went about her work, pretending nothing had changed since yesterday. She tried to appear calm and in control. But on this first day of declared peace, she was frantic with uncertainty. Her stomach was at war, and she grasped it in pain throughout the day. She was queasy and frightened, like a passenger on a ship adrift in roiling seas, with neither rudder nor captain.

She wondered who would govern Germany now. When would she know? Would there be a lot of new rules? How would Germany be punished? How would *she* be punished, just for being German, just for having a relationship with Josef? Would Josef come back? Was he still interested in her? Did she want him to come back?

~୭୧୦~

Two days later, Josef returned to see Ella. She answered the doorbell when he rang it.

"Hello, Josef." She did not hug him, or touch him at all.

"May I come in?"

"I think it would be better if I come outside."

Ella grabbed a wrap from the closet in the hall and joined Josef outside. They walked around the house to the garden in the back and sat together on a wrought iron bench.

"It's over, Ella. We can be together now."

She sighed, and raised her eyebrows.

"I don't know, Josef. I don't know what to do."

"We love each other and the war has ended. What more do we need to know?" he said, somewhat impatiently.

"Somehow, I don't think it is all that simple."

"Why not?"

"Don't you have to register with the Allies to let them know who are you? Won't they make an effort to send you home to Poland?"

"I've already let them know who I am and where I am staying. I even offered my services to them, for pay, of course."

"Which soldiers are they?"

"French."

"Good," Ella sighed. I haven't seen any soldiers, yet."

"There aren't that many here, so far. The ones we spoke to told us to stay at the barracks for now. They wrote down our names and nationalities, and said they will be letting us know what we should do next."

"Does anyone have work for you to do?"

"It's too early to tell. I don't think they know what they're going to do with us, right now. I guess if they are going to set up camps—they call them displaced person's camps, or DP camps—I can do whatever work they would need. They told us they would be providing food, clothing, and medical help, and will be implementing the process of repatriating us with our countries."

The color drained from Ella's face.

"Only I'm not going."

"Do you mean you are not going to the camp or you are not going to Poland?"

"Both. I have no intentions of moving to a camp for people like me, a camp that takes me away from here."

"Do you really have a choice?"

"I will make sure I have a choice, Ella, no matter what!"

"Oh! And how are you going to do that?"

"I have no idea."

She laughed at his bravado.

"I'm serious, Ella. I want to be with you."

She looked at him, but didn't say anything. Her silence made him uneasy.

Gesturing to her with open palms, he asked, "Do you still love me, Ella?"

She sighed, "Of course I do. I just don't want to break any rules."

He laughed. "What rules? There are no rules right now."

"We've heard radio broadcasts, Josef. There will be rules, and we will most likely be governed by the French or Americans."

"Thank God it won't probably be the Russians," Josef said, relieved.

"I agree, yet nothing is certain right now. Even if it is the French or Americans, I don't know if we will be allowed to see each other."

"What do you mean, Ella?"

"There are rumors that no one is to socialize with Germans."

"They are only rumors. Why don't we wait and see what the rules really are? Then we can figure out how to break them. Really, I don't care about rules any longer. Something is always *verboten*, and if the Americans or French move in, things will still be verboten, but then they'll be called *forbidden* if the Americans take over, or *interdit* if the French take over. What's the difference? I'm sick of it."

"There's a big difference. Whatever new regulations the governing country will enforce will be for your benefit, to get you settled into your new life, whatever...whenever...wherever that will be."

Ella looked at Josef uncertainly, her head tilted, and her eyes wide, she repeated, "wherever that will be." She continued, "And I think some of those regulations will also punish me and the other Germans."

"You haven't done anything wrong, Ella."

"Neither did you. You were punished just because you are Polish; it is only logical I will be punished in some way just because I am German. Will the Allies be any better to me or Willie and Frau Mirz because we know you or helped you? I don't think so."

Ella leaned her head against his shoulder as he put his arm around her, gently touching his lips to her hair. They rested silently together in this embrace for a few minutes, and then Ella looked up at him and softly ran her hand across his cheek.

"What are you thinking?" she asked.

"I don't want to sneak around. I want to be out in the open. Don't you want to walk together, holding hands during daylight, in the park? Don't you want to take a boat ride with me on the lake?"

"You know I do. I am just saying this might not be the right time. But maybe, soon."

"So, what's next then, Ella?"

"Let's find out what the Allies want us to do or not do, and try to follow their regulations."

"I'm not good at that," Josef grinned, and looked directly at her, removing his arm from around her shoulder, and then holding both her hands.

"You're hopeless," she teased. "You'd better go; the rest of the house staff might be getting suspicious of my absence." She stood up and faced him.

"Seriously, Josef, let's try to follow the regulations. It might be easier for us to be together in the long run if we just comply with everything for a while, even if we can't see each other right away."

He didn't answer her.

"*Now* what are you thinking? I've never seen you so quiet!"

"I am thinking about the irony of it all...," he said edgily, his voice sharp, "about the irony of obeying regulations. Consider how far blind compliance with rules and regulations has taken Germany and its citizens down a path to destruction."

"Yes," she barely whispered.

Again Josef was silent. He finally stood up and gave a deep sigh, "Ella, we'll do what the Allies expect of us for a while. But if they keep us away from each other for too long, I am going to rebel. I no longer want to have to obey anybody's rules."

"Josef, don't do anything foolish. You survived the war. Now be sure you survive the peace."

He smiled at her comment. She was right. *It might be more dangerous now than during the war. Yes, it just might be.*

"It's decided, then," he said. We'll figure out what's expected of us and we'll try to be compliant."

"Yes, it's decided. Let's do that." She added, "I love you."

"I love you too, Ella."

They parted with a lingering hug and a tender kiss, not knowing what the rules of life would be in the coming months.

~~~~~~

Over the next few weeks, Ella spent her time tending to her chores, making only an occasional trip out of the house to try to find food in the poorly stocked shops. They saw a few French soldiers who, for the most part, ignored them.

The vast majority of people in the world did not know what had transpired at the Yalta and Potsdam Conferences, where the Allies prepared for the end of the European conflict. During the negotiations, British, American, and Russian authorities thought France did not expend equivalent blood and treasure in the war to warrant the privilege of governing a section of Germany. But with the persistence of Charles De Gaulle, the French occupied some of southern and western Germany, including Stockach.[25] But it didn't happen immediately. Between May 8 and early summer of 1945, everyone lived in limbo, and effective governance didn't actually exist for anyone.

A French military contingent finally arrived to govern the town, and as they entered the larger squares, the Germans looked on in curiosity and resignation. Many retreated to their houses, shuttered the windows, and waited for whatever would come. French troops commandeered lodging in homes,[26] simply by walking in and demanding a room, usually in the grandest houses. Frau Mirz's house was not palatial enough to warrant housing any member of the French military. The French approach to housing was somewhat more humane than the methods used by the other Allies, who simply evicted people from their homes, giving then an hour or two to collect any necessary belongings before they were cast out into the streets. Those unfortunates had to find shelter with distant friends or families, or camp in vacant, bomb-damaged, barely inhabitable buildings.

It turned out some of the French soldiers, mostly those from French colonies, were almost as vengeful as the Russians, with no woman safe. Ella was extremely fearful being outside on her own, and her employer arranged to have supplies delivered to the house via courier, before the curfew the French had imposed. Eventually, the French command ordered soldiers to behave themselves and punished rapists with a death sentence.

Sometimes freed slave laborers jeered at Germans in the streets and also raped German women. Looting of shops was common. And everyone, whether German citizen or victim of Germany, fretted about food.

The Allied soldiers had their hands full dealing with people streaming into and out of Germany. The authorities set up temporary holding facilities for the war's human casualties, and appropriated entire buildings for those displaced by the war.

The commanders of the occupying forces made sure those who were Germany's victims received food and medical care first, and many soldiers shared their own rations. Germans were the last to receive anything.

During this same time, Josef, Michael, and many other former laborers were formally listed as displaced persons, or DPs. They presented their assignment booklets and wore their outer jackets with the "P" patch. The French soldiers asked the people in Josef's barracks to stay where they were as a temporary DP camp, but they were free to come and go within curfew guidelines. DPs finally had some freedom to make decisions. Some opted to move from place to place, looking for relatives or friends from home. Others searched for work. Josef offered his carpentry, machinery, and handyman services to the French.

Everyone looked for food, and stealing was commonplace; trespassing on farms and taking food or milk was a constant activity. The scarcity of food fueled a black market where, for the right price, food could be purchased. Cigarettes became a form of currency[27] and the Reichsmark was almost worthless.

Josef and Michael had shelter and each other. There had been no bureaucracy fully implemented yet to handle not only DPs, but also Germans returning from formerly conquered lands, prisoners-of-war, and concentration camp survivors. Everyone waited for direction, for structure, for order. And for food.

There were few roads and intact railroads to bring supplies into Germany. Logistics were a nightmare.

And there was an atmosphere of revenge, with many of the victors and liberated peoples demanding punishment of the German people.

Hitler escaped it all by committing suicide as the Russians succeeded in taking Berlin. His people would now spend the next few years in deprivation and near-starvation, and leave the next generation of Germans with a burden of guilt it did not earn.

22 - French Occupation

Everyone stumbled through the first year of life in post-war Germany.

Since 1943, the UNRRA organization, (United Nations Relief and Rehabilitation Administration) had been planning for the care of refugees—concentration camp survivors, people displaced from their pre-war homes, former slave laborers, and all other war survivors. Although it was founded by forty-four countries, seventeen of them had voting power, with the U.S. being only one of them, despite its substantially large financial backing. Seventy-five percent of the funds came from United States.[28]

But planning, by itself, didn't immediately build structures to house displaced people. Instead, the war survivors had to find shelter anywhere they could. Nor did planning instantly provide food or sanitation for thousands of slave laborers; only concrete action on location would do that. Planning could not make instantly available medical care for anyone, including the profound human catastrophe liberated from concentration camps. Nurses and doctors had to be deployed to the areas of Europe where the devastated masses congregated.

Reality involved people moving about the country, like a ceaselessly flowing brigade of insects; the land itself seemed as though it was crawling.

People were seeking relatives; ethnic Germans living in eastern lands, many for generations, had been fleeing the advancing Russians for many weeks before the end of the war. They returned to what was left of Germany, the only place that would accept them. Refugee camps were set up for different categories of the displaced. Many were open air facilities until shelters could be built, and some were in barely standing buildings, many of them partially destroyed by bombing.[29]

Those who did not have to move to a camp right away, like Michael and Josef, stayed where they were.

Then came the rules. Initially, they were just as restrictive as German rules posted in the barracks during the war. The new, Allied set of rules included a ban on fraternization with any Germans, and prohibitions against sharing food or clothing with any Germans, including children. A curfew was still in effect and had to be respected.[30]

It was as though someone just flipped a switch and placed the Germans on the receiving end of harsh treatment—not that it mattered who should get more food and who should get less. There wasn't enough food for anyone, and acquiring food by any means became an obsession. Concentration camp survivors and former slave laborers were allotted almost twice the number of calories per day as German citizens. Yet, too much food, or even the wrong foods, could kill someone who had endured starvation[31] or extreme malnutrition.

The black market, if you had some money or something of value to trade, offered a conduit for obtaining sustenance or other goods. Reichsmarks were almost worthless, and cigarettes became a coveted currency. Clothing and shoes were sorely needed.

Fortunately, Stockach was not far from the northwest end of Lake Constance, across from neutral Switzerland. Unlike large, industrial, German cities, it did not endure relentless Allied bombardment. Surrounded by vineyards and farmland, there was some food available, for a price. People from all strata of tattered German society traded whatever valuables they had for milk, a piece of meat, or flour. Jewelry, gold, clocks, antiques, and anything else desired by farmers, served as trading currency. As a result, many German farmers kept their own bellies satisfied and grew financially comfortable at the expense of their countrymen.

Josef spent his time doing odd jobs for the French. He helped build shelters, repair motors, do whatever was needed. It was not unlike the work he did for the Germans. He earned both money and cigarettes, which he could then trade for food and goods. He wanted to feel secure and to help Ella, Sonya, and Willie.

When the Nazi Party was in power, he took chances: broke curfew, shared meals with Germans, and dated a German girl. Since the occupation, he didn't break any rules. It was not like him to be so accommodating, and his own actions surprised him. He didn't know why he had suddenly become so meek.

Maybe Ella was right.

He recalled her words the last time they met, a few months ago: "You survived the war, now be sure you survive the peace."

What the hell is wrong with me? Since when do I care about rules?

The only answer he could come up with was he had too much to lose now. *Maybe, I am just a little wiser than I used to be.*

One late afternoon in early September of 1945, when the entire war—including the conflict with Japan in the Pacific—had ended, he and Michael sat outside their barracks and enjoyed a warm afternoon on a wooden bench. Josef hadn't seen Ella since June, when the French issued the ban on fraternization with Germans.

"So, Josef, what are you going to do about Ella? You haven't seen her in months. Is it over with the both of you?"

"No, it's not over. We just mutually agreed to obey the rules," he said a bit sharply. Michael's question unnerved him. *What if Ella is no longer interested in me? I have to find out.*

"I need to go see Ella soon. I miss her."

"We aren't supposed to see any Germans, let alone get romantically involved with one." Michael responded.

"I know, but I have to find a way to see her. And what about you and Stephania?"

Stephania, like Michael, had been transported to Germany from Poland as a slave laborer. Since the end of the war, she and Michael nurtured their once forbidden friendship, and it had now turned into a romance.

"We are going back to Poland together, as soon as we can."

"When do you think that will be?"

"Probably later this year, or maybe in early 1946. You are more than welcome to come home with us. What do you say?"

"Michael, I have to first figure out what is going on with Ella and me."

Josef had been saving some of his non-perishable food to offer as gifts to Ella, Willie, and Sonya—dried fruit, chocolate bars, and some cigarettes they could use for bartering.

Everyone was still hungry. There continued to be a serious food shortage, and help from outside was slow in coming. Allied powers estimated tens of thousands of people would die without adequate food; some wanted all Germans to suffer, and to suffer seriously, believing they were happily complicit in the atrocities executed by Hitler and his chief minions.

But rules written on paper, and in-person encounters with the starving have never meshed. It didn't work when Sonya was feeding Josef, and it didn't work now, when Allied forces saw starving German children in the streets. By October, many of the rules forbidding contact with Germans had been lifted.

The timing was perfect for Josef. He had neither seen nor heard from Ella in almost four months, and was beginning to doubt their love.

On a bright mid-autumn Saturday, with no work to do and some food in his pockets, he set off to visit Ella and the Mirz family. By now he could walk without much of a limp, but had to rest often on his half-mile trek. His artificial leg had become a part of him, although a hefty one. Since he received regular medical attention from the French, he no longer needed to see Herr Doktor, who still practiced medicine in the town.

He made his way to the Mirz house, first. When Sonya let him in, he immediately noticed she and Willie were quite thin. Sitting in the parlor, Sonya offered him some tea; he gave them some raisins and biscuits.

The three friends shared a simple snack.

"Willie, how is work?"

"I am still busy. War or not, people get sick, although there are no new war wounds to tend to now...at least not physical wounds."

"And Helga? Are you still seeing her?"

Willie was surprised Josef remembered he had been dating Helga. Only once or twice had he mentioned her in the past, when Josef was still living in his house.

"Yes, I am still seeing her."

"Is she 'the one' for you?" Josef taunted.

Sonya smiled at Josef's question, and waited for Willie to answer.

"Yes, she is. We plan to marry when things calm down."

"Good, Willie! Do you have a date yet?"

"No, not yet."

"Will you let me know the wedding date?"

"Yes, of course. It will be a simple affair."

They sipped their tea.

He turned his attention to Sonya. "And how are you, Frau Mirz?"

She sighed at Josef's question.

"It has been very hard. Our stomachs are never satisfied, and I am embarrassed, right now, to be German. I don't want to complain, though. Too many people have suffered. What that monster did to people is unbelievable."

With clear venom in her voice, she was referring to Hitler. Both she and Willie were proof enough for Josef that some Germans did not strictly adhere to all the regulations meant to create and maintain a master race. Both of them had kept him alive, and broken many rules they were supposed to obey in the process. They had put themselves at risk of punishment for helping him; so did Herr Doktor and Ella.

"And you, Josef?" Willie asked.

"Me?"

"Yes, you—what about the girl next door, Ella?"

Josef's head snapped, "You know about Ella and me?"

"We haven't been blind," Frau Mirz chimed in with a smile and a patronizing laugh. Josef thought she was amused at his now obviously erroneous assumption no one knew he and Ella were seeing each other.

Josef could feel his face flushing, "We are serious, but we decided to keep apart until the regulations were relaxed by the French."

"That's not typical of you," replied Willie, grinning.

"We didn't want to jeopardize anything."

"That is probably a good idea," Frau Mirz responded. "Are you going to see her today?"

"I intend to stop at her house a little later. Since the French forbade us to socialize, until now, I certainly plan to spend more time with her."

"Ah, the French!" Sonya replied with a sigh. "It is always the French, everything about the French! The newspapers are full of stories about France: French art, French literature, French food, French architecture, and French achievements. The radio plays only French music all the time."[32]

"It will pass," Willie said, trying to console her. "We have been subjected to only German culture for so long; I find it refreshing to be exposed to something else."

"I don't want German culture to be suppressed forever!"

Willie nodded, "Neither to do I, Mother. You know the French; they think anything French is superior," he said gently, trying to placate her. "We can be as German as we want in our home. And besides, I do not think occupation is going to last forever."

Josef suspected the proliferation of everything French was a sore point for Sonya and Willie, and one they discussed frequently. He couldn't imagine how Sonya felt, but he did understand the French efforts to push anything Germanic into the background for a time. It was almost as though a wound had to be opened and the decay within it had to be drained, regardless of how painful it might be for the patient. At the end of the treatment, the hope would be to retain what was good and pure.

Preparing to leave, Josef asked Willie and Sonya, "Is there anything I can get for you?"

He knew this was a hard question for Sonya, a proud woman.

Neither she nor Willie responded immediately. They shook their heads in unison, "No, there is nothing we need, Josef," Willie answered.

Josef reached into his shirt pocket for five cigarettes. "I would like to give you these cigarettes. I have more, and you might be able to acquire something you need, or want, with them."

Very likely, they would use them to secure food, and not some nicety, he knew.

Willie took the cigarettes.

"Thank you, Josef. They will be exchanged for something we can use, I am sure."

Sonya's eyes were rimmed with tears.

"I should be off, then, to see Ella."

They stood up. Willie grasped Josef's hand and shoulders, and Sonya hugged Josef.

As the door to the house closed behind him, Josef fumed.

They don't deserve to be treated like Nazis!

Josef

French Officer Greeting Former Slave Laborers

This photograph shows a high ranking French officer, during the period the French occupied part of Germany after the war. The officer is shaking hands with former slave laborers. Josef is second from the left. The date is November 11, 1947.

Courtesy Monica Walkow Dudzinski

23 - Love, No Longer Forbidden

His anger abated a bit as he walked around the corner to Ella's house. For the first time, he rang the doorbell like any normal person would, rather than hide in the bushes or meet in a secluded corner of the garden.

A maid, dressed in a black outfit covered with a crisp white apron, opened the door.

"May I help you?" she asked coolly, looking critically at Josef's oversized jacket.

"I am Josef. I am here to see Ella."

The maid nodded. "Come in. Wait here."

She turned and walked to a door at the far side of the entrance hall, opened it, and slipped quietly into another room. He heard the door latch solidly behind her.

Josef stood alone in the quiet reception hall and admired its highly polished dark wood floor, ornate plaster ceiling moldings, and gilded mirrors. A vase of dried flowers was centered on the round, dark, wooden table in the center of the foyer. The table was supported by an elaborate pedestal carved with grapes, and it smelled like lemon oil had just been used to polish it. Lace curtains filtered the late afternoon light coming through the long, narrow windows flanking the front door. It was a grander house than Willie's, and he wondered if any French officers had billeted themselves there since he last saw Ella. The silence was broken first by the rhythmic tick of a tall clock standing on the floor against a wall adjacent to a double-door entry into what was probably a parlor, and then by the unmistakable sound of a door latch opening. It was the door the maid who let him in had gone through a few minutes ago.

Ella walked into the foyer.

She smiled and held out both of her hands to him, and kissed him on the cheek.

"I have missed you so much," she said.

"May I hug you?"

"Make it quick, Josef, we're right in the middle of the foyer."

Josef hugged her, but it wasn't quick. He held on to her and buried his nose in her neck, kissed her shoulder, her ear, and then her lips. Her hair smelled like rose water. It was as though he had endured a parching thirst for months and she was the only fountain capable of quenching it. She clung to him, felt the weight of his chest against hers, and the pressure of his arms around her small frame. How she had missed the way he held her!

She broke their embrace. "Come, Josef. Let's go into the kitchen and talk."

She was wearing a simple brown dress, sensible shoes, and a bright white apron, the kind that covered her from her chest to her knees.

They sat together at the large table in the kitchen. No other household staff was present, and there was a pot of meatless soup cooking on the stove.

Light-heartedly, she looked at Josef. "I am so glad the French are allowing us to see each other, finally!"

Any doubts Josef had about her still wanting to be with him dissipated. He had been worried, but her warmth and demeanor did not indicate she wanted to part ways with him.

"How have you been, Josef? You look well."

"I am fine. Michael is planning to return to Poland as soon as the French get some transports going. I hope to remain here— that is, if we have a future together."

"Are you afraid I no longer love you?"

Josef sighed, "I am afraid of what the aftermath of the war has done, or could do to us. I know it has been very, very difficult, especially for German women. How have you been, Ella? I have thought about you so many times and hoped everything with you is fine, that you have enough food, and that you are cared for here."

She looked down at her lap and barely whispered, "Yes, I have been fine." When she didn't look up, Josef cupped his hand under her chin, and, wondering if she had been a victim of rape, he simply kissed her.

That's when she began to cry. He held her tenderly until the crying stopped. He had no idea if she was crying because of what might have been done to her, if she was tired, or if she was just glad they were together. Not that it mattered; he just wanted to be with her.

Finally, she composed herself. "I'm sorry, Josef. Where are my manners? Would you like some tea? We do have tea, although not much else."

"No, I don't want anything other than to see you."

Ella added, "I don't know why they are keeping me on as a cook when there is so little food to prepare. Even the soup I am cooking has only water, some potatoes, onions, and carrots. Would you like some?"

"No, no tea, no soup, thank you. I see your employer keeps both you and a housemaid. They must be very well off."

"I do much more than cook and perform light housework now. I also get up early in the morning, and if it is chilly, I make the fires in all the fireplaces. Sometimes I have to go into the woods to pick up kindling and find larger branches. But it is dangerous to go out, even in the company of others."

"Has something happened, Ella?"

Silent a moment, she ignored his question.

"I also do some dusting and polishing, and I wash the floors."

"So what does the house maid do, then?"

"She tends to my employer directly, serving tea, answering the doorbell, and helping them with their clothing. Part of her job is to give the false impression everything is fine, even though everyone knows *nothing* is fine."

"How do you get paid?"

197

"Food, and a little money, that's all. And, of course, a roof over my head. The more of us who are in the household, the easier it is to pool whatever supplies we are allotted or can find."

He asked again, "Has something happened, Ella?"

Again she ignored his question.

"Ella, is there anything you want to talk about?"

"No, I don't want to talk. I just want to be here with you."

She rested her head on his shoulder and he wrapped his arms around her. They stayed like that a few minutes, and she closed her eyes.

"I have something for you!" Josef said, as he reached inside his jacket pocket.

"What is it?" she asked as she moved away from his arms.

Josef teased her by wiggling a box of raisins in her face. Her eyes popped open when she saw them, and wider yet when he also produced a bar of chocolate. But when he handed her a stack of ten cigarettes, she let out a little shriek. Those cigarettes were gold.

She opened the raisins, and placed one in her mouth. She closed her eyes in bliss as she savored the intense sweetness and texture of the humble, wrinkled, dried fruit.

Josef enjoyed her delight in the tiny morsel.

"How did you get these, Josef?"

"We are allotted more food than German citizens, and whatever supplies are brought in, we get some of them. I've also been doing odd jobs for the French, whatever they need done, and they pay me in food and cigarettes, and occasionally some Reichsmarks. But the cash is worth almost nothing."

"The mistress of this household has been selling some of her antiques and jewelry to local farmers in exchange for food. It has kept us alive, and I even bartered a thin gold bracelet for a pair of used shoes from a farmer's wife. It is so hard to find any clothing."

She fed Josef a raisin and relished another one herself.

"I have to tell you something, Josef."

"What is it?"

"I told my mother about us. I wrote her a letter about four weeks ago. Since the mail service is so slow, I don't know if she received it yet."

"What do you think she will say about us?"

"I don't really know. It may be odd, but I don't care what she thinks. I want to be with you."

"I would like to meet her sometime, when we are free to travel to Heidelberg," he said, as he brushed a lock of her hair away from her face.

"Yes, let's do that."

Josef stood up.

"I'd better get back. There is still a curfew."

"I know," she said, as she stood and embraced him. "When will you come back?"

"In a few days, Ella."

She walked him back through the foyer to the front door. As she opened it, she kissed him again. He hugged her, and she did not resist. Lost in the scent of her hair, Josef realized they were free to be together now. Something in him relaxed for the first time in years, and the warmth of contentment spread through his body.

"I love you Josef," Ella whispered.

"I love you, too," he responded aloud.

Before he turned his back to exit the door, Ella put her hand on his shoulder, "It's nice you came through the front door."

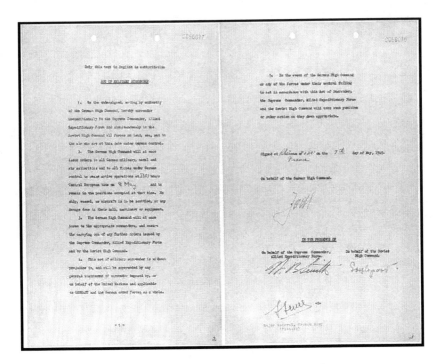

German Instrument of Surrender

This is an image of the initial instrument of surrender executed between Germany and the Allies. It was signed at Reims, France on May 7, 2015 at 2:41 a.m., and the definitive document was signed the following day, May 8, in Karlshorst, a borough of Berlin. May 8 was declared Victory in Europe (VE) Day. German General Alfred Jodl signed for Germany.

Document is in the Public Domain

24 - Adieu, Sonya

The winter of 1945-1946 was one of the coldest and most brutal in Germany, colder than the previous winter. Thousands of people in the cities starved. In the country, farmers became richer and richer as their fellow Germans traded whatever they had for food. Farmers kept the best provisions for themselves, whether it was milk, meat, vegetables, grain, or flour, and traded what they didn't need for jewelry, gold, silver, antiques, services, and anything else of value their countrymen had.[33] Resentment brewed against them, and many Germans thought farmers should be sharing more of their food, and at lower prices, with their fellow Germans.

Josef and Ella continued to see each other, and Josef grew steadfast in his decision to stay in Germany, while Michael anticipated his return to Poland, with Stephania. The authorities expected repatriation would occur sometime in the spring of 1946. For displaced persons, the food situation gradually but fitfully improved, due to shipments from western countries. The Germans were kept on a subsistence diet of barely 1,300 calories a day.[34] The Allies felt the Germans should suffer, but the extent of the suffering should be contained in order for it to not be perceived as cruel. They also wanted to ensure the Germans would not turn to the Soviets to feed them. Hunger can make for strange bedfellows, and the Allies did not want all of Germany to turn Communist. Josef did what he could to help Frau Mirz, Willie, and Ella.

In late January of 1946, Josef spent an afternoon with Willie, and noticed Sonya appeared distracted, her skin color was gray, and she had dark circles under her eyes. Josef gave them some food, which they gratefully accepted.

"Mother is worn out from the war, as well as from the aftermath of the war," Willie volunteered as he and Josef spoke in the parlor that night. Sonya had gone to bed, and that action contrasted sharply with her behavior from past nights when she would sit in a corner of the sofa and do her mending while the two young men talked.

"Sometimes, I think she has given up, Josef."

"Now, when the war is over?"

"Almost everything she treasured is gone—my father, Gunther, some of her favorite belongings, her country. Not even my coming marriage to Helga in the spring seems to cheer her. The thought of grandchildren doesn't move her either. She once told me if I have children, she hopes they would not be boys. They'd just be killed in some war."

"Oh, Willie, I am sorry she is feeling so despondent."

"I wouldn't be surprised if she soon passed away, Josef. I don't think she can, or wants, to cope with anything ever again."

"Don't say that, please, Willie! She is like a mother to me."

"When you were here she had a mission. She wanted to help you get well. It gave her a spark. When you left, she missed you, but I know she was happy to see you adjusted so well to your leg. When the war ended, I don't think there was a person happier for you than she. I think she wants the pain of all the loss she has experienced to end. Really, I feel she would not mind dying."

"I hope you are wrong."

"I hope so, too. Maybe brightening her spirits will be easier with the wedding this May. Helga and I can get her involved; she'll have something to look forward to."

But Sonya never saw the wedding. In late March, during a night where the air hinted of spring, she suddenly and quietly slipped away in her sleep. There were no theatrics, no long-drawn goodbyes. She died as she would have wanted to, with dignity. No one knew what took her life.

Ella sent a note via messenger to Josef at the barracks.

"Come quickly. Willie needs you. Sonya has died. She will be buried tomorrow."

Josef crumpled the note in anger and broke down in tears. In the absence of his own mother, Sonya had nurtured him and nursed him back to health. Whatever physical ailment may have resulted in her death, Josef knew the underlying reasons were a broken heart and a mortally wounded spirit.

Ella, Michael, and all the surrounding neighbors came to the funeral. After Sonya was buried beside her husband, Hans, and the few mortal remains of Gunter the German army returned to her, Willie stood at the open grave with Josef beside him.

"She was a compassionate lady, Willie," Josef consoled, "a dignified lady. I will always miss her."

Willie wiped tears from his eyes with a handkerchief. Bitterly, he heaved, "She didn't deserve what the war did to her!"

"No, she didn't," responded Josef, so softly. "None of us did. Not she, not you, not me, not Michael, not Ella, not Gunter, not your father."

"You're right," Willie said. "What a stupid waste!"

"I remember the day she found the extra bread in my night table drawer at your house. I was saving it for Michael. Do you remember that incident?"

"Yes, she hated vermin," Willie smiled.

"I brought some bread crumbs along, Willie. May I sprinkle them on the grave?"

Willie broadened his smile. "Yes, go ahead. I think she would find it amusing...and touching."

Josef sprinkled a scant handful of breadcrumbs into the open grave and prayed silently, *Hail Mary, full of grace, the Lord is with thee. Blessed art thou among women and blessed is the fruit of thy womb, Jesus. Holy Mary, Mother of God, you know what it means to be a mother. You know the pain of losing a child. Please pray for Sonya and keep her safe. She was a caring woman and a great lady, even if she wasn't royalty. And she was kind. So, so kind. Amen.*

He turned to Willie and touched his elbow, "Come, let's go back to the house. I understand the neighbors have prepared some food."

Willie walked from the cemetery to the house, a distance of about a half-mile. Josef, who had bartered some food for Gunter's old bicycle a few weeks earlier, had learned to cycle despite his artificial leg. He rode slowly beside Willie, while Helga, Michael, and Ella flanked the grieving young man.

Michael stayed at the house for a few minutes to offer his condolences. About an hour later, Ella and Josef also bid farewell to Willie.

"You'll come to the wedding at the end of May, won't you?" Willie pleaded to Josef, with Helga sitting next to him on the sofa where his mother had spent many quiet nights, mending.

"You know I wouldn't miss it. Your mother would want you to be happy, Willie. She loved you very much. It was constantly in her eyes. You must know that."

"Yes, I know it," he nodded.

Josef clasped his friend's hand with both of his.

"I will see you soon."

As he turned to leave, he looked back at Willie, and said again, "Willie, your mother would want you to be happy."

25 - Beginnings

It was 1946—a busy year for romance.

Before Willie's wedding, Michael and Stephania married in Germany, rather than waiting until they returned to Poland.

As Josef watched the minister perform the matrimonial rite, he knew it was now only a matter of time when Michael and his bride would be returning home. Transports of displaced persons were leaving regularly for Poland, and his brother had let the French know he and Stephania wanted to be on one soon.

Josef's mind wandered. *We've been through so much together. But he has Stephania now, so he is not alone. I hope they will be happy. But when he leaves, will I ever see him again?*

The wedding was simple, with Josef and Ella and a few friends from the barracks in attendance. Everyone pooled their resources to prepare a celebratory meal and provide the couple with a joint gift—enough food for a few weeks, arranged nicely in a large basket, along with some cooking utensils. The couple moved into a part of the barracks complex that had recently been designated as quarters for couples.

Willie and Helga married in late May. It, too, was a simple affair, with wild flowers on the tables set up in Willie's garden and whatever hors d'oeuvres could be created with available food. Josef offered a gift of a dozen cigarettes, earned by his working for the French. Ella tied them together with white kitchen string and placed them in a glass bowl. The package was wrapped in a crisp white dishcloth and tied with white string, a wildflower entwined in the knot.

Helga moved into Willie's house, and they saw Ella and Josef frequently, often sharing whatever they had.

Despite Helga's graciousness, Josef keenly felt the absence of Sonya in Willie's house each time he visited. The house wasn't the same without her.

Food and clothing were still major issues, and everyone wondered when, and if, sufficient aid from the other countries would arrive.

At one of their get-togethers, Willie teased Josef, "So when are you and Ella getting married?"

"As soon as Josef meets my mother," Ella responded, before Josef could say anything. "We have asked to travel to Heidelberg to visit her, and we might be able to go in August."

Yet before Ella and Josef could visit Heidelberg, Michael and Stephania had confirmation of their return date to Poland. It would be mid-July. Josef acknowledged the date sadly.

~~~

A few nights before Michael's departure, Josef spent time with his brother.

"What will you do when you get home, Michael?"

"I am going to try to find everyone...Pyotr, Mother, Father."

"I will miss you. Our being together made the whole ordeal of the war bearable."

"You have Ella. Maybe you'd better marry her soon, or she may get away!" Michael teased. "You can still come with us, if you want to. I am sure the French will grant you passage."

"You know I want to stay here, with Ella. But I also don't want to lose you."

"You won't be losing me, little brother." He touched his hand to Josef's heart. "I'll always be *there*." Josef realized Michael seemed happier than he had in all the war years, and he attributed his brother's lighthearted mood not only to his imminent departure home to Poland, but also to Stephania.

He deserves to be happy. I want him to be happy. Only his leaving will be awful for me.

Every time Josef thought of Michael's approaching departure, he felt a lump in this throat and he had to fight back tears every day.

206

His thoughts raced, *Will I ever see Michael again? I guess this is what it means to grow up. You have to say hello to new people and goodbye to others.*

⁓ঙ⅄৶ঙ⁓

On the morning of Michael's departure, the two brothers clung to each other for as long as they could before Michael had to board the train, loaded with Poles going home. Neither of them could contain their tears. Along with orders from Josef for Michael to hug Pyotr, and if he saw them, to also embrace Mother and Father on his behalf, they agreed to write to each other often. They made a commitment to meet again in the future, whenever and wherever that would be. Michael admonished Josef not to let Ella "get away," and boarded the train with Stephania.

Slowly, the train pulled away. Josef stood at the side of the tracks until the train evaporated from sight in the distance, like a dissipating, shimmering mirage. The train, with Michael in it, gave Josef the impression it moved into another dimension of existence.

The idea of seeing Michael again in the future seemed like a fantasy.

When will that be? A year? A decade? Never?

He found himself stumbling along the track, calling "Michael! Michael!" to the air. But he could not run, and when his legs couldn't sustain him any longer, he stumbled, pulled himself to the side of the tracks, and sat beside the rail. Convulsed in tears, and his head hung low, he made futile attempts to stop sobbing, but did not succeed. "Michael" was all he could say, over and over, between gasps of grief.

An elderly man came over to him and placed his hand on his shoulder. There was no need to say anything. He, too, was crying and staring into the distance where the train had disappeared out of sight.

Josef remained in place, sitting near the rail, not caring if another train ran him over. He pressed his chest where Michael had touched it just a few nights ago and said, "I'll always be there." *Will I ever see him again? Please, please, God, don't make this our final farewell.*

He felt he was the only person in the world, and he heard only an overwhelming, engulfing silence.

Michael was gone.

As if he had been in a trance, Josef's slowly became cognizant of the world around him. He did not know how long he had sat next to the rail. The elderly man who so kindly consoled him was gone. Children were playing in a field alongside the tracks. They made happy sounds, as children do at play. A slight breeze played with Josef's hair, and it reminded him of when Ella ran her fingers through it. He pushed himself up from the trackside, straightened his back, and walked through the field. He plucked wildflowers now and then, enjoyed their scent, and then tossed them to the ground. He felt a little guilty, knowing wildflowers could endure harsh environments, but once you plucked them, they died quickly, barely lasting a few minutes.

Michael is right. I'd better not let Ella get away.

In the following days, Josef found the barracks barren without the comforting presence of Michael, and he had let the French know he was willing to take on more work. Keeping busy was best for him, but he found himself looking for the familiar face of his brother, although he knew he would never find it there again. The only time he had felt so alone was when he was first sent as a laborer to the mines in Poland, and that seemed another lifetime ago.

I'm on my own now, for the rest of my life.

He visited Ella more frequently, always bringing a gift of some food.

After trading cigarettes for two train tickets, in mid-August he and Ella made the trip to Heidelberg so he could meet Ella's mother. This spur of the rail line was working and had not been heavily damaged during the war. Ella's letter had reached her mother, and Frau Zimmerman responded that she was looking forward to seeing her daughter and her Polish boyfriend.

Josef enjoyed the trip, especially the views along the Neckar River as they approached the city. It was in the American zone of occupation, and at the train station they had to present their papers, their itinerary, and who they would be visiting. They did not encounter any resistance from the authorities, and managed to hitch a ride from the train station to a location a short walk to the home of Ella's mother. Josef was nervous approaching the house, and he squeezed Ella's hand often. His hands were sweating, and he felt his heart pounding.

"Just be yourself, Josef. Don't worry."

"Suppose your mother doesn't like me?"

"I can't think of a reason why she wouldn't like you."

"Have you forgotten I am not German?"

"It doesn't matter if my mother likes you or not. I like you. Have you forgotten that?"

"You certainly have a mind of your own," he commented. "You've got spirit. That's sexy, you know!"

"Stop it!" she tittered.

Frau Zimmerman was a lean, dark-haired woman. She wore a dark, gray dress with a white lace collar, some eye makeup, and lipstick. Her hair was arranged in an updo. Josef thought she might have wanted to make a good impression on him, because Ella once had told him how her mother rarely dressed up. As Ella remembered it, her mother was always busy, running a household of Ella's three younger half siblings—two teenage girls and a younger boy.

Frau Zimmerman greeted her daughter with a brief hug and then turned her attention to Josef. The imposing woman looked intently at the young Pole, examining him from head to toe, like one would look at a horse before buying it.

Uncomfortable in the stillness, Josef tracked her eyes as they rested on various parts of his body.

"This is the young man my daughter told me about in her letter?" Frau Zimmerman asked, looking at him, then at Ella, and again at Josef.

"Yes, it is nice to meet you," he said, as he extended his hand. She reached out to shake his hand. He expected it to be as cold as ice, and its warmth surprised him.

"Come, sit in the parlor."

It was really not an invitation, but an order. He thought of Frau Mirz.

The three of them sat on separate upholstered chairs. Josef was expecting an inquisition, and a bombardment of questions was hurled at him immediately.

"You are a Pole, are you not?" the woman inquired. It seemed to Josef she asked this question hoping the answer would be "No, I am not a Pole."

"Yes, I am. I was a slave laborer."

He had no idea if she felt any remorse for her country's use of slave laborers. He didn't know if she had been a member of the Nazi Party. She showed no visible empathy or regret for the situation he had been in through the war.

"How did you meet my daughter?" she demanded.

Josef relayed the story about the barrel accident, losing his leg, recuperating at Frau Mirz's house, sighting Ella, and their romance. Listening intently and without interrupting, Ella's mother seemed to tightly grasp the arms of the chair she was occupying as Josef described the key events of the past few years. He noted her knuckles were white as he described the accident, the extent of his wound, and the resulting amputation. It was the only hint of emotion he saw.

"And this Frau Mirz and Willie Mirz you mention...they took care of you when you were ill?"

"Yes. I would not have survived without their care."

"And they are German, you say?"

"Yes. Loyal Germans. Frau Mirz's younger son and husband were killed serving in the German Army during the war."

Frau Zimmerman raised her eyebrows.

"And you remain friendly with Frau Mirz and Willie?"

"Frau Mirz has since died. Both Ella and I are friends with Willie and his wife, Helga."

Josef didn't know if Frau Zimmerman was thinking about how unusual it may have seemed for him to have been helped by Germans during the war. Maybe she felt Sonya and Willie had acted like traitors. Maybe she secretly found honor in their actions. It was hard to read her.

When Josef was almost finished talking, Frau Zimmerman abruptly asked, "What are you intentions with Ella?"

"I want to marry her, Frau Zimmerman."

"And how old are you?"

"I am twenty. I will be twenty-one at the end of September."

"And how will you support Ella?" she challenged.

"I do odd jobs: carpentry work, machine work, watch and clock repair; anything that is needed, really."

Eagerly, Ella leaned toward her mother. "He is really good at fixing things, Mother. Everyone knows his reputation."

The woman may have heard her daughter's comment, but ignored it.

She pushed forward in her chair, and more gently than anything she previously said, she asked Josef, "Why aren't you returning to Poland? Isn't your family there?"

"That's easy. I am staying here in Germany because of Ella. My brother Michael was also a slave laborer and he recently returned to Poland. I won't leave Ella, though." He paused and took a deep breath, not knowing how Frau Zimmerman would react to what he was going to say next. "I don't know how *you* feel about Communism, but I have decided I do not want to live in a Communist country, which Poland has become."

He thought it best to let her know right away about his distaste for Communism, as well as his love for Ella. He knew he had nothing to lose. Ella said she would marry him whether or not her mother approved of him. To his surprise, Frau Zimmerman agreed with him. I can understand, Josef. It is always best to choose your own path, if you can."

Given her decision to send Ella as a maid and cook into someone else's household, he was a little confused by her statement. Ella had wanted to study more, to be a librarian. But he let it pass.

Looking first at Josef, and then more piercingly at Ella, Frau Zimmerman cautioned them.

"Have you given any thought to children?" She didn't wait for an answer.

"Your children will be neither Polish nor German, but a mixture. It might be difficult for them, and for both of you, too. Aren't you concerned about it?"

Neither Ella nor Josef had seriously thought about it, although they briefly discussed it. In the optimism of youth, they were certain their love would conquer any problem.

"No, Mother. We haven't really thought about it. But we think we can give children a good life. Isn't that right, Josef?"

A little embarrassed about talking about children he had not yet fathered, Josef nodded in agreement. "I am not afraid to work hard to support a family. And Ella is a very special girl. I will take care of her."

Frau Zimmerman sat silently. Josef noticed it was so quiet he could hear a clock ticking somewhere. *Why doesn't she say something? What is she thinking?*

Then Josef clearly heard the rustle of her dress as she slowly got up and approached him. Towering above him, he had to raise his head to look up at her.

What the hell is she doing? He stood up.

"I cannot challenge your earnestness or your love for Ella. Although I would have preferred she fell in love with a German, you seem to be an honest man, and you certainly appear to love my daughter."

She extended her hand to Josef.

"Welcome to the family."

She embraced Josef's hands with both of hers.

Josef was disarmed. *She seems so severe, yet her hands are warm. Frau Mirz had seemed stern and reserved at first, but she was a warm-hearted woman. Is Ella's mother the same way? Was her generation taught to be aloof to the degree where they appear cold and judgmental?*

"I think it is time for you to meet the other children—Ella's brother and sisters! I am warning you, though. They are a lively bunch."

Ella beamed.

Frau Zimmerman called to the other members of the household present that day. Her husband was not at home. Ella's two half sisters and half brother bounded into the parlor, happy to see Ella and to meet their future brother-in-law. There were hugs and handshakes, and then one of the sisters tugged at Josef's hand.

"Let me show you the rest of the house and the garden."

For the first time that day, Josef relaxed and smiled broadly. The boisterous children led him from the room. The worst was over, at least for him.

"Are you coming, Ella?" he asked over his shoulder.

"No, I want to spend more time with Mother. We have some things to talk about."

"What do you have to talk about?"

"Just mother and daughter talk, Josef. Go ahead, I'll meet you outside later."

Josef and the children headed toward the back door.

"Don't rush him," Ella cautioned. "He has a wooden leg."

Her brother immediately bent down and reached to lift up both of Josef's pants legs to see the artificial limb.

"Stop that!" Frau Zimmerman commanded.

But Josef let him knock gently on his prosthesis. Within a moment they left the room, and as soon as they were gone, Ella approached her mother.

"Mother, would you please write a letter giving your permission for me to marry Josef? I am not yet twenty-one and I don't know what the age is for marriage any more. Just in case, I'd like to have the letter."

"Well, Josef isn't twenty-one either!"

"We won't get married until October or November. He'll be twenty-one in September; remember he told you that?"

"Yes, of course I remember." She cocked her head toward the small writing desk in the room.

"Come, sit by me. Ella's mother sat in a straight-backed chair at the desk, took out a pen and some paper, and started to write.

"How do you spell Josef's last name?"

"W-A-L-K-O-W," Ella spelled out for her.

"So, Ella, you will be called Ella Stichler Walkow," mused Frau Zimmerman, without looking up from her writing. "That has a nice ring to it. People might think *you* are Polish. Are you aware of that?"

"Yes...yes, but it doesn't matter to me, Mother. I love him."

"I can see that Ella. Be good to each other. The world could use more love," she remarked matter-of-factly as she wrote. Ella could hear the pen scratching on the paper.

It was a simple letter, stating who she was in relation to Ella, and mentioning she gave her full blessing for Ella Stichler, her German daughter, to marry Josef Walkow, a Pole and former slave laborer.

"I think it would be best to have this letter notarized by an official," she mentioned to her daughter. "Let's take a walk to the town hall."

Frau Zimmerman poked her head out the door to the garden and told the rest of her brood to entertain Josef while she and Ella walked to town, a distance of about a kilometer. Again, Ella told Josef they were just doing some mother and daughter things and would be home in a couple of hours. She noticed Josef was playing, tossing a ball with her brother. Until now, she had never seen Josef play.

The notarization process was easy and on their way home, Frau Zimmerman mentioned her daughter was looking well, though thin. Then, she suddenly asked, "So you truly love him?"

Ella responded, "Yes, I've loved him for some time, now."

"Have the two of you been intimate?"

Surprised by the question, Ella nonetheless could not lie to her mother.

"Yes...and...well...I'm...I'm also going to have a baby this coming winter."

Frau Zimmerman suddenly stopped walking and turned to face her daughter. She placed her hand firmly around Ella's upper right arm.

"Are you sure?"

"Yes, I am sure! I went to see a doctor and he confirmed it."

"What does Josef say?"

"He doesn't know yet. I haven't told him."

Frau Zimmerman stared at her daughter. "Is it *his* child?"

"Yes, of course it is."

"Are you certain, Ella? Could it possibly belong to anyone else...a foreign soldier, perhaps?"

"The timing is right. The baby could only be Josef's," replied Ella, curtly, almost angrily.

They walked a few steps in silence, and then the older woman stopped abruptly once again, facing her daughter.

"Do you still read, Ella?"

"Yes, of course I still read. I love to read. You know that."

Ella thought it was an unusual question, given the topic of the conversation they were having.

"Be sure you read anything that instructs you on how to be a good wife and mother. Read about people, about distant places, about ideas different from your own."

And then Frau Zimmerman added, for emphasis, "Never, *never*, give up reading, no matter what."

Ella wondered if this statement was her mother's apology for thwarting her dream of becoming a librarian.

As though Frau Zimmerman could read her mind, she asked, "Just because you are not a librarian doesn't mean you have to stop loving books, does it? And tell me, does Josef read German?"

"He can read some, and you heard him speak German in the parlor."

"Yes, he can speak some German. Can you help him become more fluent?"

"I think so."

They walked, this time more quickly, and Ella thought it was going to be a long trek back if they continued to stop so often.

Suddenly, Frau Zimmerman stopped again, gave a deep sigh accompanied by a smile.

"I met my future son-in-law today and learned I am going to be a grandmother...my first grandchild. This has been quite a remarkable turn of events for a day that seemed like any other day."

"You aren't angry?" Ella asked timidly.

"I am happy for you, not angry, but just a bit disappointed. I always envisioned a big wedding for my daughter, a German son-in-law, and a long courtship where the whole family would get to know your *fiancé*. But the war altered everything; it ended or changed everyone's hopes, dreams, and feelings of safety."

They started walking again.

"Mostly, Ella, I just want you to be happy and cared for by a good man."

"Josef *is* a good man, Mother. And we love each other."

"I can see you do. Regardless, tonight, you are staying in the bedroom your sisters share."

"Mother, is that really necessary?"

"Yes, it is. Josef is sleeping on the couch."

Ella sighed, knowing it was a futile and foolish endeavor trying to convince her mother otherwise.

"That's fine, Mother. Josef will sleep on the couch!"

At supper that night, Frau Zimmerman never mentioned the pregnancy, realizing Ella needed to let Josef know about it before it was announced. And everyone was delighted there would be a wedding.

~~~

When Josef and Ella parted for Stockach the next day, they were laden with towels and bed linens from her mother.

"You have a nice family, Ella," Josef said on the train ride home. "I feel very comfortable with them."

"They will be your family, too, Josef. And there's more."

"You have other brothers and sisters?"

"No, no more brothers and sisters! But next year we are going to have a son or daughter of our own." Her comment didn't register with him immediately, but then he just stared at her, his mouth agape.

"What? How did that happen?"

"*How*?" teased Ella. "*How*? In the usual way, Josef."

"But we only made love a few times!"

"It only takes one time, if the conditions are right."

Neither of them spoke for a long minute, and the sounds of the wheels on the track provided something they could focus on.

"When is the baby due?"

"The doctor says late February or early March of next year."

He looked at her, "I am going to be a father!"

"Yes, and a good one, I am sure."

"We should get married soon, Ella."

"Yes, we should."

For the remainder of the trip back to Stockach, Ella nestled into Josef's right arm. He stared out the wide window.

Michael, I wish you were here. I have such good news.

217

Frau Zimmerman

Frau Zimmerman (previously known as Frau Stichler, during her first marriage) was Ella's mother. She remarried and had three other children—two daughters and a son, Ella's half siblings.

Courtesy Monica Walkow Dudzkinski

26 - Newlyweds

Ella and Josef looked for a place to live as soon as they returned from Heidelberg. Eventually, they were connected with Frau Wilkesmann, a lady who rented rooms in her house, and one of only a handful of landlords who would rent to mixed nationality couples.

A few of the flats were outfitted for cooking, and Ella and Josef's was a ground floor unit, consisting of two rooms. One was used for food preparation and everyday living, and the other was a small bedroom. The bathroom in a hallway was shared with other tenants. In exchange for the apartment, they paid a modest rent and Josef took care of maintaining the property. Ella retained her job as a cook for as long as she could, and Josef also continued doing handyman and machine work throughout the village.

They married on a crisp fall day in a no-nonsense civil ceremony at the town hall, with two friends as witnesses. Ella wore a simple green dress which, despite her pregnancy, still fit her. Her groom loved the smooth, satiny dress. Josef wore his best blazer, a brown tweed. He gave Ella a corsage of one giant yellow chrysanthemum from Willie's garden, and he wore a smaller one in his lapel.

For several days before the wedding, Ella prepared a few soups and made small sandwiches for the reception. She obtained some ersatzkaffe since it was still hard to find real coffee. Helga made a wedding cake with white icing and some pink roses as part of her and Willie's wedding gift. Ella's employer allowed her to hold the wedding celebration in the house. Their friends and Ella's family offered both their good wishes and unpretentious gifts: a few pots and pans, dishes and glasses, bowls and food, kitchen linens, and some cigarettes. Willie was especially happy, and hugged the newlyweds several times throughout the celebration. Josef wished Frau Mirz could have seen this day, and he longed to see Michael. Despite their absence, it was a light-hearted affair and laughter filled the rooms.

Ella and Josef had made friends with a few couples who were in a similar situation as theirs, where the woman was German and the man was a Polish DP. Several of these couples attended the wedding reception. Over time, thousands of couples like Josef and Ella would emigrate from Europe, but in the years immediately after the end of the war, they were all getting married, having children, and starting fresh.

Ella took a moment to observe her husband circulating around the room. This was their wedding reception! Josef was laughing with people, joking, and enjoying himself. She had never seen him so happy.

He would glance at her as she opened gifts and chatted with friends. She looked so beautiful in her dress with the bright yellow flower contrasting against her dark hair. She was now his wife.

My wife, he said to himself, his heart full.

It seemed to him the weight of the long war was finally lightening. *My wife...our wedding reception.*

～๑๑๑～

Ella was constantly hungry. She had always burned calories quickly, but with a child on the way, she was insatiable. It was the worst time to be pregnant. Josef gave her the bulk of whatever food he earned or was provided due to his DP status, but it was never quite enough.

One afternoon, Ella decided to follow a farmer who was plowing his field. Her intent was to salvage any pieces of leftover potato, or beets, or whatever vegetable was being harvested. She kept a distance of about 200 meters, but the farmer saw her anyway, ran toward her, and gruffly yelled at her as he chased her away. Her pockets were full, though, and she enjoyed more hearty sustenance that day.

She told Josef about the incident, and he was incensed the farmer would chase and scare off a pregnant woman. He wanted to confront the farmer, but Ella begged him not to do it.

"What would I do if you get arrested?" she shrieked in fear. "Think of that. Please, don't do anything!"

But he could not let the episode rest. He played it over and over again, and it kept him awake that night. He imagined how the farmer might have bullied her. He visualized her stealthily picking pieces of potatoes and thought how uncomfortable she must have been bending down time after time with her growing belly. The more he pictured the scene, the angrier he became, the tighter he clenched his teeth.

The following day, armed with a thick, large stick, he rode his bicycle to the farm Ella mentioned. When he saw the farmer, he confronted him with the stick raised.

"What do you mean scaring off my wife like that?" he screamed. "She is having a child and is hungry. You let the discards from your plowing rot in the field! Why not just let her have them?"

"They're not hers, sir. They are mine. She has no right to them! She didn't offer anything for them. That's called stealing, isn't it?"

Unable to contain his fury, Josef whacked him across the right side with a hard, deliberate blow to his arm. The farmer reeled back and called out to his family. As Josef took another swing at the man, the farmer's wife and children came running and Josef realized he was outnumbered. He swung the stick like a wild man, but they subdued him, and as he fell to the ground, his wooden leg became visible and everyone froze.

He sat on the dirt, breathing hard. He looked up at the farmer breathlessly, "My wife needs more food and she is German, just like you."

"I ought to have you arrested!" shouted the farmer.

221

Josef got up by balancing on his natural knee, then raising his body with his hands. He stared the farmer in the face.

"You want to have *me* arrested? Really? *Really?* I was a slave laborer for your country. I was nearly starved. I lost a leg. And you are going to have *me* arrested? *You* are the one who should be in jail. *Your* country made me a prisoner. *You* probably used slave labor yourself to help out with the farm, didn't you? *You* are the one who has all the food you need while those around you go hungry. *You* are getting rich at the expense of others, trading your food for whatever people have to offer. *Shame on you!*"

He brushed the dirt from his pants.

"You greedy, selfish man. Don't ever approach my wife again. Do you hear?" he shouted as he pointed at the farmer. Josef was shaking all over.

"Get off my land, *now*," the farmer shouted.

The farmer and his family walked away from him and Josef heard them utter words like "lunatic" and "stupid Pole." He returned to his bicycle, and felt nothing but shame at his loss of control. His whole body was shaking, and he realized he hadn't accomplished anything to help Ella. He vented his rage and prayed Ella would not find out what he did.

It was a small town, though, and within a day or two the news was circulating. Ella casually met her former employer's housemaid at the butcher shop, both of them trying to purchase some meat. The maid mentioned the incident to her.

"Josef, are you stupid or just stubborn?" Ella asked angrily, while preparing supper that night. She removed a stirring spoon from a pot of soup and slammed it down on the stove. Her lips were tight.

"Ella, I am sorry. I couldn't help it. He had no right to treat you like that."

"It's my fight, Josef. Not yours."

"It *is* mine," he said bitterly. "You are my wife and you are having my baby. It is definitely my fight!"

"And what good will you be to me and the baby if you are in jail?" she yelled. "Have you thought of that? *Have you*, Josef?" she shot back at him. "You are lucky the farmer didn't press charges."

"That's because he knew I was right!"

"No, Josef, that's because he may feel guilty about your losing your leg, not because you were right."

They ate in silence.

Josef took the plates to the sink to wash them, while Ella prepared for bed. She turned her back to him when she slipped into bed, but he leaned over and kissed her on the head, nonetheless.

For a few days the atmosphere in their little apartment was icy, yet they couldn't stay angry at each other for very long. One night as they were clearing the table after supper, Josef, though still tentative to approach her, stood behind Ella and wrapped his arms around her. He playfully rested his chin on her shoulder and kissed her ear.

"You have pretty ears," he said.

"You just want me to not be angry with you any longer," she retorted with feigned annoyance.

"That's right. Give me a kiss."

"No!"

"Why not, don't you love me?"

She rolled her eyes, as though to call him an idiot.

"Don't you ever do that again!"

"What, kiss your ear?"

"Don't act ignorant. Please, don't ever attack anyone again. I need you to be *here*, not in prison."

"I'm sorry."

"I mean it Josef; don't be so hot headed!"

"I said I am sorry, Ella. Just kiss me."

She turned to him and kissed him, then broke away from his lips. "I'm still angry at you."

"I know you are," he smiled.

"Really Josef, I'm still angry. So don't smile."

"Don't be angry anymore, Ella. I've already told you I was sorry at least twice."

And Josef kept a boyish, impish grin on his face.

⊸ᏋᏋᏋᏋᏋᏋ⊸

The Christmas holidays came, and the new year, 1947, was celebrated with some friends hosting a baby shower for Ella. Diapers, which were still hard to get, were provided if anyone had any to spare, as well as used baby clothing, and a few blankets. The third week of February, Franz Josef was born in their bedroom, with a midwife in attendance. When she placed the infant boy in Josef's arms, he thought the baby was the most beautiful being he had ever seen. But the infant was not robust; his bones were not as straight as they should have been, and he was weak. The young couple did not know if the baby was going to be healthy, and they worried about him all the time.

Josef let the authorities know a new baby was now part of his household, so they would increase the young family's calorie allotment. He, Ella, and the baby presented themselves at French headquarters to prove it, and a few days later Ella broached the subject of religion.

"Josef, I would like to have Franz baptized as an Episcopalian, like me."

She got no response, at first, other than a cocked head and a quizzical look from her husband.

"I would like him to be Catholic," Josef said firmly.

"I want him to be Episcopalian, like me and so many other Germans. If we have a second child, he...or she...can be baptized as a Catholic. Don't you think that would be fair to us both?"

Josef wanted his son to be Catholic. But after the lunacy of the war, the current instability of the world, and his love for Ella, the choice of religion was a relatively minor concession.

"Fine, Ella," he said. "Franz will be Protestant."

Within a few days they visited the local Episcopalian church where they were advised they would need to be married in a church ceremony, despite their having already been married in a civil ceremony. Josef was given some rudimentary instruction in the differences between the Catholic and the Episcopalian religions, and then he and Ella were privately married before a minister and two witnesses.

As they exited the church, Ella remarked, "I've married you twice, now, Josef. I must really love you."

They had a good laugh about it, and within two weeks, at a Sunday service, Franz was baptized.

Josef, however, did not abandon his Catholic faith. It was part of who he was, like a hand. He already knew what it was like to lose part of himself—his leg—and he would not allow his faith to be lost, also. He continued to practice his religion, sometimes going to Mass. At the baby's Protestant christening he silently prayed, *Hail Mary, full of grace, the Lord is with thee. Blessed art thou among women, and blessed is the fruit of thy womb, Jesus. Holy Mary, Mother of God, please bless my son, Franz Josef. Keep him safe from harm, and guide him through his life. May he never know war. Shield him from evil things, and always be with him. Amen.*

Ella and Josef Walkow

The date of this photo in not known. It was probably taken in the late 1940s or early 1950s.

Courtesy Franz Walkow

27 - The Boys

The baby breast-fed for several months, and during this time it was really Ella who needed more food. Josef did everything he could to find additional work and augment their food allotments; but Ella, with an exceedingly fast metabolism, was still undernourished and hungry.

As though fate was at war with the young couple, Ella also developed a serious case of mastitis and was hospitalized with abscesses and flu-like symptoms. Ella's condition was severe enough for the doctor to advise her against any further breast-feeding, which was an accepted part of the treatment at the time. Josef performed chores for a farmer and was able to obtain extra food and fresh cow's milk as payment. Their landlady agreed to look after the baby while Josef was out during the day. After a few days, Ella returned home. She looked pale and drawn.

"What are we going to do to feed Franz?" she cried, shaking and inconsolable, wiping her nose and eyes with the back of her hand.

"You just get well," Josef responded, his hand on his wife's shoulder. "I am working for a farmer and he has given me some food and milk."

"This is the last thing I ever expected to happen," she sobbed. "I never thought I would be unable to feed my own baby."

Josef had been holding Franz and handed him to Ella, along with a bottle of warm milk. The baby fussed a bit, as he had when Josef first bottle-fed fed him during Ella's hospitalization. But Franz settled down, and looked into his mother's eyes as he drank.

Ella's eyes dried. There was nothing more beautiful to her than the child in her arms. She calmed down, and caressed her tiny boy.

"My little Franz," she whispered, as she held him.

Franz continued to drink cow's milk. Ella did some laundry for people, and Josef did his handyman projects, often repairing farm machinery. Willie would occasionally stop by and bounce Franz on his lap, happy to have a young one to dote on and spoil. He and Helga had not yet had children.

Josef wrote often to Michael and they shared stories of their young fatherhoods. Michael and Stephania had a little girl. Josef wrote of Franz; Michael wrote of life in Poland and his daughter. Letters were sporadic. It might take a week, a month, or longer for a letter to go either way. Despite advancing post-war reconstruction in Europe, postal services had not yet stabilized to the point of predictability.

Josef learned from Michael that their parents remained in what was now the western Soviet Union—the Ukraine region.

How Josef missed Michael! He wanted his older brother to know Franz, and he wished he could meet his niece. In Michael's absence, Josef nurtured his friendship with Willie.

As 1947 drew to a close, there was some aid from the west trickling sporadically through Germany, and occasionally Josef and Ella received some packages of food and clothing. They had read about a plan the United States was spearheading to offer massive aid to Europe, including Germany. It had not yet been approved within the U.S. It was called the European Recovery Plan, and eventually would be known as The Marshall Plan. But at the end of 1947, it was just a wishful rumor.[35]

A few weeks before Christmas, Josef and Ella were eating a simple supper of bread, soup, and a little bit of chicken.

"How was the baby, today?" he asked Ella as they ate.

"He was crawling around, but the floor is cold."

Ella cooked with a stove fueled by wood. Her supply was running low, and it was time to gather more from anywhere they could find it.

"Josef," Ella asked, "before it snows, why don't we bundle up Franz and the three of us go for a ride in the forest to gather some wood?"

They both had bicycles, and Josef had rigged up a basket on each one for Franz.

Josef responded, "We will have to keep riding farther and farther out of town—the wood close in has all been gathered. Let's collect what we can—it will keep us warm when you use it in the stove."

"I miss having a gas stove. Cooking with wood is much harder."

"You'll have a gas stove someday, Ella. I promise. You take the baby in the basket on your bicycle, and I'll use my basket and the back fender to carry any wood we find."

"That's fine. But it won't work next year."

He looked at her, his eyebrows scrunched.

"What are you talking about?"

"Next year, we will need the basket of your bicycle for the new baby."

He spoon froze in mid-air.

"Another baby?"

"Yes. And don't ask 'how,' Josef! It happened the same way as Franz happened."

They both smiled.

He reached across the table to take her hand. "When do you think the baby is due?"

"August, next year."

"They'll be just eighteen months apart, won't they?"

Ella nodded as she swallowed a spoonful of hot soup. "It makes me tired just thinking of running and scrambling after *two* of them," she said. "I hope the baby is a girl, Josef. We would have one child of each sex then. Wouldn't that be nice?"

Josef didn't say anything. Ella plunked both hands on the edge of the table with a thud, frustrated by her husband's continued silence.

"Josef, are you here? Are you listening to me? Did you hear what I said about how nice it would be for the new baby to be a girl and that we would have a daughter then?"

"A daughter would be wonderful. But Ella, I prefer the baby is a boy. I want Franz to have a brother."

Ella was silent. She knew how Josef cherished his brother, and nodded in consent.

"I just hope the baby is healthy and we have food."

"Me too," he said. "But I really hope the baby is a boy. Franz should have a brother...yes, he needs a brother."

"Two boys will be quite a handful," Ella smiled.

—◦√◦√◦—

As Franz grew out of infancy, he required wooden supports to brace his legs, so they would grow straight. Ella and Josef were glad there was a remedy for his bones, but they hated to see their little boy wearing braces for months.

"If this is the only thing wrong with him, I think we are lucky," Ella said to Josef one evening.

"He probably won't remember he had to wear braces, Ella. Let them do their work, and I think he will be fine. I know he will be fine. He is a happy, bright baby."

Ella or Josef would go to a local farm to obtain milk for their son. On one occasion, Ella traded another small piece of jewelry for the precious liquid. When she returned to their apartment, she poured the milk from its many-times-used glass jar into a drinking glass, placed the glass on the kitchen table, and then carried Franz into the bedroom to change him and put him down for a nap. During that brief interval, Josef walked into the room, and seeing the glass of milk, drank it.

Ella emerged from the bedroom holding her index finger in front of her two closed lips to signal Josef the baby was sleeping. She peeked back into the bedroom one last time and stared for a moment at her slumbering son, never tiring of seeing him asleep, never tiring of seeing her baby, her son, at rest.

Josef had seen her do this final check on their sleeping child many times, and he loved these quiet moments when his wife gazed at Franz. He was a good baby, not fussy, even with his leg braces.

She always looks so tender, so soft, when she stares at Franz. Her eyes flood with love for him. If this is family life, then I couldn't be more content than I am right now.

Ella silently closed the bedroom door and turned to face the kitchen. She noticed the glass she had previously filled was empty, coated only with a white film of milk.

"What did you do?" she hissed at him, pointing at the empty drinking tumbler.

Josef was taken aback, alarmed.

"I drank the milk," he simply said. "I thought you left it on the table for me," he said, his voice quivering a little.

"That was for Franz, not you!"

"Oh, I'm sorry."

"Sorry? You're sorry?" she yelled, her eyes wide.

"Yes, Ella, I am."

"You're selfish—*that's* what you are!"

"Ella, Ella, please, let's not fight."

But Ella was fuming. He had never seen her quite so angry, not even when she confronted him about hitting the farmer who had chased her away from his field the day she trailed him to pick up potato scraps.

Her voice was full of rancor.

"How *could* you do that? How could you drink *his* milk? What's wrong with you?"

She didn't wait for an answer.

"I never thought you could be so selfish, denying your own son a glass of milk that is incredibly hard to get. What were you thinking?"

Her face red, her heart pounding, she turned her back on Josef, headed toward the bedroom, opened the door, and then slammed it behind her, not caring if the noise awakened Franz.

Josef stood in the kitchen, dumbfounded, and then he heard the lock click.

"Sleep on the floor, tonight!" she tossed at him from the bedroom, her jaw tight.

Josef chastised himself. *Why did I think that milk was mine?* He hated when he and Ella had a spat.

Meanwhile, Franz had awakened, and Ella picked him up and cuddled him with a tenderness in stark contrast with the fury she held for her husband. The closeness of the baby against her chest soothed her. She dozed off as she sat in bed, and when she awakened, still holding Franz, she pictured Josef with his one leg, sleeping on a cold floor. Placing the baby on the bed, she unlatched the door, tiptoed into the kitchen, hoping her husband had heard the click and would come to bed. But Josef slept soundly on the floor. But the floor was very cold. Ella smiled gently, covered him with two blankets, tenderly tucking them around him, and then placing a small pillow under his head.

The months leading to the new baby's birth in August were eventful for Germany. At the end of June, 1948, two months before the child was born, the Reichsmark (RM) currency was officially replaced by the Deutschmark (DM) in the western occupied zones of Germany. Individuals were each given a total of DM 60 in two installments.[36] Once the new currency was created and became the official payment method for goods and services, prices stabilized, hyperinflation deflated, and the black market collapsed. The shops filled up with stock, and though nothing was cheap, goods slowly became more available. The currency reform was done in conjunction with the release of funds and the delivery of supplies, mostly from the U.S., through the Marshall Plan, designed to help Europeans rebuild their industries, infrastructure, and agricultural output. In addition to the obvious humanitarian objectives, it was thought a strong Europe, with a good economy, would be the best defense against encroaching Communism.

When Walter Michael was born in a hospital in August of 1948, the milk situation had been resolved. Powdered milk had become available, and people no longer had to supplicate themselves to farmers for milk. As a result, Walter never did drink the milk from the same cow as Franz did.

When it was time to baptize Walter as a Catholic, the priest insisted Josef and Ella have a Catholic wedding ceremony first. The couple dutifully followed this advice, and for a third time, they married. They laughed about it often, realizing there were not many couples who married each other three times.

The Sunday of Walter's baptism, little Franz wore his best clothes. Still wearing his wooden leg braces, he stood next to his parents as cool water was poured over Walter's head, and sacramental prayers were recited. Josef, as usual, silently offered his own special prayer:

Hail Mary, full of grace, the Lord is with thee. Blessed art Thou among women and blessed is the fruit of thy womb, Jesus. Holy Mary, Mother of God, please keep my son, Walter, safe. His middle name is Michael, for my brother. Please let him and my older boy, Franz, have a close and loving relationship, as I enjoyed with Michael. Guide them and keep them safe. Let them live in a world without war. Amen.

There was a glimmer of hope in Germany now. Josef and Ella's lives were full. Josef was rarely without work; the toddler and infant kept Ella busy all the time. At last, life seemed to be settling into a dependable pattern.

Ella returned from doing errands one Saturday, with the two children in tow—one in her arms and the other holding onto her arm. She clutched a cloth shopping bag half-filled with some groceries.

She placed the bag on the kitchen table and settled the boys, as Josef helped.

"Is this all you could get? Some bread and eggs?" asked Josef.

"Yes. That's it. No one wanted to sell me anything. I went to the German delicatessen, and they told me to go to the Polish store, since I married a Pole. So then I went to a Polish store, and they told me to go to a German store, since I am German. What am I supposed to do?"

Josef was quiet.

"Don't go whacking anyone, Josef, do you hear me?"

"Yes, I hear you. I can't believe they are doing this to you."

"Neither can I, Josef. I didn't understand what my mother said to us when we visited her in Heidelberg, before we got married. Do you remember her words?"

"No, I don't, at least not exactly, Ella."

Ella remembered them. She remembered them verbatim.

She repeated Frau Zimmerman's admonition, looking anxiously at Josef: "Your children will be neither Polish nor German, but a mixture. It might be difficult for them, and for both of you, too. Aren't you concerned about it?"

Josef nodded his head slowly, as though a great truth of the universe had suddenly been revealed to him.

Ella initially dismissed her mother's prescient concern. But now...now she completely understood what her mother meant. Frau Zimmerman had been both wise and right.

"I'll go to the Polish stores, Ella. You go to the German stores. Let's try that."

"Why should it work for you any better than it did for me?"

"I don't know if it will. Let's just try it."

Ella agreed, but vowed to fight the prejudice. She knew many Germans harbored increasing and vocal resentment toward displaced persons. The DPs had received preferential treatment since the end of war, three years earlier. Many of her German friends begrudged the guilt they were expected to feel—just because they were German—for every malevolent thing that happened during the war. A handful of Ella and Josef's friends in the same situation as they were in, were beginning to talk of emigrating away from Europe.

The thought of leaving Europe seemed radical to Josef and Ella, and yet the embers of discontent, though not fanned, smoldered quietly.

And the young couple had more pressing matters to address.

Franz was captivated by his little brother, even though the baby was too young to play with him. The young parents noticed their younger son was growing healthily, but Franz, their eldest, was not flourishing. They understood his braces were temporary, but something else troubled them. Franz had trouble gaining weight. Then, in July of 1949, several months after his second birthday, he developed a persistent cough that increasingly was accompanied by thick mucus.

The cough did not abate. In August, armed with a homemade cake as payment, they took him to see a doctor.

The doctor asked them to describe their son's symptoms, then examined Franz. He listened to child's chest, took samples of sputum, and suggested he take an x-ray.

"What's wrong with him?" Ella demanded, as the young boy sat on her lap, his head leaning against her shoulder.

"I don't know yet. But tell me, what does he eat?"

"Anything we can get—some eggs, vegetables when we can get them, fruit, jam, milk, some meat."

"Did you breast feed him?"

"Only for a little while. I had to stop." She told the doctor of her bout with mastitis.

"So, if you could not breast feed him, what milk did he drink?"

"I did some work for a farmer and he supplied fresh milk from his cow, along with some other food," responded Josef.

"Was the milk pasteurized?"

"Pasteurized?" they both said, their faces quizzical.

The doctor explained pasteurization of milk involves heating the milk to a high temperature and then cooling it rapidly so the growth of bacteria is inhibited.

"But he's never gotten sick on milk!" Ella responded.

The doctor paused for a long moment. He knew the word "tuberculosis" could trigger terror. It was an ancient infirmity, as old as humanity itself. He also knew in northern Europe it was considered more of an inherited disease, whereas in southern Europe, the disease was more correctly understood as an infectious ailment.[37] But customs die hard, even in the face of empirical evidence; no doubt, the young parents before him would feel guilty, however unjustifiably, about the condition they would think their son inherited from them.[38]

"I am not sure, Herr and Frau Walkow, but it is possible your son has an early case of tuberculosis."

Ella gasped. Josef's eyes bulged.

"We need to do some tests on him, as well as both of you. Do you have other children?"

"Yes," Josef said. "Our younger son is eleven months old."

"And has he had milk from the same cow?"

"No!" snapped Ella. "He's never had any. Since powdered milk has become available he has been drinking it. Franz drinks that now, too. We don't get milk from the farm any longer."

"Did either of you drink the milk also?"

"Yes, I did. Once," replied Josef, as he glanced sideways at Ella, remembering the night he slept on the cold floor.

"I never did," answered Ella.

The doctor nodded, "Let's test the whole family. Come back on Friday, at 2:00 p.m. I will take an x-ray of Franz's chest then and another sputum test. In the meantime, try to keep Franz away from his little brother. We know the disease, if Franz has it, spreads through contact. It is not anything he inherited from either of you. What is your younger son's name?"

"Walter. Walter Michael."

The doctor jotted Walter's name in the family file he had created during the visit.

They thanked the doctor, and gave him the cake. As they exited his office, Josef and Ella felt they had each been punched hard in the stomach.

Silently, they cycled back to their apartment, and asked Frau Wilkesmann to keep Walter for another hour. Ella prepared Franz for a nap, and once he was asleep, she tiptoed out of the bedroom to the kitchen table.

"How can this happen?" Ella cried.

She looked at Josef and whimpered in disbelief, "We could all have tuberculosis."

Josef wiped tears from his eyes; he had no words to offer.

The little jacket Franz had been wearing was draped over a chair at the kitchen table. Ella picked it up, its lining facing her. She pressed the diminutive wool piece of clothing to her heart and buried her face in it.

"Will he live long enough to outgrow this?" she asked herself. As though smelling a magnificent rose, she inhaled Franz's scent in the jacket's cotton lining.

"My baby!" she wept.

Ella hung the jacket on a wall hook and ran her hand down the fabric's length. She turned to look at Josef, and he got up from the table to walk over to her. They clung to each other in the little, homey kitchen where they thought they had made a safe haven for the family. Desperately, they clung to each other.

The wait until Friday, just two days away, would be interminable.

"Let me go get Walter," Josef finally said, breaking away from Ella, then blowing his nose in his handkerchief.

A skin test for tuberculosis was administered to the whole family. The doctor took sputum samples, too, repeating the diagnostics already in progress for Franz. He led Franz to a room in the rear of his office, and took an x-ray of the boy's chest. They were told they would have to wait a few days for any reaction to the skin test, and analysis of the sputum would take about a week, maybe two, although he had put a rush on Franz's previous sputum test. The doctor also told them he would review the x-rays with them when they came back.

Josef offered to do some work for the doctor as payment, and the doctor told him if he had some work for Josef, he would let him know. Otherwise, the services were free. They thanked the doctor again and went home to wait for the lab results and any reactions any of them might have to the TB skin test. They knew the wait would be difficult, and they tried to distract themselves with work, caring for the boys, and playing outside. For Franz, it turned out to be short wait; he developed a large, nasty, red welt within twenty-four hours of the test—a clear sign of tuberculosis exposure and an indicator he might actually have the disease.[39] The rest of the family showed only a mild reaction, indicating exposure, but not infection.

Three days later at the doctor's office, the physician looked at Franz's arm as he reviewed the lab report of Franz's first sputum sample. The results were positive. He also interpreted the x-rays of the boy's lungs for his parents. Two tiny holes in the right lung could be seen. Every one of Franz's TB diagnostic tests was positive.

Ella could not hold back her tears.

"What now?" asked Josef, his voice quivering.

"Franz needs treatment. There is a sanitarium not far from here, higher up in the mountains. Franz will need to go there for a while."

"You mean take him from us?" Ella cried.

The boys were watching their parents. Franz looked at his mother and pointed to her tearful face.

"What is the value of sending him away to a sanatorium?" asked Josef, trying to control his panic. "And we can't pay for it!"

"Don't worry about payment. TB is a public health concern, and accordingly, people are routinely sent to sanitariums, regardless of their ability to pay for treatment."

"But what is the *point* of sending Franz away? Can't he just be treated at home?" Josef inquired.

"Yes, we'd rather keep him at home, with us," Ella echoed.

"As far as the treatment goes, the tuberculosis bacteria cannot reproduce well where the air is thinner—there is less oxygen. It is thought the higher the altitude, the more positive the effect for the patient.[40] I have already called the facility. They are ready for Franz."

Both Ella and Josef were stunned. Their little boy had to go away...away from them, their home, and their life.

"When? When must he go, Herr Doktor?" asked Ella. "And for how long?"

"As soon as possible. Tomorrow, or the day after that. I don't know for how long he will need to stay; it could be anywhere from six to twelve months."

Ella and Josef were speechless, their eyes wide with fear and filling with tears. Then the anger surfaced.

"*Nine months*?" Josef bitterly complained. "That's a very long time for such a young child!"

"No, I can't give him up. *I can't*. He is staying with us. That's final," Ella declared, as she embraced Franz more tightly against her chest.

The doctor placed his elbows on the desk and weaved the fingers of both hands together. He let the young couple's fear and anger subside before he said anything.

"I cannot imagine what you are feeling right now, Herr and Frau Walkow. I can't imagine."

The words seem to have registered with them; he could see they were looking at him, expecting more.

"But your son is sick. And, you have another son who, I am sure, you wish to remain well."

They both nodded in silence.

"You will be able to visit Franz."

Ella was crying. Josef looked at her "We really have no choice, Ella. Franz needs to go."

"I know, I know," she wept. Looking at the doctor, she wiped her eyes with her handkerchief.

"How often may we visit him?" she pleaded.

"Not more than once every week or every two weeks."

"I can visit several times a week and do any volunteer work the nurses need. Would that be acceptable?" Ella pleaded.

"Frau Walkow, it is too upsetting for the children to always be subjected to saying goodbye to their parents. It is important they get accustomed to the routine at the sanitarium and learn to trust and rely on the staff."

Ella sobbed again, and Josef took her hand, "What the doctor says makes sense, Ella."

She nodded her head in reluctant agreement.

Their two sons looked back and forth between their mother and father. Franz, especially, understood they were crying.

The doctor continued, "I can take him in my car, but I want all of us to wear masks in the car. I will also give you some to take home to use right away. With the knowledge the disease is in your household, it would be best to wear them. Maybe you can make it a game with the boys. Also, it would be best to wash all linens and wipe all surfaces with strong detergent."

Neither Josef nor Ella could speak. There were no words that meant anything. They simply stared at each other.

The doctor added, "I should have the sputum tests for both of you and little Walter in a week or two. Based on your skin test reactions, though, I don't think you have anything to worry about."

"What time should we be here the day after tomorrow to take Franz to the sanitarium?" asked Josef.

The doctor looked at his appointment book. "Meet me here at noon. You may leave your bicycles in my garden while we take Franz to the mountains. I would prefer you leave Walter at home."

"We'll do that," responded Josef. He shook the doctor's hand.

As they left the doctor's office and rode back to their apartment with Franz on Ella's bike and Walter on Josef's bike, Josef imagined a giant yellow balloon hovering above. The balloon represented hope. The war was over, food and other supplies were becoming available, their family was growing, and he always had work, even though he did not make much money. The west, especially America, had a plan to help war-ravaged Europe—including Germany—become a prosperous nation again.

Everything had been looking positive. Everything.

And just like that, the yellow balloon popped and spiraled to the ground as useless strips of tattered trash.

Ella, riding slowly and silently behind Josef, kept her hand on Franz's arm. She harbored an anger she had never felt before, an anger greater than when her mother thwarted her dream to become a librarian.

"This never would have happened if we were living in Canada or Australia or the U.S., and I am *not* raising my family here!" she fiercely muttered aloud.

Josef pedaled steadily, aware of the rhythm of his movements and his artificial leg. He touched his left knee, strong now after a few years of solid activity.

Gently stroking Walter's head, he was lost in thought.

I survived losing my freedom and losing my leg. I do not think I will survive losing one of my sons.

Front Side

Reverse Side

Five Reichsmark Note

The Reichsmark was the currency used in Germany until the Deutschmark replaced it in 1948. In the years immediately following the end of World War II in Europe (June 1945 through June 1948), the Reichsmark became increasingly worthless.

Photo credit: Walter Walkow

28 - An Idea Takes Root

Two days later, Ella and Josef remanded Franz to the doctor's care. The physician drove them thirty-five minutes away to the sanitarium in the mountains. They brought along clothing for Franz and some toys.

They met with their doctor and the intake nurse in the administrative office. Franz was allowed to play in the corner with some communal toys, as well as those they brought from home, and he soon occupied himself with a wooden airplane—a bi-plane. It was a German fighter, a Heinkel HD 38, developed between the first and second World Wars. He used his arms to drive it through the air while his parents were occupied with the nuts and bolts of what life would be like for their son at the sanitarium.

Josef and Ella had so many questions.

"How long will he be here?" Ella asked the doctor, hoping the nine to twelve month duration the doctor mentioned previously had miraculously been diminished.

"If he progresses well, I would expect him to be home in about nine months," the doctor replied. "I know I originally told you up to twelve months, but it could be only nine months."

Ella reflexively placed her hand over her mouth indicating there was nothing "only" about nine months.

Still in shock with the reality of having to be away from their son, Josef choked, "That is a long time for such a little boy!" He took out his handkerchief and blew his nose. "We will miss this entire part of his childhood."

"Nine months!" Ella whimpered, her faced scrunched in sorrow, deep furrows between her eyebrows. She turned to the nurse. "What will you feed him? He can be fussy with some foods, and he doesn't like any kind of pudding. He hates it."

"The children have a very nutritious diet."

"What do you feed them?"

"Fruit, some meat, good bread, cheese, vegetables, and dairy products. He will not be hungry here," the nurse responded."

"And what happens if he is afraid of the dark and cries? What then?" Ella wanted to know.

"Each ward has a night nurse. If any of the children fuss, or need to use the bathroom, she is there to help and comfort the child."

"What if he doesn't want to do something, like go outside and play, or...or...whatever it is you make them do?" Ella wanted to know.

The nurse smiled again, "We encourage the children to take part in all the activities we have planned for them, as well as to take the rest periods we also want them to have. This is not a prison, Frau Walkow. Your child is not being punished. We want him to get well, as you and Herr Walkow do."

"May I write to him? Who will read my letters to him?" Ella wanted to know.

"The children get letters and packages all the time. We read the letters to them if they can't read yet, and they are free to respond. Being so young, Franz probably doesn't write, so we will suggest he draw you a picture and we will send it to you."

"What about his clothing? Who cleans his clothing?"

"We have a laundry on premises, fully staffed. Have you marked his clothes with his name?"

"No, I didn't," Ella answered.

"When we get to his bed to unpack his things, you can mark them." She slipped a pen filled with indelible ink into the pocket of her bright, white, starched uniform.

The nurse turned her attention to Josef, "Herr Walkow, you have been quiet. Your wife has been asking all the questions. Do *you* have any questions?"

"Lice. What about lice? Will he have lice?"

"The children bathe and have their hair washed twice a week. Mattresses are treated weekly. We have not had a lice problem."

244

"Is the water warm? Who bathes them?" he inquired.

"Why yes, we have hot and cold running water. The nurses bathe them. Youngsters are never left unattended in a bathtub or shower."

Ella asked, "What about the room he will be in? Is it kept clean, and is it warm? Are the sheets clean?"

"Yes, it is spotless and it is comfortable, but not overly warm. We have good blankets and crisp, clean sheets on the beds, too. We change the sheets once a week and more often, if necessary."

Josef cleared his throat, "How often will he see a doctor?"

"The doctors here are specialists in lung diseases. He will be seen once or twice a week, and after a few weeks, they will redo his sputum tests and x-rays. We will send the results to your doctor."

"I want to see where he will be staying," Josef said, firmly.

"Let's do that now," the nurse said, as she rose from her chair at the desk.

"Franz, come," said Ella.

"May I take the plane with me?"

Ella looked at the nurse, who nodded in agreement.

But Franz placed the Heinkel back inside the toy box and took out another airplane. This one was metal and a more recent aircraft, with American insignia. He grabbed it and fingered the letters, "Douglas A-20 Havoc."

"That's a nice airplane, Franz. It's from America," his father commented. He didn't say it was probably a model of one of the planes used to defeat Germany. He wanted to protect his son from anything to do with war.

Franz asked, ever so slowly, "A-me-ri-ca?"

"It is a place far away from here," his father answered.

The nurse escorted Josef, Ella, and Franz to the ward where the child would stay. On the walk there, through a maze of hallways, Josef thought about Franz's accommodations. *It had better not be like the cold barracks I had; there had better not be lice, and they'd better be sure they keep him clean!*

245

The doctor stayed in the office to fill out some documents about Franz's tests results, thus far.

Franz, the nurse, Ella, and Josef walked through the building into a large, airy room with ten beds and several large windows.

"Look, Franz, this is going to be your room for a little while. There are other children here, too, and what a nice window you have right near your bed! You can see outside, look at the birds, and watch clouds go by," Josef said, feigning cheerfulness and envy. Ella held onto Franz who leaned against her with his back to her, and she placed her hands around his face, trying to memorize the feel of his smooth, young skin and the curve of his cheeks.

With the Havoc still in his hands, Franz broke away from his mother's embrace and placed the toy on his bed. He then rushed to the window and threw the top half of his body onto the window's deep sill in order to sit on it and see outside. He turned to his father, "Poppi, Poppi, tree..big tree. Look...tree," as he pointed at the window.

"Franz, I wish I had a tree like that to look at!" Josef teased. Franz returned to his bed and retrieved the airplane from the bed and once again flung himself onto the windowsill. He flew the American bomber across the spotless glass of the window, and Josef helped him. They were like two little boys, but Josef's heart was breaking as he played with the airplane.

Ella sorted through the clothing she had brought for Franz and marked each piece with his name. She clutched each small garment tightly, not wanting to let any of them go as she furtively glanced around the room. Some of the beds held patients too sick to be outside, and each bed, including Franz's, was assigned to a child. Her heart ached for them; it ached for their mothers.

The nurse showed Ella where to place Franz's clothing, shoes, and toys in his cabinet that also served as a night table and dresser. Ella asked Franz, "Would you like to place your toys in the dresser?"

He nodded his head in agreement and arranged his toys from home in the lowest of three drawers. He was still holding the Havoc as the small troupe toured the rest of the facility that was opened to the public. They saw the dining hall, the pool, visitation rooms, the chapel, the medical exam rooms, and the playground with a few swings, a slide, some seesaws, and a jungle gym. When they returned to the intake office, the doctor had finished his paperwork, and Ella and Josef had to sign some of them, attesting to Franz now being in the care of the sanitarium. The doctor left to wait in the car for Josef and Ella.

As they prepared to leave their son, the young couple faked enthusiasm. They wanted Franz to feel like he was going to have a wonderful time at a kid's camp, and they needed to convince themselves of the same thing.

When it was time to say goodbye, they took turns hugging and kissing Franz, and assured him he would have lots of fun, and would play games outside with other children. They told him they would see him next weekend, even though he didn't know what "next weekend" meant.

He cried, no, screamed as they left him in the care of the nursing staff. The child was inconsolable.

"Mami! Poppi! *Nein*, come back. Mami!" he wailed. As the nurse shepherded him down the long corridor to his room, the little boy tightly grasped his airplane in one hand and tried to extricate himself from the nurse's firm grasp on his other hand. Josef and Ella could hear his ragged, frantic gasps of "Mami! Poppi!" over and over again, the sound becoming muted as the building swallowed him within its cavernous passageways.

Outside, Ella leaned against the doctor's car, sobbing. Josef cradled her shoulders, tears streaming from his face, his nose red and full of mucus. All they thought of was the receding sound of Franz's cries.

The doctor had witnessed this heartrending scene more than once over the course of the years he practiced medicine. As he approached them, he tried to ease their sadness.

247

"He is not suffering from an advanced case, Herr and Frau Walkow. With the reduced oxygen at high altitude and the cool, fresh air, I hope he can return home quickly; quickly, that is, for TB. It takes time for the lungs to heal; that's why we think it will be about nine months, more or less."

"Nine months!" Ella whimpered, covering her face with both hands.

"I know this separation is difficult. I don't think it may help you feel any better, but you are not the only parents having to cope with a sick child. We've learned of several other children who contracted TB and we have traced their illness to the same cow, on the same farm. The animal will be destroyed."

It didn't make the young couple feel any better, but the doctor again assured them the cow would be destroyed.

The two distraught parents returned with the doctor to his office in town. There was little conversation, and each of them was lost in thought. Ella and Josef rode their bicycles home from the doctor's office. During the ride, Ella felt as though something had been ripped from within. Josef thought of Franz, of the first time he held him; and he thought of Frau Mirz and her aversion to lice. When they arrived home, they scooped Walter from Frau Wilkesmann's arms. They hugged him closely, smothering his neck and head with kisses. The delighted baby giggled at the attention and ran his hand over his father's nose and his mother's lips, flailing his arms in unfettered joy.

Ella and Josef said little the remainder of the day, but Josef couldn't stop thinking about Franz: *Was he crying? Did he eat? Was he in bed already? Was he lonely? Was he getting affection and adequate care?* He looked over at Ella, who was preparing some supper. She looked angry, he thought. Scared. Furious. He was waiting for her to explode in rage and fear. He kept his distance and busied himself writing a long letter to Michael, explaining what was happening. He didn't know if would take a week or a month for the letter to reach Poland; he just knew writing it helped.

Without Franz's presence, there was a palpable emptiness in their apartment, and Ella did not have an emotional outburst. It surprised Josef.

For the remainder of the week, they both went about their daily routines, and on the weekend, they rode a bus up the mountain to see Franz, and took their bicycles with them for the ride back.

It was a difficult visit. Franz was happy to see his parents, and when they departed, he was just as upset as when they had initially left him at the sanitarium. Josef and Ella delayed their bicycle trip down the mountain for a good half hour, until Ella had composed herself enough to ride without crashing; Josef insisted on it.

Finally she said, "I'm ready. Let's go home."

"Are you sure you can ride safely now?" Josef asked, taking her hands in his.

She took a deep breath, "Yes."

"You lead this time. I'll ride behind you for a change." Josef wanted to keep an eye on her and see if she would falter and need help.

"I'm ready...let's go," Ella said as she mounted her bicycle and took the lead.

As one day melted into the next, they knew it was too early to determine if there was any change in Franz's condition. Josef and Ella dreaded the idea of having to repeat the heart-wrenching visit every week. And, during the winter, they couldn't ride their bicycles in the snow. They would not see their son as frequently as they would like to, and they had no phone they could use to call the sanitarium and talk to him.

As the third week without Franz at home came to a close, Ella sat at the table after supper, sipping hot tea. She poured one for Josef, too, while Walter played with a toy on a new rug placed in the living area. Ella had been unusually quiet the past few days, and Josef always wondered what she was thinking during her silent times.

"Josef, I have been too upset to talk about it until now, but I want us to consider going to the west."

He stirred a little sugar into his tea. "When you mention 'the west,' what do you mean?"

"United States, Canada, even Australia. Someplace better than here in Europe."

Josef sat back in his chair, and swallowed hard.

"Things are getting better here, Ella. We have more food than before, even more clothing. I always have work. Franz is getting the care he needs. Walter is doing well. The doctor told us our sputum tests are normal. We don't have TB."

"It's not just TB, Josef. Not just that, although I am certain if we lived in the west, Franz would never have received tainted milk."

"What is it then?"

"Our children are half-breeds here in Germany. They are not German, and they are not Polish. My mother was so right. The anger people have for DPs like you and women like me is visible in the streets and in the shops. Just the other day I saw a girl I knew from school in Heidelberg. She was here in Stockach, and when I told her we had two children and you are Polish, she stopped talking and spat on the ground at my feet, then turned her back to me. It was horrible."

"What did you do?"

"I yelled something at her."

"What did you yell?"

"It doesn't matter, Josef."

"Tell me, Ella, what did you say?"

"I said something about she must have learned nothing from the war. Her heart hadn't changed." Ella paused and looked at her husband, "We are living with many people who just don't want mixed couples here."

Josef had no answer to her comment.

More change. A huge change. That is what Ella is suggesting. She has no idea how big a change she is talking about.

His shoulders slumped forward. A suffocating heaviness pulled his stomach downward with a truth he did not want to acknowledge, a truth he dreaded. Hatred toward Poles had poisoned Ella's friend, and resentment toward DPs was increasing, breeding more hatred. Josef tried to imagine the scene where Ella met her girlhood friend. He wished Ella did not have to experience what had happened. He was disappointed.

"Ella, we will get through this. People can't stay angry forever."

"Josef, I don't want the children to grow up being despised. We can't raise them here."

Ella walked to the new rug where Walter was playing and picked him up, smoothing his hair tenderly.

It was the end of 1949 and the war had been over for four-and-a-half years. They had two children. Germany, at least in the west, was a republic, and, thankfully, not militarized. But Josef, too, had been the object of disrespect and also sensed the resentment of the Germans who seemed to wish the DPs would just go home.[41] All of Europe—not just West Germany—was tired of DPs, because too many refused to return to their homelands, including Josef. Often it was because their countries had been incorporated into the Soviet Union or were Soviet satellite countries.

"I have no idea how much it would cost to leave home and start fresh in a new country. Neither of us speaks English, Ella. That is a big concern. And what makes you think it would be better in the west?"

"I read, Josef. I read magazines and books. I listen to the radio. Immigrants of all kinds go to the west, and especially in America, they get steady work. I've read many stories about DPs who have settled in the U.S. They may have little to begin with, but it seems if they work hard and save money, they have good lives. And there is plenty of food! As for the language, we'll learn whatever language we need to. I don't see any reason why we shouldn't give ourselves the same opportunities."

Her confidence and conviction showed a hidden strength Josef had not seen before. *She seems so sure of it all, as though learning a new language is the easiest thing in the world.*

Suddenly, he thought of Michael. He hadn't seen him since 1946, but Josef enjoyed some comfort knowing they were at least on the same continent! Moving to the west would create another physical barrier between them. They would be an ocean apart, and depending on where they settled, perhaps another whole continent apart, too.

"Josef, can you inquire about emigrating...what is involved, how to do it, what it costs, which country is the best to go to, and what kind of work is available?"

He tapped his right index finger slowly on the table. Despite whatever it might cost, they simply did not have the funds. He had friends here. His skills were appreciated here. Stockach had become his home.

Something felt very heavy in his chest.

Ella added, "Some other couples like us left Germany already. Do you remember the couple upstairs?"

She didn't wait for Josef to respond. "He was a Polish DP, like you, and there was the tall German farm girl who visited him all the time. Do you remember them?"

Again she didn't wait for Josef's answer. "She would bring him all kinds of food and throw out what they didn't eat while *we* were hungry. Oh God, I hated that, Josef. They moved to America—the United States. Can you imagine that? America!"

Josef sat there, stupefied.

"I think they went through the Catholic Church or something like that."

Annoyed, he responded, "Of course I know the couple upstairs moved. We said goodbye to them and they agreed to keep in touch with us and let us know where they settle. But slow down, Ella, slow down!"

More gently, he said, "Our son is sick, and we don't know when he is coming home. This can wait, don't you agree?"

"I'm not saying we should move today. What harm is there in finding out how to relocate somewhere else? You have contacts in the DP community. Can you try to find out how it is done?"

Her lower lip trembled. "This isn't easy for me. I've spent my whole life here in Germany. It is my home, but it is the boys I'm concerned about." Her voice cracked when she said "the boys."

Josef sighed, still irritated. He didn't want to think about moving. Ella had blindsided him, and he wondered how long she had been thinking about leaving their home.

"Will you look into it, Josef?" she pleaded.

"I'll see what I can find out, but all this talk about moving has made me tired. I want to take a nap."

His comment seemed to satisfy her for the moment—she shook her head in consent, and handed Walter to him, kissing the child on the head, first.

But Josef's heart was like a lump of dense wood in his chest. He remembered how he felt the day he bid farewell to Michael and Stephania when they returned to Poland.

I don't know how many more farewells I have inside me.

He cooed to Walter, "Let's take a little nap and dream of kielbasa, bratwurst, and some sausages called 'hot dogs' in America. I had some at the barracks after the war ended, my son. They aren't as good as our European sausages, though."

Walter encircled his arms around Josef's neck and rested his head on his father's shoulder.

Josef glanced back at Ella to see if she heard him say "hot dogs," as though to tease her, but she was already engaged in another pursuit. He headed with Walter into the bedroom.

Ella took out her crochet needle and woolen yarn to launch a project she had been contemplating since Franz went away. She selected some pastel colored yarn and then made the first of many stitches that would become a small blanket for Franz's bed at the sanitarium. She didn't care if the nurse and doctor talked about how cooler, lower oxygen air helped the lungs heal. She wanted Franz to be embraced by the blanket, as though it was she who would be hugging him. Her plan was to make it as closely stitched as she could, to help keep her little boy warm, to know a piece of her would be sheltering him.

The fuzzy wool slipped quickly through her fingers, warming her fingertips as she crocheted. Tears trickled down her cheeks, and then she burst into tears. She allowed herself the luxury of crying for some time before she made herself hot tea. Then she returned to her crochet work, and the repetitive action of creating stitch after stitch soothed her.

"This isn't fair, not to Franz, and not to our little family. What have we done to him by giving him diseased milk? Did the farmer know the cow was infected? Franz getting sick would never, never, never have happened in America," she whispered to herself, her needle working furiously. "Never."

A few weeks later they visited Franz and brought him the soft, woolly, pale blue, white, and yellow coverlet Ella made.

Franz held their hands and walked around the facility. They sat outside and had some rich, hot cocoa. It seemed he wasn't getting any worse, and a battery of tests was planned, including x-rays, to determine if there was any improvement.

During the ensuing weeks, Ella continued to think of leaving Germany, but she did not bring the topic up again with Josef. She would wait until the new year.

1950 approached, and Ella, Josef, and Walter spent a quiet, snowy New Year's Eve at home with Willie and Helga. Ella made a small roast, and Willie brought beer, potatoes, and cake. Except for Walter, who was delighted with all the adult attention, their thoughts were of Franz, his absence looming large in the small apartment. They discussed the new republic West Germany had become, with a German, rather than an Allied, leader. The official name of West Germany was the Federal Republic of Germany. Konrad Adenaur, a devout

Catholic and former mayor of Cologne, became its first *Bundeskanzler,* or Chancellor.⁴² Though still subject to Allied oversight, Germany was healing, politically. They hoped Franz would heal also.

The following day was a holiday, and a welcome day off. At breakfast Josef asked Ella, "Do you think Franz will remember Walter?"

Ella placed her fork on the plate and folded her hands in her lap. "I don't know. He hasn't seen Walter for five months. I am afraid someday when we visit Franz he won't recognize *us* and think we are strangers. We can't see him often during the winter, either."

Josef sipped his tea and noticed Ella was not eating. "Ella, eat your breakfast."

She grasped her stomach, "I'm not hungry," and then gave Walter a spoonful of warm farina.

"It won't help Franz at all if you get sick."

"I lost my appetite."

They sat in silence, Josef eating, and Walter being fed by his mother until Ella blurted, "Walter will have no idea who his brother is when Franz comes back...*if* he comes back!" Little Walter stared at his mother, surprised by her quivering, loud voice.

She was on the verge of tears and Josef could see she was trying to hold them back.

Neither of them spoke until Josef thought of a possible solution.

"Willie has a camera. I am going to ask him to take photos of us and Walter and we will leave them with Franz." He looked at Ella, waiting for some comment, but none came.

He continued, "When we are with Franz, we will take some pictures of him alone and with us, and show them to Walter every day. What do you think, Ella?"

She sat back in her chair, and looked at Josef.

"Ella, don't you think the photographs are a good idea?"

She took a ragged, deep breath, "That does sound like a good idea and...and...I'll put my lipstick on for the pictures," she teased hesitantly.

Josef was happy her mood brightened, and as he brought his plate to the sink, he remembered all those nights at Willie's house. His routine then was to get up from the table and deposit his silverware, plates, and glass in the sink while Frau Mirz waited for him to slowly maneuver around her kitchen with his crutches, and then with his prosthesis. He was homesick for Poland then, and now, well, now he was faced with the idea of moving to another country and a totally different culture again. The whole idea of it wore him out.

As Ella washed and dried the dishes, Josef sank into the comfortable easy chair that came with their furnished rooms. He held Walter on his lap, and after about twenty minutes, the child cuddled into his Poppi's chest and arm, and fell asleep. Finished with the dishes, Ella gathered her yarn to crochet.

Josef relaxed deeper into the chair, stretched his arm muscles, and closed his eyes. His mind wandered to a conversation he and Willie had on a cool Saturday afternoon, not long after Ella first brought up the idea of moving.

Helga had opened the door.

"Josef, what a nice surprise!"

"It is good to see you, Helga. You look wonderful." Her blonde hair was pulled back and arranged in a bun. She was glowing.

"How are you feeling?" Josef asked.

"Just fine. The baby is due in less than four months, and everything seems to be going quite well. We are so excited!"

"You will both be wonderful parents," Josef said, grasping Helga's hands in his. "Is Willie home?"

"Yes, he is in the shed in the back."

"Ah, the shed. I know it well. May I go out there?"

"Of course, but you may not recognize it inside. Willie has made it his own private little retreat."

Josef walked through the kitchen. He would always think of it as Sonya's kitchen, despite Helga being the mistress of the house. When he opened the door to the garden, Willie saw him and greeted him with a firm handshake.

Willie echoed Helga's words. "What a nice surprise, Josef. Come in the shed. I put a small kerosene heater in there. It's nice and snug. Helga makes me keep it clean and orderly, too," he said with a smile. "How are Ella and the boys?"

"Walter is growing and seems to be a happy and healthy baby. Thank God, none of us has tuberculosis. We try to see Franz as often as we can make it up into the mountains."

"How is he doing?"

"It's too early to tell. He isn't worse, they tell us. We want him home with us."

Willie nodded his head. When Josef had told him about Franz, it was after all of the family had been tested and the sputum and skin tests were negative for Ella, Josef, and Walter. Willie thought how considerate it had been of Josef not to come to the house until he knew he was not capable of spreading the disease. His heart ached for his friend. After everything he had endured, this was not fair.

"When do you see him next?"

"We hope to get there before Christmas."

Josef fussed with his fingers.

"Is there something on your mind?" Willie asked.

"Yes, there is."

"Well, out with it," Willie commanded.

Josef sighed deeply.

"I don't know where to start, Willie."

"Just say it."

It's about moving. Ella is convinced we should leave Germany and emigrate to the west—America, or Canada, or Australia."

Willie straightened his back. This comment was the last thing he ever thought he would have heard Josef say.

"But why? Things are getting much better here."

"She believes Franz would never have developed TB if we were living in one of those countries."

"You don't know that, for sure."

Josef didn't say anything.

"Are you aware the infected cow was shot and its carcass burned? The local authorities oversaw it. I know that doesn't make you feel any better Josef, but it is good to know no one else can get infected."

Josef shrugged his shoulders and flicked his wrists outward.

The cow being dead doesn't help my son.

"There is another thing Ella is anxious about, too."

"What is it?"

"She is concerned for our sons' futures here. They are not fully German, nor are they fully Polish. There have been a few incidents when shopkeepers wouldn't serve us. It really upsets my wife. She feels she is being rejected by her own people."

Willie lowered his head and shook it from side to side.

"Old habits die hard, I think."

"Yes, but these old habits are in force during my sons' formative years. *Sie sollen alles werden, was sie werden wollen.* I want them to be anything they desire to be. I never had that choice, and neither did Ella."

"I don't want you to go," Willie said, almost in a whisper. Looking directly at Josef, he added, "Ella may be right though, when you think of it from the perspective of your sons' futures. From anything I've read about the west, especially America, it doesn't seem to matter *who* you are or what your nationality is. What seems to matter most is what you *do*, what you accomplish."

Josef didn't respond to Willie's comment. His eyes brimmed, and to quell his tears he looked around the shed. Willie had placed some wood planks on the floor and added an area rug and an upholstered easy chair. It was the chair from the room Josef occupied when he was recuperating after his surgery.

"You need some electricity in here, Willie."

"That's beyond my abilities."

"But not mine. Let's get it done soon. You can help me with it. Then, every time you come in here, you will think of me when you use the light switch."

Willie scanned the space he had modified. It was comfortable, and Josef would always be a part of it. He turned to his friend.

"So, you're going then?" he asked timidly, "to the west?"

Josef shook his head from side to side. "I don't know, I just don't know, Willie. If we do go, obviously it won't happen until Franz gets better. Or, as Ella says, *if* he gets better."

"But you said he isn't any worse. That's a good thing, don't you think so?"

"I suppose, but what I really want is to see good test results."

There was a heavy silence between them.

"Tell me, Josef, which country will it be?"

"I haven't thought about it. I don't *want* to think about it! Some other people in our situation, you know, a Polish DP and a German wife, have gone to America. I just don't know. Ella asked me to talk with the authorities at the small DP camp in town to see how all this is done. I will do that, just to satisfy her, but my heart isn't in it."

He didn't say anything for a moment, then added, hopefully, "Maybe she will just forget about it."

Willie gave him a withering look, a look that said "You should know better."

"I know, Willie, I know. Ella will definitely not forget about it."

Josef stared at Willie's hands and smiled. He noticed Willie wore two rings—his wedding band, and the silver signet ring his brother Gunter had given him.

Willie saw the smile. "And just what are you grinning about?"

Josef laughed, "Are you aware of something we both have in common?"

"What is that, Josef?"

"Take a look at our hands."

Willie looked at his hands, and then at Josef's, "What about them?"

"We both are wearing wedding bands."

⁓ᔐᕹ⁓

Wedding bands, Josef mused as he broke his reverie and sat up in the chair. He fingered the thin band on his hand, then fondled Walter's light brown, almost blond, hair while he kissed the top of the child's head. The display of affection did not disturb the little boy who contentedly and safely slept in his Poppi's arms.

Josef stared at the boy's long eyelashes and smiled as he admired his younger son. With Walter still nestled in his arms, Josef surrendered to the softness of the chair, closed his eyes, and fell speedily into a dreamless sleep.

Ella's crochet needle stabbed the silence in the room.

Getting Cool Air at a TB Sanitarium in the Alps

Since it was thought the cold air helped heal the lungs, patients spent time outdoors. In this photograph, children at a sanitarium in the Alps are exposed to cold, crisp air.

Image is in Public Domain

29 - Making Plans

On an uncharacteristically mild Sunday in March of 1950, Ella and Josef visited Franz, toting Willie's camera with them. They had taken pictures of themselves with Walter and had gotten the film developed; their plan was to leave the photos with Franz.

When they arrived at the sanitarium and asked for Franz, the nurse in charge looked at them, quizzically.

"Weren't you told Franz is no longer here?"

Flabbergasted, Josef and Ella looked at each other, then at the nurse.

"What do you mean he's not here?" Josef asked in disbelief, clutching his hat in his hand, his knuckles white.

"He was transferred to another facility earlier this week. Your doctor should have notified you."

"No one told us anything!" Ella responded, almost in a panic. "Where *is* he? And *why* was he moved?"

"Have a seat here in my office. Let me pull out his file."

Panicked, Josef and Ella sat at the edges of their chairs across from the nurse on the other side of desk, their hearts pounding and their bodies tense.

The nurse retrieved Franz's folder from the file drawer, opened it, and reviewed several pages of information. She then opened an additional file marked "Transfers" in dark lettering on the tab, and scanned the papers inside that folder. The silence in the room roared.

The nurse cleared her throat and looked at the young couple sitting stiffly before her.

"Herr and Frau Walkow, there seems to be something amiss with these files. Let me make a few phone calls to determine what transpired."

Josef and Ella glanced at each other. Ella cried out and stood up. "What happened to Franz?"

"Franz was fine when he was transferred. But the detailed transfer information seems to be missing. Please give me a few minutes."

Ella's heart was pounding, and all the color drained from Josef's face.

They were terrified their child was taken away, never to be seen again. This was a haunting specter from the war, when non-German, Aryan-looking children in countries conquered by Germany were forcibly removed from their families to be raised as Germans, in German families. The program was a facet of the *Lebensborn*[43] campaign. Could it be happening again because Franz was so fair-skinned and blond?

The nurse telephoned the chief administrator, explaining the problem to him. After she responded to what appeared to be a series of rapid questions, she handed the phone to Josef.

"The administrator would like to talk to you."

"Hello," Josef barked.

"Good day, Herr Walkow," the administrator said. "As soon as I get into the office in the morning, I will determine where Franz was sent and why."

"Why did you take him away? Is the Lebensborn program active again?" Josef yelled into the phone.

"No, Herr Walkow. That horrible program is illegal and I always thought it was immoral, even when it was allowed under Hitler. We will find Franz. I don't know why you weren't informed, and I am quite sorry. This is not how we operate the sanitarium. We will get the problem resolved."

"Resolved? This is my son you are talking about. I want to know where he is. Now!"

Josef slammed the phone on its cradle and addressed the nurse. "We don't have a telephone. No one in the building where we live has a telephone. How are we supposed to be contacted?"

"Your doctor should have told you. Let me call him now."

She dialed doctor's number. When she relayed the problem to him, he was just as surprised as Josef and Ella. He had never been informed Franz was to be moved. The nurse repeatedly said, "I'm sorry, Herr Doktor." Before she hung up, she said, "We will find out."

The nurse sat deep in her chair and intertwined her fingers. "There is a problem with our records. We have to determine what happened, and when we do, we will call your doctor. He will get word to you. As you can surmise, he was surprised also, and quite angry."

"How, just *how* could you move him and not know where he is?" Ella implored. "How could you move him and not secure our permission first? *How*? Tell me."

"I do not know why this happened, Frau Walkow. We will find him. I am sure it is just a paperwork issue."

"My son is not just paperwork!" Josef yelled, as he got up and slammed his chair against the desk.

"I know he is not just paperwork," the woman in charge responded, as she pushed her own chair away from the desk, wary of Josef's outburst.

Ella got up and placed her hand on Josef's arm. He shook her hand off and walked toward the window, looking outside, his arms folded tightly across his chest. Ella took a breath from deep inside, knowing one of them needed to calm down. Josef was not that person at the moment, and she had never seen him quite so upset. Emotions could control her later, but right now, she needed to know how they were going to find Franz.

She left Josef at the window and turned to the woman. In the coolest, most businesslike voice she could muster, she asked, "What other sanitariums might he have been transferred to?"

"There are two within an hour's drive from here. Most likely he was taken to one of them. I can't imagine what you must be feeling right now. I also have children." She took a deep breath, "May I get you both a cup of warm tea?"

"No, no tea, thank you," Ella tersely responded. "Would you please call the other two sanitariums and find out if he is at one of them?"

The woman hesitated.

Josef turned to her.

"Call them!" he bellowed, like a master sergeant.

"Let me find the numbers."

While the nurse pulled a placard of phone numbers from her desk, Ella walked to the window to be near Josef.

"How could they do this?" he hissed.

"I don't know. I'm upset too, but let's allow this woman to call and find out." Ella's hands were shaking.

The woman dialed the first facility and then the second. Each time she hung up the phone without having talked to anyone.

"No one answers in either building," she announced. "That isn't unusual, especially on the weekends when their business offices may not be staffed."

"What now?" Ella demanded. "This is my *child* you have misplaced!"

Timidly, the woman advised them there was nothing else to be done today and to return home to wait until they heard from their doctor.

"You just want us to leave here, where our son was, and go back to our normal lives as though nothing has happened? Do you really think we can do that?" Josef asked through clenched teeth.

"Herr Walkow, I do not think there is anything else we can do today. I am sorry, I really am."

Josef and Ella stood there, as though they had been stripped of their clothes and their dignity, fearful not for themselves, but for Franz.

Without saying another word, they headed toward the office door, and as they did, the woman intercepted them. "We will find out where he was sent."

They looked at her, but did not respond, then left the room and headed into the hall, toward the exit door.

Josef and Ella sat outside in the bright sunlight at a round wrought iron table near the entrance. Although the temperature was chilly, the sunlight made them comfortable. Neither of them was ready to ride down the mountain.

"How can this happen? *How*, Josef?" Ella queried in disbelief.

Josef looked down at the new grass coming up between his shoes. It was bright and green, young and fresh. He felt ancient and worn-out. With the crushing panic he felt because no one knew where his son was, he realized his heart ached for his own parents.

How did my mother and father cope with life when Michael was captured as a prisoner of war and I was carted away from home?

Now, he knew.

How did they grieve, not knowing where their sons had been sent?

Now, he knew.

Did they survive the grief?

That, he didn't know.

"What gives anyone the right to take our son from us, even if it is for his own health? What gives anyone the right to transfer him without telling us, without our giving consent? Who do the doctors think they are? Who do all of these administrators think they are? Who?" he asked Ella, his fists tight, and his voice escalating.

Josef rarely complained, but Ella could see his anger, fear, and resentment were raw and bleeding. She felt it too, yet despite the profound dismay hounding the back of her throat, making it difficult to talk, she took long, visceral breaths, as though they came from the tips of her toes to her nose and mouth.

"I don't have any answers to your questions, Josef," Ella replied in a soft voice.

"No, I don't either, Ella." They held each other's hands across the table and fixed their glance on each other with pained, fearful eyes. Ella sniffled and let go of Josef's hands. She took a handkerchief from her purse to wipe her eyes and blow her nose, then took Josef's hands in hers again and squeezed them.

"We should get home to Walter," she said after a while.

Josef broke his grasp on Ella's hands.

"Are you ready to go, Josef?"

"Not yet."

"What are you thinking?"

"About the war, about my parents, about making decisions for myself and for my family."

She nodded her head.

He looked at her, his head tilted to the left, taking a ragged breath, "Maybe you're right about going to the west."

Before Ella could say anything, he stood hastily and walked toward his bicycle, parked under an early-budding tree near the sanitarium's entrance.

Ella followed him, saddened it took an event like the authorities losing their son to get Josef to consider life might be better somewhere else.

They mounted their bicycles, Josef out front. This time Ella would need to keep an eye on him. The road was clear and the ride home was uneventful.

The following day progressed gruesomely for the couple, and Josef worked distractedly. Neither they nor the doctor heard anything from the sanitarium. He was frequently jittery and he repeatedly asked himself, *How could they have let this happen? How could they move Franz without our permission? How could they have lost him?* Although the war had ended and reconstruction was progressing well, he was overtaken by a persistent feeling of being on the sharp edge of terror. Ella often awakened at night, and would cry herself back to sleep. Not knowing where their son was made her even more unwavering in her determination to leave Europe.

The chief administrator was unable to definitively determine where Franz was sent until they had traced all their transfer records, interviewed personnel at work for the past few weeks, and made a series of phone calls. He contacted the Walkow family doctor with updates on the task of finding Franz, and the doctor then sent a note via courier to Josef and Ella to let them know what was happening. On Monday there was still no word of Franz's whereabouts. Tuesday passed without any word, also. In the end, the chief administrator drove to the facility where Franz was reported to be, to confirm it was actually him.

By Wednesday of that panicked, disorienting week, they received another note from their doctor telling them Franz had been located. The boy had been moved to a sanitarium where they had taken more tests, and the patients were not quite as sick as in the first sanitarium where Franz had been a patient. Apparently, there had been an emergency with one of the patients, and the process of completing all the documentation for Franz's transfer was abandoned and never completed.

Very un-German, Josef thought ruefully.

Despite his relief at Franz having been found, this intolerable and inexcusable mishap—misplacing his son—finally made Josef concede to Ella's idea of leaving Europe as their best option for a normal life. He didn't tell her, though, but decided to do a little research.

He visited a local library and reviewed recent magazine articles about life in America. Josef was amazed at the photos of jet planes fighting in Korea, but he was simultaneously saddened at the existence of yet another war. It seemed the farm land and forests in America were endless. The automobile advertisements were beautiful and he wondered if someday, if he ever moved to America, he would own one.

He made an appointment to talk to the authorities at the DP camp within the next two weeks.

Before that appointment, though, he and Ella took a bus to the new sanitarium. It was a longer ride than to the first sanitarium, and the fare cost them more, which took a bite out of their food budget. The doctors told them Franz's tests were very good. A new set of x-rays showed the holes in his lungs were closing; he had gained weight and was very active. His leg braces had been removed, and his bones were straight.

Their son would be home in a month or two. When they saw Franz, they ran to him and held him tightly. The boy looked better—much better. And Ella and Josef were delighted his leg braces were no longer needed.

And he remembered they were his parents.

They had borrowed Willie's camera again, and a staff member took pictures of the three of them to show to Walter. In each photo, Franz held the Havoc American bomber he had played with at the first hospital. They allowed him to take it with him when he was transferred. It was his favorite toy, and he took it everywhere he went. Ella and Josef showed Franz the photos of Walter they had taken, calling the child in the photo "your little brother."

Because "month" or "a few weeks" did not mean much to the three-year-old Franz, they promised him they would visit four or five more times before he could come home. When they kissed and hugged Franz before departing, the three of them experienced another difficult farewell.

Departures never got any easier.

Before they boarded the bus to return home, Ella took her husband's hand. "I still want to move."

Josef sighed and simply nodded his head. Once they were seated on the bus, Josef turned to her. "I know you want to move. This week I am seeing the authorities at the DP camp to find out how it is done and how much it will cost."

Ella looked at him and gave him a small smile. "Good."

"Good? Is that all you can say?"

"Yes, Josef, it's good you will find out about moving."

That's it? Good? Is that all she has to say? Does she have any idea what is means to move to a new country?

Ella had the film from the camera developed and showed the pictures to Walter. She told him the boy in the photographs was his big brother who was sick in a hospital and would be coming home soon. She did not know if Walter understood what she was saying, but he pointed at the images of the boy in the photographs, repeating "Franz" each time. Ella also showed him pictures of he and Franz together, when Walter was a baby.

By the end of February, the doctor had sent them a letter telling them Franz could come home sometime in June. They were ecstatic, although they wondered how the homecoming would play out between the two children.

Ella made some new clothing for Franz, and they continued to prepare Walter for the return of his brother, and for sharing toys and his bed. Josef often sat on the area rug with Walter, playing with him and his toys, pretending to be a little boy, pretending to be a big brother, pretending to be Franz.

～ຊາຊ～

The discussion with a relocation counselor at the DP camp turned out to be long and informative.

Josef was told it was not at all unusual for mixed couples like them—a Polish man and a German woman—to emigrate. Prejudice still existed at home, and some Poles had no homes in the east to return to. Quite a few refused to live under the Soviet regime.

The relocation counselor told Josef there was neither stigma nor defeat in the desire to move. It was probably the wisest choice, and he advised Josef about different country's quotas and timeframes for accepting refugees. If he was interested in the United States, which was generically called "America," it would best for the family to be in a queue as soon as possible, to meet an immigration deadline for the following year, 1951. Josef was concerned about Franz having had TB. He was advised of the health processes. As long as Franz's medical records indicated he had been cured, there should be no problem. Josef's most pressing concern was the cost. He and Ella simply didn't have the money to move.

The question of money turned out to be the easiest to resolve, however. An organization called Catholic Relief Services would either find a sponsor for them or act as their sponsor, and pay for the family's passage. The agency was very well-prepared to accept refugees. They had a network of small business people and farmers in the U.S. who registered with them for workers who had the skills they needed. When the refugees entered the U.S., they were housed in a hotel until they were employed and able to secure other lodging.[44] A man with Josef's skills would be in demand, the official believed.

"How much does it cost?" Josef asked.

"Catholic Relief Services pays for your ship passage."

"I still want to know how much it costs."

"It will cost 250 American dollars, per person.[45] That would be $1,000 for your family of four."

Josef stared at him, his mouth opened in shock. It was a fortune. $1,000 equalled over DM 4,000.[46] The amount was beyond his comprehension. He and Ella had only DM 150.

"It will not be possible for me to ever pay back that much money."

"You do not need to pay it back, but Catholic Relief Services also gives you some initial spending money, about $300."

Josef's eyebrows shot up.

"You will need to pay that back. Chances are you will make much more in America, and you will have many years to repay the loan."

Josef was now quite curious. "How much does a house cost in the United States?"

The official removed a sheet of statistics from the middle drawer of his desk. It was titled *U.S.A. 1948-1949 Statistics.*

"A pre-owned home, on average is less than $2,000, but that cost increases or decreases depending on where you would settle. A new home is about $7,000."

$7,000 was so far out of his reach that he ignored it.

"And a car...how much does a car cost?" Josef asked. He remembered the glossy, gleaming autos he saw in the magazines at the library.

The relocation counselor smiled. Everyone wanted to know how much a car would cost.

"It varies with the kind of automobile. A new car would cost about $1,400, but a used car would be considerably less, and gasoline is about seventeen cents a gallon."

"How much money could I make?"

"That, too, depends on the work you would do and where you live. I would say you could expect to earn from seventy five cents to a little more than one dollar per hour, to start.[47] Life in the city is more expensive than the country, but there are more opportunities to work in the city."

Josef fidgeted in the hard wooden chair facing the counselor's desk, and he wanted more information. "What does the $250 transportation cost per person include?"

"It includes travel from your home to the port of Bremerhaven in the north, your passage on a ship, along with your meals while onboard, travel to your hotel in the U.S., and breakfast each day at the hotel. And, as I mentioned already, you will receive a loan of $300 for incidental expenses."

Josef stared at the ceiling. *How will I ever be able to pay back $300? Or eventually get a car? I would love to have a car someday.*

He cleared his throat, "And do you really think I will be able to find work quickly?"

"Probably, yes."

"How long do we need to stay at the hotel?"

"Just until you are able to find an apartment and make enough money for monthly rent and food. Some people have family in the U.S. and move in with them, but you don't; you might be at the hotel for several months. The important thing to know is you and your family will not be without a roof over your head or food to eat."

Josef could feel his heart beating. He had a roof over his head now; he had food now, although the memories of scarcity still haunted him and especially, Ella. But his sons were the focus of their relocation—his sons and their futures. They were the real reason why they were considering moving.

"When do you need to know my decision?"

"As soon as possible. Within the next week. If you are serious about moving to America, I want to get your name on the list, along with your wife and children."

Josef nodded his head, "I will talk it over with my wife."

Josef left the office and splurged a little by taking a bus ride home. During the war he was not allowed to use public transportation, but that was behind him now, and he had the same rights, officially, as anyone else.

When he got home, Ella greeted him with a big kiss. It made their toddler Walter laugh and clap his hands.

"The doctor sent us a letter. Here, read it, Josef. It's great news."

It was the best letter in the world. It informed them Franz was scheduled for release from the sanitarium on June 15th, just a month away.

Josef bent down to pick up Walter, then snatched Franz's photo from the top of a cabinet.

"Your brother is coming home soon. You can play with him and have lots of fun!"

"Franz?" Walter asked, as he pointed to the photo with the boy holding an American bomber plane.

"Yes, Franz. You can play with him all day if you want to."

Walter would be almost two by the time Franz returned, and they were certain Walter would not remember his brother in the flesh. They were trying to make it sound like it would be an adventure when his older brother came home, and the world would be right again.

"I have news, too, Ella."

"What is it? I hope it is good news."

"I found out about moving."

Ella's stomach plummeted. She had wanted this move, and now, faced with the potential reality, she became both happy and terrified all at once.

"Tell me," she said matter-of-factly, trying to hide her ambivalence.

274

Josef told her everything he knew, so far, and Ella did not interrupt him as she prepared the evening meal.

When Josef told her how much it would cost, she placed the bowl she was holding on the little kitchen table.

She held onto the bowl's rim, "That's a lot of money, Josef. How can we ever pay it back?"

"We have to pay back only $300, over time...years, I was told."

"Josef, I am very uncomfortable owing anyone money."

"I am, also. But it is the price we will have to pay if we want to live somewhere else...in the west."

As she spooned food onto the plates, Ella realized it was now Josef who was more enthusiastic about moving. But bitter memories of her girlfriend spitting at the ground, the bigoted shopkeepers, and the reality of her children's mixed nationalities reinvigorated her resoluteness about moving.

"Where should we go, Josef?"

"Everyone wants to move to America, the United States. This is our chance."

She sat at the table and took a bite of her meal. "I looked into a preschool for the children, today. When Franz comes home, both of the boys can go. It will be good for them, and I can walk them to school from here."

"Ella, why are you changing the subject? Do you *not* want to move now?"

"No, I just need to think about everything you said, Josef. I'm a little scared."

"So am I."

They finished their supper. Ella took Walter into the bedroom to get him ready for bed. Josef sat in his soft, upholstered chair. He opened the day's newspaper, which he liked to read after supper each night, but his thoughts drifted elsewhere—to America. He thought of the many pictures he had seen of the faraway country. People looked healthy; they looked happy; they looked rich.

When Ella exited the bedroom, Josef motioned for her to come join him. She sat on a low stool next to him, her back against the side of his chair. He stroked her dark brown hair.

"What do you think?" he said.

"I think I want to go, but part of me wants to stay. My sisters and brother won't really know their nephews if we move, and my mother won't know her grandchildren well."

Ella had lived apart from her mother a long time and their relationship was strained, but she kept a framed photo of Frau Zimmerman on the bedroom dresser. Ella rarely saw her sisters and younger brother, and letters were not frequent, either. She knew the family that mattered most was Josef, Franz, and Walter.

After a long silence, she leaned her head backwards against the arm of the chair, her face up.

"Josef, kiss me!" she taunted.

He leaned over and kissed her, his lips upside-down on hers. They both laughed. She turned her head to face his directly. "Kiss me properly!" she demanded. He did. It was a long kiss, a passionate kiss.

She pushed away and twisted her body around, facing him and holding one of his hands.

"Josef, let's go to America."

30 - A Full Family

Willie's son was born in April of 1950. Not long after, Josef and Willie spent a sunny weekend day in the shed together while Ella and Walter stayed in the house with Helga and the new baby. Willie had purchased all the electrical materials and fixtures Josef told him to buy when they had previously talked about adding electricity to the shed.

The two men dug a trench from the house to the shed, laid insulated electrical wire in it, and then buried it with dirt. Walter came outside to stomp on the dirt laid over the trench before getting bored and going back into the house. Josef then installed a light switch inside the shed for the overhead light, added two wall outlets, and hung the ceiling light.

As Willie flipped the switch for the first time, Josef opened two bottles of beer, and the two friends toasted the success of the project. Willie freely admitted it would never have happened if Josef hadn't done it.

"Well done, my friend!" he toasted Josef.

"I told you it wasn't an overwhelming job, didn't I?"

"For you, maybe; you know I am hopeless with these things."

"We all have different talents," Josef replied diplomatically.

They located good spots for two table lamps, or maybe a table lamp and a radio which Willie said he intended to buy or requisition from the house.

Each drank another beer.

"Your son is a handsome little fellow, Willie."

"That he is. So are yours. And when is Franz coming home?"

"Soon...about six weeks from now. He is doing very well. They had originally said he would be away up to twelve months, but it won't be that long."

"I am so glad for you and Ella. It must have been quite a trying time for you both."

"You have no idea."

Willie relaxed in the upholstered chair, and Josef settled into a wooden chair.

The beer was room temperature, as they liked it, and Willie had a full supply of it on hand.

"Josef, have you given any more thought to moving?"

Josef nodded his head, "We have decided to go to America."

"You mean the United States, right?"

"Yes. I have done some research. It seems like the right place for us, and my relocation counselor at the DP center thinks my skills will be in demand there. You know, it is amazing how organized everything seems to be in the U.S. All across the country, relief agencies, and in particular Catholic Relief Services, have let the word out from the pulpit, in civic, farming, volunteer, and business organizations, as well newspapers and magazines, about DPs like me.[48] Anyone who needs a worker registers with the relief agencies and sooner or later we get matched with one of the employers."

Willie brushed a piece of lint from his slacks. He was thinking about how the relief system Josef just described was like the slave labor system in Germany during the war, when German businesses or farmers could draw on a pool of workers. The key difference, though, was Josef would be doing the work voluntarily in the U.S., and he would be paid a decent wage; he could decide whether or not he wanted to take a specific job. He knew freedom was very important to Josef. Hell, it was important to anyone! He got up and opened a cardboard box.

"What do you have there, Willie?"

"Something for us to play with."

He slipped a black and beige dart board out of the box along with two sets of darts. One set had feathers in white, the other in blue.

"How about a game of darts?"

Josef had never played darts, but he said, "Sure, I'll try a game."

Looking around the shed, he said, "Why don't we hang the board on the wall over there?" as he pointed to the right. "You can hang it, can't you?" he teased Willie.

"That, I think I can manage," Willie laughed as he walked toward the wall. Josef got up and handed him a hammer and a big nail. After estimating the right height for the bulls-eye dartboard, Willie hung it. He stood a distance away and hurled a dart at the board. It missed completely. Then Josef tried. His dart bounced off the board's metal frame.

"Oh, that is bad...but I hit the board, Willie!"

"Really? Where's your dart?"

"On the floor."

"We're even then. Josef, how about another beer?"

Each young man took deep gulps of his third drink.

"You take the blues, and I'll take the whites," Willie said as he passed the darts to Josef.

"What are the rules of the game?" Josef inquired.

"I have no idea. There's a set of instructions in the box, but I just want to see how close I can get to the center. You go first, Josef."

"Where should I stand?"

"Here," Willie pointed to a spot on the floor he knew would definitely be considered too close to the dart board.

Josef looked at the position Willie suggested and then asked, "Shouldn't we stand back more?"

"Not yet. Not yet, Josef. Let's stand here until we get good at it. Then we can move back."

Josef aimed a dart and released it. It missed and stuck in the wall to the right of the dartboard.

Willie readied himself and aimed his dart. It landed to the left of the dartboard. He scrunched his eyebrows together in mock seriousness. Slurring a bit, he pursed his lips at Josef. "If your dart went right and mine went left, then statistically, I guess we landed somewhere in the middle—a joint bulls-eye, even though both darts are sticking in the wall."

Josef found his statement quite amusing and laughed his way a few steps back to put more distance between the tips of his fingers and the board on the wall. He aimed and released the dart. This time, it landed on the dartboard.

They continued playing, and within a few shots, most of the darts actually landed on the board, rather than in the wall. Each time a dart lodged in the board, both men inspected how close it was to the bulls-eye and measured the distance to the millimeter with a ruler, jotting down the numbers on a piece of paper. After nearly thirty throws each, it seemed Willie was winning, as the total distance to the bulls-eye of all his throws was the lowest. This was their own way of keeping score and they didn't care if it bore any resemblance to the scoring instructions on a white sheet of paper in the dartboard's box.

"Josef, let's swap darts. I'll take the blue ones and you can have my white ones. Maybe you'll do better with my darts."

"Don't be so smug, Willie. I'm not changing darts!"

"How about another beer, Josef?"

"I would like that, but I have to relieve myself, first."

Willie stood still and silent, as though pondering some great philosophical truth. "That sounds like a good idea. We can go behind the shed."

The two friends positioned themselves behind the shed, hidden from view, and proceeded to urinate, commenting on who had the stronger stream.

"Time for more beer," Josef joked as he and Willie returned to the shed.

It seemed their inebriation actually improved their aim, and within an hour the two friends decided to completely ignore the dartboard and aim for the spines of specific books on the bookcase in the room. Finally growing bored with that particular endeavor, they both collapsed into chairs.

Willie opened two more beers, handed one to Josef, and took a deep drink. He looked straight ahead rather than at Josef.

"Where will you settle in the U.S.?"

"I don't know yet. It could be anywhere."

Willie chuckled, "Maybe you are going to be an American cowboy, Josef, wearing a great big hat, just like we see in all the magazines now."

"Can you see me rounding up cattle somewhere in the Wild West? If I can't catch them, I'll just throw my wooden leg at them and stun them!"

Fully tipsy by now, both men laughed loudly and frequently.

"So when do you think you will leave?"

"For sure by the end of next year. The government in America has extended the immigration quotas for DPs until the end of 1951. The quotas may be extended in the future, but we aren't going to chance it."

"What is it that finally made you decide to go?"

Josef sighed and leaned back in his chair, cradling the bottle of beer between the palms of his hands.

Suddenly, he lifted the bottle to toast Willie, "We're going to get in trouble with the women."

"I'm sure of it!"

They both took another sip of beer.

"So, what forced the decision?" Willie probed.

"Do you remember I told you the people at the sanitarium lost Franz?"

"Yes, how could I forget?"

"When that happened, I experienced something more than fear, more than anger. I felt disrespected. It was the last straw in a series of events that preceded it: trouble with shopkeepers; general resentment about DPs having received preferential treatment; and an incident Ella told me about a friend of hers who spat at her feet when Ella told her she married a Pole."

"I'm sorry about those incidences. No one should be treated in that way." Willie continued, "Josef, something really bad is happening."

"What would that be? I can't think of anything worse than not knowing where my son was."

"Something almost as bad."

Willie pointed to Josef's beer bottle. "Your beer bottle is empty." They burst out laughing and Willie opened another beer for Josef. Josef knew he was drunk, and he found it easier to open up, to talk about things.

"You would think after all the years I lived as a captive, it would not bother me so much. After all, I have food, a place to live, medical attention when I need it, and good friends—you being the best, of course. Oh, and I forgot to tell you...I am getting a new leg at the end of the summer!"

Willie let his head slump down and smiled, "I'll never forget my mother stuffing old socks in your prosthesis so your stump would be well-cushioned."

Josef also smiled at the memory and patted the top of his artificial leg.

Willie looked at his friend, "I will miss you, Josef."

"And I, you."

"We'll just have to drink a lot of beer together by the end of next year." Willie laughed.

Meanwhile, after admiring Helga's baby and playing with Walter, the women prepared a meal of ham sandwiches, tomato salad, and soup. Walter played with a toy. Helga's baby slept.

As they set the kitchen table for supper, Ella said, "Helga, Josef and I decided to move to America."

Helga stopped what she was doing. "So, you made your decision. Willie told me he and Josef talked about it not too long ago. You know we will miss you terribly."

"I feel the same way, but it's best for our boys."

Helga approached Ella and took her hand. "I know. When will you leave?"

"We need to be on a boat by the end of next year, but we don't have a date yet."

"That will be quite a voyage for all of you. But I am glad we will have time together before you leave," Helga responded as she smiled at Ella.

"Speaking of time together, it's time we should call Willie and Josef inside to eat. I'll get them," Ella said, as she headed toward the kitchen door that opened onto the back garden.

"I'll finish setting the table," Helga responded.

Ella called across the garden to the men, who were still in the shed. She heard a muffled something like "We'll be right there" emanate from Willie's little haven and she returned to the house. As the two men worked their way to the kitchen, one of each of their arms was splayed around the other's shoulders. In unison, as they practiced a few times before leaving the shed, they slurred and hiccupped their greeting as they walked into the house, *"Guten Abend, schöne Frauen, der Schuppen ist elektrifiziert."*

"Don't 'Good evening, fine wives, the shed is electrified' *us*," scolded Ella. She looked at Helga and held up her hands in surrender. Both women simultaneously shook their heads in amused disapproval of their husbands' intoxication, as if each had another child on her hands.

Six weeks later, three-year-old Franz came home, cured. Ella and Josef took a bus to the sanitarium, and the nurses and doctors hugged Franz or shook his hand as he left. The staff allowed him to keep his favorite toy, the airplane. He looked at the scenery outside the window on the bus ride home, commenting on everything. Once back at the apartment, Franz shyly looked around and then took out the photo of Walter he had in his pocket.

He looked up at Ella, "Mami, where is Walter?"

"He will be here in a minute. You stay with Poppi."

Ella climbed the stairs to another apartment where Walter was drawing a picture under the watchful eye of their landlady.

"How is Franz? May I see him tomorrow?" Frau Wilkesmann asked.

"Of course, and he looks good. His pants are too short now!"

Hearing the word "Franz," Walter cocked his head and looked up at his mother from the table where he was drawing some pictures on butcher paper.

"Let's go see your brother," Ella said. Walter abandoned his crayons and got up to leave.

"Wait, Walter. You should thank Frau Wilkesmann for playing with you," his mother admonished.

"Danke, und Gutentag."

Both women smiled at the boy.

Frau Wilkesmann responded, "Good day to you, Walter."

"Let's go downstairs," Ella said.

On the stairway, Ella suggested to Walter that he run over to Franz and hug him. Walter shook his head from left to right, a clear indication of "No!"

As Walter and Ella entered the apartment, Franz was sitting at the kitchen table. He turned to look at his little brother, then at the picture he was holding. He held it up and pointed to it, saying "Walter."

Walter had been clinging to Ella's side, and when he saw Franz, he ran to the table, picked up a picture of Franz, and pointed to it, saying "Franz."

Recognizing his cue, Josef retrieved two wooden toy trucks from a drawer. He had purchased them used, cleaned them, and made any necessary repairs just for this moment. As he gave one to each boy, he said, "Go ahead and play with your trucks." The two boys—almost strangers—retreated to the rug in the living area and played with the trucks. Franz still had the American bomber, and Walter was more interested in the airplane than he was in the truck.

"They are very polite to each other," Ella whispered.

"That's because neither of them has figured out brothers fight. Give them time," Josef whispered back.

"I can't wait," Ella said, with joyful sarcasm. "It will make the house seem normal when these two little brothers actually have a fight."

Ella and Josef stood, cemented to the floor and transfixed by the scene before them. Both their sons were together, safe, and playing.

In the following months, the boys played together more and more, and Franz became comfortable in the family once again. Walter had to adapt to another child in the house, and inevitably, sibling rivalry reared its head from time to time. Neither Ella nor Josef minded, though. It was normal. Josef and Ella needed normal.

In the fall, the boys attended preschool, which was offered for free by the government. They attended school five half days a week, where they played games, learned many German folk songs, fables, and participated in alphabet and counting activities. Ella loved to get them dressed up each morning. Their absence for part of the day afforded her a few hours alone. She used the time for house chores, cooking, baking, mending, and running errands.

The plans to move to America were taking shape. Both Ella and Josef gathered all the required documentation. Josef's status as a DP was not in doubt, so one hurdle had already been surmounted. The authorities did not have to conduct any further research on Josef's DP qualifications. The family would make the 1951 deadline—the end of December.

By late autumn of 1950, Ella and Josef saved enough money to finally take a boat ride on Lake Constance, and lightheartedly referred to the excursion as their long overdue honeymoon. It was a beautiful, clear day. Josef felt unsteady walking on the boat's deck and held onto the rail as he struggled to keep up with Ella and the children. The boys wanted to explore every corner of the boat, and Ella accompanied them, with Josef in slow pursuit. Josef purchased warm Ovaltine for the family at the boat's refreshment stand, and all of them enjoyed it with the lunch Ella brought along for the day. After the boat ride, Josef took Franz out in a rowboat, while Ella and Walter stayed ashore and scoured the shoreline for rocks and other treasures.

For Christmas Eve, 1950, Ella invited friends to enjoy supper with them in their tiny apartment. Each family brought part of the meal, and the gifts were simple. After everyone left and the boys were in bed, Ella and Josef burned some additional wood in their wood-fired cooking stove to keep the room warm for a while yet.

"That was a nice gathering, don't you think so, Ella?"

"Yes, it was. Do you realize it will be our last Christmas here? That makes me sad."

"Yes, I realize it." He paused, and then asked, "Ella, will you make us some tea?"

"That's a good idea."

Ella made tea, brought each of them a cup, and sat across the kitchen table from Josef. As she added sugar to her cup, Josef cleared his throat.

"Ella, I'm concerned. Are you having second thoughts about going to America?"

"No...No...We should go, for the boys. I'll just miss our friends here."

"I will miss them, also."

"In the spring, I want to take the children to Heidelberg to visit my family. It may be the last time we see each other for a long time."

"We don't have to go anywhere, Ella. We can stay here in Germany if you wish. That has always been an option for us. You know that, don't you?"

"I know, I know. But all the reasons we decided to leave still exist. We need to go."

A few days later, on a cold, clear New Year's Eve, Ella and Josef bundled up the boys for a ride into the nearby forest to gather small twigs and branches for the kitchen stove. Walter rode with his father, whose bicycle towed a small cart to hold the wood. Franz rode with his mother. Everyone picked up some kindling and tossed it into the cart, singing songs in the silent, moonlit woods.

Both Ella and Josef were lost in their thoughts on the ride back to town, and each held on to a drowsy boy.

It was their last New Year's Eve in Europe.

Winter eventually gave way to spring, when the family visited Ella's family in Heidelberg. There, Josef announced their decision to move to America, much to the bafflement of everyone. Ella and Josef stated their reasons for moving, and although her family didn't understand the decision, they respected it. On the return trip to Stockach, Ella imagined members of her family shaking their heads in confusion.

The following day, Josef checked in with the relocation counselor, who confirmed an early September departure date. From Stockach, they would need to report to the relocation camp at Bremerhaven in the north, their port of departure. It was time to tell Michael about the move.

Josef's wrote him a letter, outlining the reasons why they were moving, as though he was seeking his brother's permission, or at least, his blessing. He included the address of Catholic Relief Services where mail could be sent, and then forwarded.

As he reread the letter before placing it in an envelope and taking it to the post office, Josef noted he had asked Michael to pray for him, and he realized he had not said many prayers since Franz was diagnosed with tuberculosis. Sealing the letter, he prayed, *I am sorry for being so angry, God. Thank you for making Franz well. And Mary, please help us with the decision to move.*

Throughout the late spring and summer, Ella busied herself with determining what should be packed for the trip to America. It was a daunting task, since the family was allowed one trunk plus an additional suitcase for each person. They devoured magazines showing images of American life, and they watched movies. Everything they read and saw showed vast forests, endless expanses of open plains, mighty rivers, gleaming cities, and snowcapped mountains. The distances seemed limitless—so different from Stockach, with its main street, a few shops, and a population of fewer than ten thousand people. Josef and Ella showed the photos to the boys many times, and Franz, who was now over four, seemed very interested in them. They all got their inoculations.

Josef wanted to give Willie a farewell gift. He had been to visit Willie several times since the day they electrified the shed, played darts, and consumed too much beer. Since then, he noted Willie had added a radio to his hideaway, so he didn't need to get him one. Instead, he decided on a nice table clock.

He scoured secondhand shops and finally found a clock he could afford. The fact it didn't work didn't concern him. Before he purchased it, he opened it to see what the problem was. Convinced he could get it working, he bought it and promptly proceeded to repair and refurbish it. The clock measured six inches wide and eight inches high

Josef once again visited with his relocation counselor. Finally, Josef was handed an envelope with four train tickets to Bremerhaven and a set of instructions as to what to expect at the DP relocation camp at the port. As Josef departed the relocation office, the counselor wished him well and told him not to hesitate to drop by if he had any more questions.

When he placed the envelope on the kitchen table, Ella opened it and drew in a deep breath. She stared at the tickets in her hand for a long time.

"Is something wrong?" Josef asked.

She moved her head back and forth, to say "No," and whispered to herself, "This is what we wanted."

31 - Farewells

As soon as Ella told her friends about their moving date, the need for Josef and Ella to host a party evaporated. One friend organized a farewell gathering for them. Each invited friend gave them a useful gift. There were bowls, sheets, kitchen gadgets, English dictionaries, small toys for the children, preserved foods, and a crystal candy dish among the gifts. Not knowing if they would see any of their friends again, Ella and Josef were tearful at the end of the party, and overwhelmed by the generosity of their friends.

It was now late August. The trunk and suitcases were laid out on the rug in their sitting area. The boys played with them, and Walter's third birthday was celebrated among the luggage.

A week before their departure, with the clock cradled in his arms, Josef made a Saturday morning visit to Willie.

Holding her son, Helga opened the door. "Hello, Josef."

"How is the baby, Helga?" Josef said, as he caressed the little boy's cheeks with his free hand.

"Getting bigger every day."

"Is Willie home?" Josef asked.

"Yes, he's in the kitchen."

Josef followed Helga into the kitchen. Willie was at the table, reading a newspaper. "Good morning, Josef, it's good to see you."

"I have something for you."

Josef removed the piece of cloth covering the clock.

"That is beautiful!" Willie beamed.

"I noticed you do not have a clock in your shed. "This is for you. It doesn't need electricity, either; all you do is wind it."

"That's really lovely, Josef, and too nice for the shed. Willie, let's keep it on the mantle above the fireplace," Helga suggested.

"No, no, this goes in my shed!" Willie responded. "Hands off," he teased Helga.

With Helga smiling behind their backs, the two men departed for the shed, and the first thing Willie did was offer Josef a beer.

"Thank you, but just one. I have chores to do today, Willie."

Willie was still holding the clock. He looked around the room and then placed his gift on the bookcase.

"What do you think? I can see it when I sit in my easy chair. Is this a clock that was a broken-down wreck you magically made new again?"

"No, it wasn't a complete wreck, but it did need work."

"I am sure I will enjoy it for a long time. Thank you, Josef. We met over my wristwatch, remember?"

Josef felt odd. Suddenly, he was uneasy around Willie and found he didn't have much to say.

"Yes, I remember. That wristwatch eventually saved my life."

"No, your ability to fix the machinery in the barrel factory is what really saved your life."

"Oh, and you had nothing to do with it?"

Willie smiled sheepishly, "Well, maybe a little."

"Maybe a lot," Josef retorted.

Josef sat in the wooden chair, and Willie sat in the easy chair. The chairs were angled so the two men could see each other, yet also see the bookcase across the floor. They each took another sip of beer. It was as though there was an unspoken force between them, sabotaging their efforts to make small talk.

"Goodbye" was something they did not know how to handle.

"Josef, I have a farewell gift for you, also."

"Willie, you don't have to give me anything; your friendship has been enough. Don't you know that?"

"No, I don't know that, and besides, I will not be talked out of giving you the gift I want you to have, young Josef," Willie said in a mock commanding voice. Both of them laughed.

"Helga and I talked about what we could give you, and although she was resistant to my idea at first, she finally agreed."

Curious now, with an eyebrow cocked, Josef looked at Willie.

Willie wiggled in his chair and looked down at his hand. He placed his beer bottle on the floor, then slowly removed the signet ring his brother Gunter had given him, and handed it to Josef. Willie looked lovingly at the ring as he tried to pass it to his friend.

"This is for you, Josef. You have been like a brother to me. I want you to have it."

Josef recoiled. "I cannot take your ring! It's from your brother and your initials—WM—are engraved on it. Please keep it for yourself. I completely understand why Helga had misgivings about giving me the ring. She is right. It is something you should *never* give away!"

"No, no, Josef. It's yours. Please, open your hand."

Josef resisted at first, keeping his hands grasped around the bottle of beer. But when he saw Willie's eyes had moistened, he relented. He extended his hand to Willie.

Willie carefully placed the silver ring in the cupped palm of Josef's right hand.

Josef was speechless. He did not want to take the ring.

"Try it on, Josef."

Josef slipped it on his right ring finger. It fit perfectly, and bore the warmth from Willie's body. Josef's eyes reddened and he could feel the sting of salty tears.

Neither of them said a word. Josef took a deep breath and stood up. He shook Willie's hand warmly and firmly, and the two men squeezed each other's shoulders tightly, then pushed each other away, looked long at each other, and grasped shoulders again.

Josef turned hurriedly and left. He walked through the kitchen and waved farewell to Helga without looking at her.

He could not speak.

Willie's Ring

Willie gave Josef the silver ring in this photograph. It was Willie's farewell gift to Josef when the young Walkow family moved to America. It is engraved with a "W" in the foreground and an "M" in the background—Willie's initials.

Photo Credit: Walter Walkow

32 - Coming to America

The entire process of choosing what to pack for the trip to America was confusing; they did not know if they were making the right choices.

The single steamer trunk allotted for their household items was soon filled with necessities. Ella packed and re-packed blankets and sheets, pillows and towels, essential cookware, a few cook books, and one or two mementos from home. She changed her mind many times as to *which* frying pan to pack, *which* soup pot to pack, *which* towels to pack, *which* sheets to take. Josef vacillated many times with his choice of hand tools, an axe, and a horseshoe for good luck. Each time Ella repacked the trunk, both she and Josef tried to fit in just one more item. What's more, the trunk had to be shipped separately, and would meet up with them in America a few months after their arrival.

In each flimsy suitcase—they were allowed one per member of the household—Ella packed clothing and whatever other household items she could squeeze in. Each of the boys also selected two toys. What didn't fit in their suitcases, they would have to carry in a small fabric pouch Ella made for each of them.

Josef and Ella prepared the boys for the coming trip as best as they could. They described the all-day train ride to the pier and the camp they would live in for a little while in the port at Bremerhaven, in northern Germany.

"Look here," Josef would say as he spread a map on the kitchen table while the boys gathered in his arms. He pretended his fingers were a ship, and traced their route across the North Sea, then across the North Atlantic to New York in America. "This is where we live now," he would say as he pointed a finger to Stockach, "and this is the way the train will travel to Bremerhaven." Josef mapped the trip many times for the boys, and, little as they were, they were both able to locate Stockach,

Bremerhaven, the North Sea, the Atlantic Ocean, and New York on the map. If Walter made a mistake, Franz corrected him.

Ella would stand over them, reminding them of the route, just as Josef had reminded them. "From Bremerhaven we then go all the way across the North Sea, then the Atlantic Ocean to New York," she said as she, too, used her fingers to trace the route across the Atlantic. Her fingers stopped at New York. The boys ran their fingers across the blue sea.

"Will it be a long trip on the ship, Mami?" Franz asked.

"It will take nine or ten days."

"Where will we sleep? Franz asked.

"We will have hammocks or cots to sleep on inside the big ship."

Walter responded, "Hammock?"

Ella explained what a hammock is.

Franz asked, "What is a cot?" and Josef explained it.

Franz also asked, "We are going on a big train, too, right Poppi?"

"Yes, a very long train with many cars."

During the weeks leading to their departure, Josef and Ella repeatedly described the trip to the children. It was as though pre-living the trip helped to allay their own fears, also. Every night, both Ella and Josef used the English phrase books and dictionary given to them by friends to practice their soon-to-be-adopted language. Franz and Walter especially liked to look at the children's picture dictionary they had received as a gift, and both Josef and Ella also used it.

On a glorious September morning, they bid farewell to their neighbors and took a taxi to the train station. After checking their suitcases, they settled into their seats, and as the train rolled slowly forward, Ella and Josef looked at each other. They reached for each other's hands across the space between their facing seats. The boys excitedly pressed their faces against the train's windows, leaving nose prints, as Walter jumped up and down with delight when the train gained speed.

Josef finally told Walter to sit down. The rhythmic clack of the train's wheels on the rails lulled the boys to sleep, with Ella nodding off soon after, but not before she wondered where their trunk full of household supplies was. It had been shipped two weeks earlier. Alternating his gaze between his family and the German countryside, Josef absorbed the almost-autumn scenery and harvested fields and, for the first time in a long while, offered a silent prayer.

Hail Mary full of grace, the Lord is with thee. Blessed art thou among women and blessed is the fruit of thy womb, Jesus. I don't know if we are doing the right thing. I don't know what lies ahead. It made so much sense to move, but now I am not so certain. Please help me provide for my family, and keep us healthy. Please help us make friends and a find a good home in America. Holy Mary, Mother of God, pray for us sinners now and at the hour of our death, Amen. And Mary, please forgive me for not praying to you more frequently. I know it may seem ungrateful, but I really need your help and guidance. Amen.

The train pulled into Bremerhaven early in the evening, and a bus transported all the emigrants from the train to the relocation camp.

The camp was full of people making their way to a new life.

"Mami, where are we?" Franz asked.

"We are at a place where we have to wait until we are given the name of a ship to go on."

"When will that be?"

"We don't know yet."

"Will it be tomorrow?" he asked.

"Probably not. Other people are ahead of us," Ella replied.

Josef presented the family's documents to the authorities and the four of them were each examined by a physician in the medical building on site. All except Franz were approved to go aboard a ship.

"But I have all his papers! They indicate he has been cured of TB!" Josef protested to an official.

"Yes, I see that, but the physicians want to make sure he remains free of TB. We will do another x-ray on him in a few days, and decide if he can be approved then. Until then, just settle yourselves here at the camp."

Josef felt a lead weight hit his chest, and Ella just looked away and shook her head.

"And what if he isn't approved?" Josef demanded.

"Then you will need to decide if he will remain behind with relatives, or if only two of you go to America, or you may decide none of you will travel."

Josef hadn't anticipated a change in plans. It couldn't happen!

"Sir, I have some phone numbers here. One belongs to Franz's doctor and the other will allow you to contact the sanitarium that released him. Will you please write them down and ask the physician who examined us to contact them?"

Josef handed a sheet of paper with the phone numbers to the camp official, who wrote them on a new piece of paper.

"Please, sir, please...give them to the physician right away," Josef implored.

"I will, and in the meantime, we have accommodations for your family here."

Obviously flustered, Josef protested, "Sir, I can't afford to pay for accommodations; may I help out here at the camp, instead?"

"There is no additional charge for a room and half board. Any additional food you will need to pay for."

"Yes, yes, I forgot that. Thank you, but do you need any work done in the camp? I can repair things. I'm good at it, I'm told."

"I'll keep you in mind," the official said, as he handed Josef the family's building and room assignment.

They walked slowly to their assigned building, using one of the carts available in the camp to haul their luggage.

"What now, Josef?" Ella asked, deflated.

"I can't think right now, Ella. Let's get settled first."

Their room included two beds and a sink. Towel hooks were attached to the wall on both sides of the sink. The bathroom was in the hall. In an adjacent building they would find the mess hall where breakfast and supper were served daily. There was a wide, well-worn dirt playground beyond it. It had a small field, swings, a human-powered merry-go-round, and a slide.

At supper, three-year-old Walter asked, "Poppi, big boat?" as he craned his neck to see a ship through the window, a ship anchored in the harbor, waiting for its cargo of refugees.

"That boat isn't ours, Walter. We have to wait a few days. And since it is a very big boat, it is called a ship."

"Why isn't it here?" Franz asked, gulping a sip of milk.

Ella admonished, "Don't talk while you are eating, and let your father enjoy his supper."

Ella and Josef made casual conversation with others like themselves...DPs, mostly Polish men and German women. They were not alone, and took some comfort in the similarities of everybody's stories about their post-war experiences.

In bed that night, Ella whispered to Josef, "There are a lot of people like us here. Some of them have to wait, like us, also."

Josef cradled her in his arms.

"It will all work out, Ella."

"How can you be so sure, Josef?" Ella whispered.

"I'm not sure, but I have faith it will work out. We can't have come so far for it not to work."

"You may have faith it will all work out, but I want solid signatures on real paper saying we are all cleared to leave."

"So do I," Josef responded.

"We are going to have to think about what to do, just in case they won't let Franz get on the ship. I'm not leaving him here and I don't want to split up the family!"

"We won't split up the family. I promise you. We will go back to Stockach if we must."

Ella took a deep breath and kissed her husband's cheek before she closed her eyes.

Josef raised his arms above his head, resting them on the pillow. He was exhausted, but couldn't sleep yet. *We can't have come this far to be turned back. We just can't!*

Josef prayed, *Now what, Blessed Mary? Please help us get through this; please make them approve Franz to board the ship. Amen.*

The remainder of the week was carefree for the children; they spent time in the playground and enjoyed a fruit they had never eaten before—a banana.

Ella made friends quickly with some of the women, while Josef earned extra money helping out with maintaining the camp. He repaired hanging door hinges, stuck windows, tilting steps, plumbing, anything. One of the ships anchored in the harbor was loaded with hundreds of camp residents. When it departed, Ella and Josef felt they had been left alone, in a desert, to fend for themselves. Except they weren't alone; new people arrived daily by train to await departure on another ship, and the young couple felt a special camaraderie with those detained for health reasons. They read newspapers and magazines, practiced some English words and phrases with others, listened to radio, and even watched some movies played at night in the mess hall. It could all have been delightful, but for the nagging fear they might never make it to America.

And then the unthinkable happened.

The boys broke out in a rash, and they were diagnosed with measles. They would not be allowed to board any ship as long as they had measles, and they would have to be separated from the rest of the population of the camp. Both boys were together, along with other children, in the quarantine building. Ella and Josef explained why they had to be separated, and it would be for only a short time.

Franz cried, "No Mami, No!" Walter then whimpered, but he did not have the memory of having been separated from his parents for months. Ella and Josef hugged their boys, and told them they would see them every day, which they did, through the playground enclosure.

298

The earliest the family could leave was two weeks from the beginning of the quarantine period, assuming all went well with Franz's x-rays.

From the relocation camp, Ella and Josef looked out at the three remaining ships moored in the Weser River channel—the entrance to the North Sea—wondering if they would ever board one of them.

On September 25th, the day Josef turned twenty-six and the air had a definite freshness and the nights were already cold, the medical officials summoned Franz for another exam. Their promise to examine Franz a few days after he arrived turned into a few weeks due to the measles outbreak. The infectious phase of measles had passed, and the two boys were back with their parents.

Leaving Walter in the care of a family with young children who also had waning cases of measles, Ella and Josef took Franz to the medical building where the physician listened to his lungs, and an x-ray was taken.

"How do his lungs sound, Herr Doktor?" Josef asked.

"His lungs sound good. I will review the x-rays later today. You should know by tomorrow if he has been approved for travel."

Ella was simply unable to control her anxiety. "Tomorrow? *Tomorrow?* I can't wait any longer! Please, please, can't you look at the x-rays now and tell us? We need to move forward with our lives. It has been such a long journey—not only the train trip and the stay here at the camp, but the entire last ten years, the war, the aftermath," Ella said, her voice cracking as she sniffed back her tears. "We need to know if we can go or if we have to stay here in Europe."

"Ella, we can wait another day," Josef said softly. "We have waited so long already."

"Josef, I just can't wait! I can't."

Franz looked up at Ella and nestled against her side. The physician looked at Ella intently and relented, relaxing his hands over Franz's paperwork. "Give me a few minutes. Please wait here."

The physician left them in the room.

"Am I sick again, Mami?"

"No, Franz. You are well. The doctor just needs to look at the picture of your lungs on the x-ray."

"I don't like x-rays."

"They didn't hurt, Franz," Josef responded.

"I just don't like them," he said, shaking his head side-to-side.

Ella was combing Franz's hair with her fingers when the doctor opened the door to the room.

God! Please let it be good news, Josef prayed, barely breathing. Ella turned white.

"Wonderful news! Franz's lungs look quite healed; his paperwork looks in order, and yesterday I talked to his doctor in your town as well as the staff at the sanitarium. The information we have in Franz's file and the new x-ray indicate your son is clear of tuberculosis."

"Thank God!" Ella exhaled. Josef tousled Franz's hair, which Ella had just combed.

"Are we approved to travel now?" Josef asked.

"Not until both boys have passed the two week mark since their measles diagnosis."

"We know that, but is Franz cleared to go, regarding his tuberculosis?"

"Yes, I have signed all the required documents. See the person at the intake desk outside my office. She will tell you what happens next." The doctor smiled as he handed Josef a packet of papers and tousled Franz's hair. Franz pulled his head back, as though he wanted everyone to leave his hair alone.

"Thank you, Herr Doktor, thank you!" they both responded, their words tripping over each other's.

"Have a good life in America," the doctor said.

"You see, Franz, I told you so. You are no longer sick with TB," Ella said as they exited the room.

"But Mami, I still have measles...look at my spots. Walter has measles, too."

"The spots no longer matter. They are going away."

∽∾∽

The lady at the intake desk gave them a sheet of paper with official seals, signatures, and stamps indicating Franz was free to travel once his measles cleared. She provided similar paperwork for Walter. The next step was for Josef to bring the official paperwork to the camp's central administrative office. When the officials had the required documentation in hand, they would assign the family to a ship.

Ella placed all the treasured, officially stamped, properly sealed and signed-in-ink papers in her purse. Their official look comforted her. As they turned to leave, the woman at the intake desk smiled at Franz. "*Bon voyage,* young man," she said.

"Say '*Danke,*' Franz," Ella quietly whispered.

"*Danke,*" Franz responded.

As they walked back to their building, Franz tugged on his mother's hand, "What is a bon voyage?"

As she laughed, Ella realized how downtrodden she had felt, and how the aura of heaviness had now lifted.

"It means 'have a good trip,' in French," she said.

"When are we going on the ship?" he asked.

"The big trip comes next...the trip on the big, big ship."

"But when are we going?" he insisted.

Josef answered, "We will know very, very, soon."

"May I go to the playground, Mami?"

"Yes, go, go have fun." Franz tore for the playground.

Ella and Josef walked arm in arm through the camp to a juncture where Josef headed to the administrative office with all

301

the papers from Ella's purse tucked in his shirt pocket. They kissed gently as they parted, and Ella picked up Walter from the family who was looking after him, then took him to the playground to join Franz.

As suppertime approached, Ella had the boys wash their hands and faces in their room. Josef walked in, beaming, as he tossed a packet of paper on one of the beds.

"October 10th, October 10th! That is the day we leave for America." He spread all of the tickets fan-like on the bed and deposited a stack of instructions next to them. "It is happening. It is really happening. We are going!"

Franz and Walter plopped themselves on their parents' bed, drawn by Josef's excitement.

"Franz, Walter, look. Look at the tickets." He pointed to each one, showing them their names on their tickets.

Ella and the boys were assigned berths in the large forward hold of the ship, in the women's quarters. Men were housed aft, but due to his infirmity, Josef was given a shared cabin higher on the ship. It was feared he would not be able to navigate the ship's ladders with his prosthesis as the ship pitched and rolled.

Ella had not planned on being separated from Josef during the ocean voyage, and was not happy with these arrangements. But she was determined to make the best of it, and so was Josef.

The four of them ate a hurried supper, shared their good news with the other refugees, and then returned to their room to read the packet of traveler information.

Sheets of rules and regulations made it clear the trip would not be a relaxing vacation cruise. Women would be conscripted to help prepare food in the galley and clean up after meals, as well as keep their immediate living quarters tidy and maintain the women and children's heads. Men would be responsible for ensuring all men's washrooms and living quarters were kept clean and they were expected to scrub the decks and bulkheads each day. The passengers were to select among themselves who would do what and on which day.[49]

The routine was similar to what soldiers had to do on these transport ships.

Once their departure date was set, the family could finally unwind for the remainder of their stay at the relocation camp. They made new acquaintances, and the children played all day. Their days were almost carefree. Time seemed to stop, and responsibilities ceased, rather like a calm before the tempest of the voyage, and the challenges of the future.

Josef wrote to Michael to update him on their travel plans, and Ella wrote several letters. One was to her family, another to a girlfriend, and one was to Willie and Helga.

As they boarded the *USNS General R. M. Blatchford,*[50] a converted American troop transport ship, on October 10th, 1951, and verified their names on the ship's manifest, Ella noticed she was listed as a Pole, since her husband was Polish. Once aboard, they settled into their assigned quarters. Josef shared a four-person cabin with lower and upper berths; he took one of the lower berths. The cabin was on a deck that did not require him to navigate stairways often. There was a closet for his clothing, and the head was down the hall.

Ella and the children descended below decks to a large compartment outfitted with multi-layered hanging stacks of fully-extended, bright, white, canvas hammocks, and some cots that pulled down from the bulkhead. The space seemed jammed with people and luggage.[51] A few scattered portholes let in some light. All of the heads were in the hallway. "This is a dungeon," Ella thought to herself.

She identified their sleeping quarters—three pull-down cots— and the boys settled into theirs, placing their suitcases on the deck, right next to their cots. She knew most of the time she would be topside or on the mess deck, where three meals a day would be served. Certainly, the children would spend time with

Josef, too. She was grateful the boys considered the entire coming ordeal as a fascinating escapade. Already, they loved their beds and practiced getting in and out of them. She envied them.

Late in the afternoon, when the sun was low and the sky was turning golden-tinged red, the ship departed with a barely perceptible movement. The Blatchford headed into the middle of the Weser River. No longer tethered to Europe, the passengers—all of them refugees—waved goodbye to loved ones on the pier. Tears were abundant both on deck and on land, as the ship traveled to the mouth of the river and the waiting sea.

Although Josef and Ella had no one wishing them farewell, they remained glued to the rail, watching Germany slowly recede, aware a page had turned to a new chapter in their lives. They held hands, and each of them also held on to a son. At the confluence of the North Sea and the Weser, the ship headed northwest and the air freshened. The boys were restless and wanted to run along the deck; there was no greater excitement in the world for the youngsters.

They were on a big, moving ship, heading out to sea, led by tall people in strange, pressed uniforms, people who were speaking an unfamiliar language. Their nautical surroundings fueled their curiosity about everything: the ladders, the mess deck, the heads, the lifeboats, the portholes, the smokestacks, even the passengers and crew. The ship's initial movements made them giddy and they pretended to stagger on the deck. They were on a grand adventure and the ship...well, the ship was even better than the train!

On the deck, about midship, Ella and Josef faced east, to the land they were leaving. Franz and Walter strained at their parents' firm grasps. They looked west, toward the bow, as the ship entered the North Sea, and then sailed toward the Atlantic.

The ship was bound for New York City, where its over six-hundred passengers would be processed at Ellis Island, then transported throughout the U.S., as their papers stipulated. Josef,

Ella, and the boys were to establish themselves, initially, in Manhattan.

Just as everyone else, the family stayed on deck until they could no longer see any land. Josef then returned to his quarters, and Ella took the boys into the hold.

Every hammock and pull-down cot was assigned, and Ella estimated there were more than 350 women and children in the shared space.

She sat carefully in the center of her cot and noticed the bulkheads showed their rivets. As she visually examined the space she had to live in for the coming days, a young woman resting in one of the hammocks next to her cot became seasick.

Nor was she the only one. Vomiting was a shared activity, it seemed, and although Ella was not yet seasick, the stench made her wretch. She offered to help the woman next to her.

"It is fine, I'll clean up after myself," the young woman said. After she tidied the area around her hammock with supplies from the head, the blonde woman introduced herself to Ella. "I am Hanni. Hanni Zak."

"I am Ella Walkow and these are my two sons, Franz and Walter."

The women had much in common. Both Germans, they each married a Polish displaced person who had been a slave laborer. They, too, were planning to settle in the New York area.

"I'm pregnant," Hanni whispered. "Very early."

Ella raised her eyes. The rules stipulated pregnant women were not to travel.

"You don't show at all."

"I know. I wanted to get on this ship. The window for refugee relocation to the U.S. is closing."

Ella nodded and told Hanni about their delay due to Franz's health and the boys' measles.

Throughout the remainder of the trip, the refugees performed their chores, and almost everyone had a bout of seasickness. Although the boys had their own cots in the forward hold, they took turns sleeping with their father in his bunk in a cabin on an upper deck. Most of the time, everyone enjoyed the fresh air on deck while socializing, comparing war stories, daydreaming, and expressing apprehensions about their futures. Children aboard were treated to tours and generally indulged by the American crew. Western movies and films about the natural beauty of the United States were shown. Josef was impressed with all the forests and was glad he brought an axe, assuming he would eventually need it. Ella and Josef became fast friends with Hanni and her husband, Kasimir.

After nine long days, with the shores of America in view, everyone gathered topside.

The passengers raced to port to see the Statue of Liberty, and the captain had someone announce in Polish the people should disburse so the ship did not list too much to one side. Just as they passed the statue, the ship slowed and stopped, with Ellis Island, where they would disembark, in view.

Many of the refugees were crying. Ella and Josef each lifted up a boy to show them the statue and explain what it meant, welcoming them to a new home.

The ship remained there for hours. Occasionally, the captain made an announcement, but by the end of the afternoon, the official word was there was a longshoremen's strike that had just been initiated at the New York piers. No ship could load or unload, even a ship filled with anxious, weary immigrants. The Blatchford would be diverted to Boston, and the passengers would disembark there and then be transferred to New York City via train or bus. The announcement set off a panic among some of the passengers, who feared they were going to be rejected, or worse, thrown overboard and drowned because they were not wanted. At a minimum, there was disappointment; at the most, there was terror.

But the ship arrived in Boston harbor the following morning.

Waiting in line to be officially allowed to enter the U.S., Franz asked, "Poppi, what happened to the big statue?"

"It is in a place called New York. We are in a different city, Boston."

"Are we still in America?"

"Yes, we are. I will show you where we are on a map when we get settled."

Franz turned to his little brother and pointed a big brother finger at him, teasing, "I know something you don't know."

"What? Mami, make him stop!"

Ella admonished sharply, "Boys, stop it; stay still; we have to pay attention."

"We are in a place called Boston," Franz teasingly whispered to Walter.

"So?"

"You're a big baby, Walter."

"No, I am not!" Walter slapped back.

"Boys, stop it. I don't want to hear another word," Josef ordered, glaring at his two sons.

He diverted his eyes to Ella, giving her a half-smile. "They are just tired and excited at the same time," she said.

"Like us," Josef responded.

They slowly waited their turn to be admitted into the country. All of their papers were in order, but since Boston did not have the same facilities as Ellis Island in New York, the family, along with everyone else, would need to be transported by train or bus to New York City, and from there, bussed to Camp Kilmer in New Jersey. Camp Kilmer had been a military camp for the deployment of troops overseas during World War II and when Josef arrived in the U.S., it was used for the same reason, but for a new war—the Korean War. It had the necessary space and medical facilities to handle the ship's passengers while keeping them sequestered from the troops. Hours later, when they finally arrived, exhausted, at Camp Kilmer, there was yet another line to navigate. A physician examined each member of the family, and also reviewed their medical records. Other immigration officials checked the names of an immigrant's sponsor in the

United States. The sponsors would ensure new immigrants, like Josef and his family, would not be financially dependent on the government. For many during this late stage of DP exodus from Europe, their only sponsor was Catholic Relief Services. During the admission process, the authorities paid particular attention to Franz's records, and to the relief of a very anxious Ella and Josef, he was admitted along with the rest of the family.

Having passed the hurdle that most concerned them, the family settled into a barracks for showers, some food, and a good night's rest. It had been a grueling day, and the children fell asleep instantly in their beds. The couple took stock of their belongings. Among the four members of the young Walkow family, they had one suitcase of clothing each, a few toys, and a nominal supply of linens. Their steamer trunk loaded with household supplies was somewhere in transit. They also had their hopes, their faith, their youth, and love.

Satisfied all their worldly goods were accounted for, Ella and Josef nestled together in bed, his arms embracing her.

"We are finally here," Ella whispered. "I'm so glad there was no problem with Franz being admitted."

"Ella, I am anxious to get settled in New York, at the hotel, and find work."

"They said they'd transport us in a day or two, didn't they Josef?"

"Yes. That's what they said. Right now, everything is a blur — the train, the ship, buses, and more buses. I feel like I'm still moving."

"How does your leg feel?"

"Do you mean by missing leg?"

"You know what I mean," she cajoled. "Are you sore, Josef?"

"I ache all over."

"Me too. I could sleep for a week, but the boys won't allow it."

"They've been good sports, this whole trip, haven't they? Even when they got seasick."

"Everything is new to them, Josef; they are too young to worry about anything. All they see is an exciting set of brand new adventures—new places, new people, new foods. They don't see the uncertainty. I am jealous of them."

"Too bad we can't be more like them," Josef exhaled.

They cuddled quietly, and Ella asked, "Will you write to Michael?"

"Yes, I will, but in a few days, after we've moved into the hotel. Will you write to your sisters and maybe send a note to Willie? Your German is much better than mine."

"I will; I just look forward to the day when we will have an apartment again. Our own address."

"Let's just concentrate on each day as it comes," Josef said.

"We need to learn English, Josef."

"Yes, we do, but not tonight!"

"I can see you want to sleep," Ella tittered quietly. "Good night Josef." She kissed him on the cheek and rolled over on her side.

Josef rested with his arm over his head. He felt no sense of accomplishment—just relief the trip was over. He closed his eyes. *Hail Mary full of grace, the Lord is with thee, blessed art thou among women and blessed is the fruit of thy womb, Jesus. Holy Mary, Mother of God, please help me be strong and healthy, so I can find good, steady work. I am more frightened now than when I lost my leg; more frightened than when I was first made a slave laborer. It isn't only about me now. There are Ella, Franz, and Walter in my life, and maybe someday, another child. I ask you to be at my side and guide me, to help me learn English, to lead me to the right decisions in life. I am only twenty-six, yet I feel like fifty-six. Can you find a way to make me joyful and playful? Can you help me be resourceful and content? Amen.*

And so, on a cool October 20th, 1951, their lives began in America.

The Ship that Took the Family to America

USS *General R. M. Blatchford* (AP-153) was a General G.O. Squier class transport ship used by the United States Navy during World War II. In 1946, she was transferred to the U.S. Army as USAT *General R. M. Blatchford,* and in March of 1950, the ship was transferred to the Military Sea Transportation Service as USNS *General R. M. Blatchford* (T-AP-153). After the war, she carried displaced persons, commonly referred to as refugees, to Sydney, Australia, and New York.

Courtesy U.S. Navy, in the Public Domain

Class ___ ap ___ from Bremerhaven, October 10th, 51

USNS "GENERAL R. M. BLATCHFORD" arriving at port of New York, N. Y. 20 OCT 1951 51

NAME IN FULL / DESTINATION IN UNITED STATES		AGE	SEX	HEAD TAX ON SINGLE	RACE OR NATIONALITY	HEIGHT AND DESCRIPTION OF PIECES OF BAGGAGE	HEAD TAX COLLECTED	THIS COLUMN FOR USE OF MASTER, SURGEON, or U.S. OFFICERS
VINDASIUS	Pranas	39	Ma	Md	I-603584 Lithuanian		No	
VINDASIUS 1339 Center St, Racine, Wisc.	Marta	33	F	Md	I-60 Lithuanian		No	603
VINDASIUS 1339 Center St, Racine, Wisc.	Irene	9	F	S	I-603589 Lithuanian			
VINDASIUS 1339 Center St, Racine, Wisc.	Loreta	5	F	S	I-603587 Lithuanian		No	
VINDASIUS 1339 Center St, Racine, Wisc.	Marina	10m	F	S	I-603588 Lithuanian		No	
VOGILUS Rensselaer, Ind.	Vincas	26	Ma	Md	I-603124 Lithuanian		No	
VOGILUS Rensselaer, Ind.	Myle	24	F	Md	I-603125 Lithuanian		No	
VOGILUS Rensselaer, Ind.	Vincas	4	Ma	S	I-603126 Lithuanian		No	
WALTON 149 Madison Ave, New York NY	Josef	25	Ma	Md	J-1037743 Polish	B/1000 blanket BC Bond Newark		
WALTON 149 Madison Ave, New York NY	Ella	25	F	Md	J-1037746 Polish		No	
WALTON 149 Madison Ave, New York NY	Franz-Josef	4	Ma	S	J-1037744 Polish		No	
WALTON 149 Madison Ave, New York NY	Walter-Michael	2	Ma	S	J-1037747 Polish		No	
WIFINOSIEDER 3345 McDougall Ave, Detroit 11, Mich.	Stefan	70	Ma	Md	X-419431 Polish	B/1000 blanket BC Bond Newark		
WIFINOSIEDER 3345 McDougall Ave, Detroit 11, Mich.	Rosalia	61	F	Md	I-419432 Polish		No	
WIK	Andrzej	30	Ma	Md	I-606463 Polish		No	
WIK 3175 66th St, Cleveland Ohio	Stefania	34	F	Md	I-606464 Polish		No	
WIK 9495 Wayborn, Detroit 24, Mich.	Piotr	65	Ma	Md	I-410974 Russian	B/1000 BC Bond Detroit	No	
WIK 9495 Wayborn, Detroit 24, Mich.	Wera	62	F	Md	I-410976 Russian		No	
WOJTUNIECKI 7618 Hendrie Ave, Detroit 13 Mich.	Antoni	43	Ma	Md	I-1140421 Polish		No	
WOJTUNIECKI 7618 Hendrie Ave, Detroit 13, Mich.	Anna	30	F	Md	I-1140420 Polish		No	
WOJTUNIECKI 7618 Hendrie Ave, Detroit 13, Mich.	Renate	8	F	S	I-1140422 Polish		No	
WROBEL 5 Winston Salem NC	Mieczyslaw	29	Ma	gd	-696055 Polish		No	
WROBEL 5 Winston Salem NC	Dagmate	25	F	Md	I-696056 Polish		No	
								596

Ship's Manifest, Full Page

Ship's Manifest, Detail

Each member of the Walkow family, including Ella, is listed as Polish, even though she was German. The ages at boarding time are also inaccurate by a few months for some of the family, due to time elapsed between when they registered for resettlement and the actual date of boarding the ship. A hand-written comment indicates the passage was paid for by a relief organization. The arrival location was to be New York, but it was changed to Boston.

Document is in the Public Domain

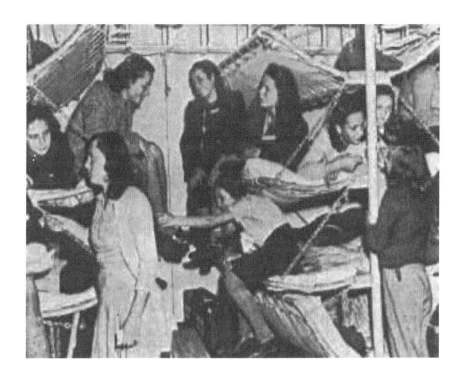

Women's Quarters on Refugee Transport Ships

This photograph depicts the accommodations refugees shared as they were transported away from Europe.

Courtesy American Merchant Marine at War. Image is in the Public Domain

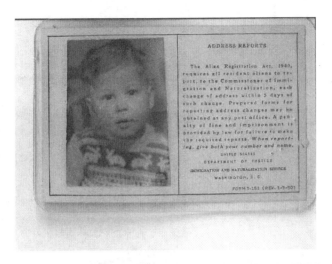

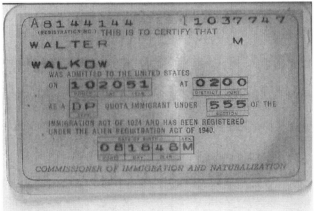

Immigration Card for Three-year-old Walter

The document above is the immigration (alien registration) card for Walter, along with his photograph. On the reverse side he is listed as a DP, or Displaced Person, subject to an immigrant quota.

Courtesy Walter Walkow

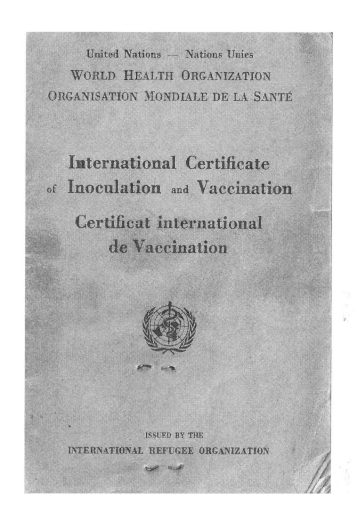

World Health Organization (WHO) Certificate of Inoculations and Vaccinations

A booklet like this was issued to each person leaving Germany to go to another country. Inside was the list of inoculations the book's owner received. This is the cover of Walter's inoculation certificate. Note the text is in both French and English.

Courtesy Walter Walkow

Smallpox Vaccination Documentation

Walter's smallpox documentation is inside his inoculation book. His name is spelled in French...Valentur. Both his birth certificate and baptismal certificate list him as "Walter." Fortunately, the difference did not cause any problems for the family as they entered the United States.

Courtesy Walter Walkow

33 - Adventures in Manhattan

"Let's go, Franz and Walter, we have to get on the bus."

"Where are we going, Poppi?" Franz asked.

"We are taking the bus to New York City. We will be moving into a hotel with other people who came here on the ship with us."

"Will we have bananas?" Walter asked. Walter had fallen in love with bananas.

Ella replied, "We can get some bananas in a day or two."

The four of them approached the bus and they placed their luggage in the hold, but Ella boarded with a tote bag containing food and drinks.

Everyone aboard the bus stretched their necks as far as they could when they saw the skyline of Manhattan come into view.

"Josef, it is so big," Ella said. "How will we ever find our way?"

As the bus exited the Lincoln Tunnel into Manhattan, the buildings loomed above them, right and left. The boys were wide-eyed. "America has big buildings," Franz said.

Josef could see Ella was getting nervous. She bit her lower lip as she removed her German/English phrase book from her tote.

"Hello, my name is Ella," she said to the air. "What is your name?" She looked at Josef. He did not respond. She prodded his knee. "My name is Ella. What is your name?"

"Josef," he replied.

They had been practicing some basic phrases and words during their voyage from Europe. Things like, "My name is...," "Where is the vegetable store?" and "I need a doctor, please."

Josef noticed Ella's face was pulled tight and her voice raised half an octave when she spoke. He tried to reassure her by holding her hand. The boys were enraptured by the sights of the city, looking up to see the tops of the skyscrapers.

"Ella, English has some words that are not so different from the way they are said in German: sauerkraut, doctor, milk, and house. Probably, you will learn English better than I ever will."

"Josef, you need to study this book, too. You need to learn more English, especially when you will be trying to find work."

Josef didn't tell her he spent quite a bit of time on the ship looking at the English/Polish dictionary and phrase book he had purchased back in Germany.

I learned German when I had to, so I suppose I can learn English also.

About two hours after leaving Camp Kilmer, the bus arrived at the hotel Catholic Relief Services used to house displaced persons who had not yet found places to live. It was a simple place, with unfussy furniture in the lobby and brown wood Venetian blinds on the windows. The floor was black linoleum with some white streaks in it. The building smelled like disinfectant. Polish was heard in the halls and public areas. Josef sighed with relief when he heard his native language.

The family was assigned a room on the third floor. They had to carry their luggage up steep flights of stairs, and another Pole who was reading a newspaper in the hotel's foyer rose from his chair and helped them. Their room had a wash sink, two full size beds, two tall windows, two well-worn tan easy chairs, and a round, dark wood table with a large lamp on it between the chairs. The sheets were thin, but clean, as were the towels. The white towels hung from a rail attached to the side of the sink, and a mirror was hung above the sink. Between the two beds there was a dark wood nightstand with some cigarette burns on it. A large clothing dresser, also with cigarette burns, was positioned against the wall across from the beds. An array of wall hooks would hold their coats and jackets. The heated room kept the autumn chill at bay. Hotel guests shared bathrooms at the far end of the hall on each floor.

Josef saw a pack of written material on the table and rifled through it.

"Josef, let's get unpacked and washed up first, before we do anything else. Besides, we should all eat something," Ella suggested.

After they unpacked most of their clothing, Josef glanced again at the Polish/English instruction papers in the room. The packet of papers identified the locations of the nearest churches and synagogues, nearby libraries, the closest public laundry facility, inexpensive restaurants and cafeterias, grocery stores, hospitals, pharmacies, and banks; furthermore, the papers contained information about the city itself, including a street map, a subway schema, and bus routes. Josef was both excited and overwhelmed. He ran his hand over his hair. *My God. This city is so big and there is so much to learn.*

After they ate a supper of sandwiches, Ella prepared the boys for bed, but the room was noisy. The shrill blare of taxi horns came from all directions, and city buses stopped to discharge and pick up passengers, their brakes making a whooshing sound. The entire night was punctuated by approaching and receding police cars and fire engines, their sirens blaring. Ambulances wailed along the broad avenues. Voices from people on the busy streets below floated into their room. Bright streetlights and thousands of illuminated windows in the office buildings cloaked the night's stars while simultaneously flooding their room with harsh, bright light. Josef drew the curtains to offer some respite from outside.

Once the boys were in bed, Josef and Ella opened the map of New York City and located their hotel by cross-referencing their address with the written material in the room. They pinpointed the nearest stores, which were only a few blocks away, and counted their money. They had only eight dollars left. Catholic Relief Services would soon be giving them the promised loan of $300, which they were expected to pay back when they could, but the money had not arrived.

Josef knew he would need to find work, and quickly. The bulletin board in the lobby listed employers who were looking for workers. Catholic Relief Services needed DPs to become independent as quickly as possible.

"Ella, I am going downstairs to the lobby. I want to look at the list of workers needed tomorrow."

"Don't leave me for too long, and please don't go out! I do not want to be alone here with the boys."

Ella walked him to the door of the room and kissed him on the cheek. He reciprocated, then headed for the stairs and descended them while carefully holding onto the wooden banister that gleamed with the oil from thousands of hands.

In the lobby he glanced at the list of jobs tacked onto a bulletin board. It showed workers were needed on the following day for carpentry assignments, janitorial jobs, and factory work. Some of the listings mentioned the employer would send someone to the hotel to pick up the workers; others gave the address of the job and the required reporting time.

But I am not going to tell anyone I have only one leg, he said to himself. As he ascended the stairs, he stopped when he reached the fourth step, turned around, and returned to the lobby. It was just too enticing. He exited the hotel, turned right, and headed toward the corner. There was a delicatessen on the way and he saw late-night diners eating huge sandwiches of either corned beef or pastrami. *The sandwiches are enormous.* A Chinese storefront restaurant next to the delicatessen displayed red lanterns and the aroma of roasting garlic wafted onto the street. A few doors down, a pizzeria was selling mozzarella-smothered pizza by the slice for only fifteen cents.

Food is everywhere! I want to try all of it. I have to get a job. He returned to the hotel and stood outside the door, drinking in the sights and sounds of endless traffic, the faces of people walking by, and the fusion of aromas permeating the air. He stood there with his arms folded across his chest, fascinated and terrified. About twenty minutes later, he reluctantly returned to the lobby and climbed slowly upstairs. He almost inaudibly opened the door to his room, so as not to wake the boys, and entered. "Josef, do you think there is some work for you?" Ella asked, almost in a whisper. She was sitting at the table looking at the orientation materials. She had placed a towel over the light on the table, so the children would not be disturbed, but the subdued light made it hard for her to see what she was reading.

"It looks like there are some jobs I can do. I have to be downstairs at 7:30 a.m. The hotel offers coffee, rolls, some orange juice, and bagels for breakfast. They stop serving at 9:00 a.m., so you need to get down there with the boys before then."

"How much does it cost?"

"The sign on the wall says it is complimentary."

"Thank God," Ella sighed.

As Josef settled into bed, he kissed Ella goodnight and thought about the next day. Ella had set their little mechanical alarm clock for 6:00 a.m. That would be enough time for Josef to get up, attach his prosthesis, wash, walk downstairs, and eat breakfast. But Josef had trouble falling asleep, afraid he would not wake up, despite the alarm.

The next morning, he awakened on time, and Ella reset the alarm for 7:30 a.m. She walked Josef to the door of their room, wished him good luck, and then returned to bed. The boys had been jolted awake by the alarm but readily fell back to sleep.

Ella looked at her boys.

"How will I look back on this day when I am old?" she wondered.

Josef watched the other men split the hard crusted rolls and fresh bagels, toast them, and then spread butter and jam on them. He did whatever they did, and ate both a roll and a bagel. He also poured himself a cup of coffee and joined three other men at a wooden table in the tiny breakfast room in a little alcove off the lobby. They introduced themselves to each other. Three of them spoke fluent Polish and one spoke Ukrainian and a little bit of Polish. Another also spoke some English.

They told Josef each of them had found day jobs for three days a week, and he was heartened by the prospects for work.

There was a bowl of apples on the breakfast bar, and he slipped one in his pants pocket for later during the day.

At 7:30 a.m., some American men showed up to select day workers. One of them chose Josef and two other men to prepare a renovated suite of offices waiting to be rented. The men got into the car driven by the man who chose them, and they were taken to the work location about ten blocks away. The entire day Josef cleaned and polished floors and elevator doors, dusted, and placed trash pails at all the desks in the suite. His boss called him "Joe" all day, and Josef understood it was a shortened version of his name.

Joe. I like that. It sounds American and is not too different from Josef. The "J" was not pronounced like the soft "Y" in Polish. In English it was a hard and strong sound.

At noon, he ate his apple and took a long drink from the water fountain. The other two men asked if he wanted to join them outside at one of the street vendors to get a hot dog. Josef had a dollar in his wallet. His fifteen-cent hot dog had been boiled in water, slathered with mustard, and topped with sauerkraut. Instead of ordering a drink, he simply used the water fountain again when he returned to the building. Josef had enjoyed American style hot dogs in Germany, but he still referred to them as frankfurters. On this first day of work in America, he decided to use the phrase "hot dog" in the future.

The men had to make their way back to the DP hotel on their own. They could walk or take a bus, but Josef wanted to save the fare. He walked the ten or so blocks, and drank in all the sights, sounds, and scents of one of the busiest cities in the world. He waited at each corner and crossed streets when other people crossed them. He stopped at a fruit stand and purchased four oranges, marveling at the abundance of food. A few times he rested against deep, granite window wells, where he could sit and take the weight off his legs.

New York City is really busy. And crowded. People walk fast here. After taking a few more steps, he added, *and it's loud.*

He walked south toward the hotel, with the city map in his pocket. When he was only three short blocks from the hotel, he found himself short-breathed and anxious. *How will we ever find a place to live here?*

His heart was thumping as he held the brown paper bag containing the four large oranges. *But I have more money now than when I left the hotel with just one dollar this morning.*

Josef had eight dollars and sixty-five cents; he was paid eight dollars in cash for the day, and had sixty-five cents left over from the dollar he had in the morning, after he paid for his hot dog and four oranges.

Wait until I tell Ella my new American name.

When he returned to the hotel, he placed a nickel in the contribution box at the hotel desk. The money deposited in it helped pay for some of the breakfast items offered each morning. It was strictly voluntary to contribute to the kitty, and Josef felt he could afford five cents. He now had eight dollars and sixty cents—a comfortable sum for a day's work, he thought.

Back in his room, he was alone. Ella and the boys were out and left a note saying they would be back at 5:00 p.m. It was after five already, but before he had a chance to worry where his family could be in the enormous city, they barged in with a rush of air coming through the doorway.

"Poppi, Poppi!" the boys yelled with glee as they rushed to him. He cradled the boys in his arms, and then hugged Ella, who was carrying a brown bag of groceries.

"Josef, how was your day?"

He told her all about the car ride to the office building, the hot dog, his walk back home, and his stop at the fruit stand. He opened the brown bag he had carried home and pulled out three beautiful, large oranges. "This one is for Franz," he said as he handed his elder son the piece of fruit, and "this one is for Walter." The boys sniffed the oranges and tossed them to each other, like balls.

"We will eat these later, for dessert," Ella said, as she gathered the oranges from the boys and placed them on the round table in the room.

"Ella, this orange is for you." It was the largest one, and Ella admired it. Finally, Josef took out the last orange, "This one is for Joe," he declared, emphasizing the English "J" and wondering what Ella would say about the shortened version of his name.

Ella looked at him, puzzled, her mouth half open. "Who is Joe?"

"Me. 'Joe' is my American name. It is short for Josef."

"And who called you this name?"

"The man who offered me work this morning."

"Do you like it?"

"I don't know. I'll have to see how it feels."

Ella rummaged in her brown grocery bag. "Okay, Joe, look what I purchased!" she replied as she exaggerated the "J" sound.

Ella took out some paper plates, cookies, a loaf of bread, a quart of milk, a pound of sliced ham, and a bunch of bananas.

Josef blanched. "How much did all of that cost?"

"Three dollars. How much did you make today?"

"Eight dollars."

"With the food here at the hotel, I'll make sure the boys eat a big breakfast, have a small snack during the day, and then a good supper; that way we don't have to spend too much."

"We can get a hot dog each—it will cost us only sixty cents for the four of us, and you can get it with sauerkraut, too, for no extra charge."

"Better yet," Ella said. "A representative from Catholic Relief Services came to the hotel today, and gave me the $300 they are lending us." She removed a stack of singles, fives, tens, and twenties from her purse and waved them in front of Josef.

Josef gasped. It was more money than he had seen in a long time.

"You shouldn't be walking around with all this money, Ella. Why don't you hide some in the room?"

"I don't know, I'd be afraid someone might steal it."

They stared at each other, not sure of what to do.

"I think I will sew it into my coat. It should be safe there," Ella said, "and I'll sew an extra inside pocket into your jacket, so you can have some of it, too. We need to keep track of every single penny. I'll write down how much money we have in the morning, how much money you come home with every day, and how much we spend."

As they ate their sandwiches that night, Ella couldn't stop talking. She raved about the vegetable sellers, the fruit vendors, the churches, the restaurants, and the stores that sold anything you could ever want, if you had the money. She and the boys had walked dozens of blocks, and all three of them feasted on New York with their eyes. Eventually, they wore themselves out. Ella told Josef she consulted the map she had picked up in the hotel's lobby and plotted the shortest route back to the hotel. Finally, they enjoyed their oranges, and Ella took the boys to the washroom to prepare for bed.

The next morning, Josef repeated his breakfast routine and was selected for more day work, this time to help a plumber. He came home with more money in his pocket and gave most of it to Ella for safekeeping. For three weeks, he took a different job every weekday, stashing away as much money as possible with Ella, and keeping no more than a dollar or two in his pocket for his daily expenses. He never spent it all. Ella kept track of their spending and earning. On the weekends the family walked to nearby parks. They found a church to attend on Sundays. Back at the hotel, Josef relaxed with other families who spoke Polish. Their friends, Hanni and Kasimir, who they met on the ship, were housed at a different hotel, and one Sunday the two couples and two boys went out to supper, to try American pizza.

Kasimir and Joe compared their daily jobs and the women shared information about the shops.

Ella spent her days exploring the city, finding inexpensive stores and secondhand shops, letting down pants legs for the boys, and finding all kinds of inexpensive treats for their mid-afternoon snacks. Some days it was a piece of fruit; some days it was a couple of cookies, or a chunk of cheese; always, there was a carton of milk for them to share. She located a fabric store and purchased a remnant to make inside pockets for all their coats. On some days she, Hanni, who was becoming visibly pregnant, and the boys explored the city together.

By the end of the fourth week at the hotel, a Jewish gentleman, not too much older than Josef, came to find a worker for a longer-term assignment to help in the plastics factory he owned with his family in lower Manhattan. His business was making plastic display boxes for baby supplies like bottles and pacifiers, as well as for other products.

"The machines need to be maintained properly," Mr. Levy said to Josef. "Can you do work like that?"

"Yes, I can; I've worked on the banding machines for barrels in Germany during the war. I've repaired pumps, heating equipment, small appliances, and clocks. Given the right equipment and materials, I can fashion machinery."

"The Germans must have appreciated you."

"I was a slave laborer, Mr. Levy." And, after a pause, he lifted his left trouser leg. "I lost my leg in an accident at the barrel factory."

Mr. Levy looked at the prosthesis, and then fixed his gaze on the face of the man before him.

"I lost much of my extended family in the concentration camps."

Josef nodded, "I'm sorry."

Both men shared a quiet, pensive moment.

"When can you start, Josef?"

"Right away, and you can call me 'Joe' if you prefer."

"Good. I'll offer you a trial position at fifty-five dollars a week, for a five day workweek. If it goes well, then I will offer you a permanent position, with an increase in pay."

When Josef told Ella about the job, she was delighted, and silently hoped it would work out.

Josef worked for Mr. Levy for about six weeks, and then became a permanent employee. He not only maintained the machines in the factory, he also helped anyone else who needed assistance on the assembly line. After a few weeks of work, he could practically run the factory.

On his way to work each day via city bus, he looked out the window and still marveled at everything he saw.

I can't believe I'm here. There are so many people here, so many neighborhoods. Where will we settle?

Having a permanent job offered the family a degree of security, although they could not comfortably afford to pay rent and utilities, leave a security deposit on an apartment, and buy furniture. Their steamer trunk of household items still had not arrived at the hotel, and Josef learned through talking with others that sometimes it took six months to reach them. The boys were growing, and Ella had to spend some of the $300 on clothing for them.

The housing issue resolved itself when a plumber he had once worked for as a day laborer asked if he would like to be the superintendent of an apartment building he owned on 9th Avenue. The second floor apartment they would live in was partially furnished, so they wouldn't have to buy kitchen items or furniture. But there were no beds. Nonetheless, they moved in right away. The owner gave them mattresses to sleep on, and over the coming weeks, they bought some beds. The family would receive free rent and a small stipend. All utilities were included, and Josef could keep his day job at the plastics factory and maintain the building in the evenings and on weekends. Ella would keep the public spaces like the hallways, stairs, banisters, and shared bathrooms shiny and clean.

The trunk with their household items arrived within six weeks of their moving into the 9th Avenue apartment, and they were happy to have things from home...their European home.

The three-story apartment building was configured into six apartments, and each floor had a hall bathroom shared by the tenants on that floor. In addition to keeping the public areas clean, and maintaining the plumbing and heating systems, Josef and Ella collected rent, handled the trash for garbage collection day, and did general repairs. It wasn't a home they owned, but it was their apartment, rent-free, with central heat and a gas stove.

Between his job at the plastics factory and his work maintaining the building, Josef kept busy and easily made friends with all the tenants. His English slowly improved, and at night he would read the *New York Daily News*. Living in the city, he sometimes looked at the axe he brought from Germany, wondering if he would ever use it. One of the tenants had a small black-and-white television, and the gentleman regularly invited the other apartment dwellers to watch programs. That television opened the world of a still alien American culture to the family. It provided endless entertainment for the boys, and was an excellent tool for learning English.

Sometimes Josef would stop doing, doing, doing, and reflect on his new life, although it had been only months, and not years, since he left the pier at Bremerhaven.

He had purchased an inexpensive box camera and, the gadget lover that he was, he enjoyed using it. Ella wrote to Willie and to her family, and enclosed snapshots of their weekend outings in Central Park, an oasis of hundreds of acres of green in the middle of Manhattan. Because Josef and Ella sorely missed the lush greens of the countryside, Central Park became their favorite haunt. Josef wrote to Michael and Pyotr, and also included snapshots. Most nights, before he fell asleep he said a simple prayer: *Hail Mary full of grace the Lord is with thee. Thank you for all you have given me, for my job, a place to live and a healthy family. Holy Mary, pray for us sinners, and keep us safe. Amen.*

They walked wherever they could, and Josef increased the distance he could travel without discomfort. Now and then they rode buses and subways, enjoyed the Staten Island Ferry, and embraced much of what the city offered. But they still missed seeing trees, grass, and flowers outside their windows.

Ella handled the bills and mail. Sometimes she needed assistance with English, and Mrs. Dinato, an Italian-American woman who lived upstairs, helped her.

The time went quickly, and the boys were strong and energetic. By the end of summer, 1953, Franz was six-and-a-half and Walter was five.

They were old enough and curious enough to create some serious mischief.

Ella had to do some grocery shopping one day and didn't want to take the boys. She learned early on it was best not to take them—they wanted everything they saw. She left them with the babysitter, Mrs. Dinato. The two boys, however, told Mrs. Dinato they wanted to play in their own apartment and do some chores in the house for their mother. She agreed and said she would check in on them every fifteen minutes.

The boys really did want to help their mother with chores. But unfortunately, the chore they chose to do required more skill than they possessed. Within a few minutes of leaving Mrs. Dinato's, Franz and Walter decided to wash the kitchen floor. Not knowing how to do it, they decided the simplest way would be to pour a bucket of sudsy water on the linoleum floor, and then swish the water around with a mop. When they saw the first bucket of water was not sufficient for the whole floor, they dumped another bucketful of water on the floor, then another, and another, and another, until the tenant below them came rushing up the steep flight of stairs, yelling. He owned a used furniture store and the water had poured through the ceiling below.

Mrs. Dinato ran to the boys' apartment to see what the fuss was all about.

"We wanted to wash the floor for Mami," they explained.

When Ella came home, she was quite upset, yet thanked the boys for trying to help her.

"Boys, when you are older, you may wash the floor, and I will show you how. Thank you for trying to help, but don't ever do that again," she said.

The furniture in the storefront below their apartment was not soaked through and dried well. Josef helped the shopkeeper dry everything. Furious he had extra work to do, he was nonetheless amused at his boys' resourcefulness.

When the boys were old enough, they attended elementary school in the public school system. At P.S. 52 they received formal instruction in English and excelled in Mathematics. After school each day they participated in children's programs either at St. Paul's House or Hartley House, which were both within walking distance of their apartment. They settled into a routine of school-St. Paul's or Hartley House-homework-supper-time with Mami and Poppi-bed.

A year or so after the wash-the-floor incident, Ella and Josef needed to go to the grocery store one evening. They decided to leave the boys alone, with some books and toys in the parlor as babysitters. The boys loved their trucks, airplanes, sailboats, building blocks, and books. They especially adored cowboy toys like hats, guns, and holsters. Their favorite, though, was anything relating to Roy Rogers and Dale Evans, whom they fell in love with from the television at their neighbor's apartment. The boys had learned to behave themselves when their parents went out, and they had become responsible little fellows, avoiding any house chores unless there was adult supervision.

While Walter remained in the parlor, playing, Franz decided to wend his way through the railroad style rooms in their apartment to reach the kitchen. He wanted something to drink. It had gotten dark and he flipped the light switch.

The next thing he knew, Ella was crouched over him, shaking him, and crying "Wake up, wake up, Franz!"

There had been an undetected natural gas leak near the stove, and when Franz switched the light on, the windows in the parlor, where Walter was still playing, exploded onto the street. Plates rattled off shelves in the kitchen where Franz was. The concussion knocked terrified Walter off his feet, and it knocked Franz out. Ella and Josef, their arms full of groceries, were approaching the building when the explosion occurred. They dropped their groceries in the hall, and ran upstairs to the boys, terrified they had lost their sons.

It turned out both boys were fine and luckily, the shattered window glass did not injure anyone on the street.

Josef, angry at himself, had the gas company make an emergency visit. He called the plumber who owned the building, and the two of them applied plywood to the naked spaces that used to be windows, until new windows could be ordered. As the landlord, the plumber paid for the wood, had new windows installed, and deeply apologized for the mishap.

Ella and Josef redoubled their efforts to save every penny they could, so they could buy their own apartment building. If he was going to spend his limited time replacing windows and repairing water damage, Josef wanted it to be in his *own* building.

Life in a new country, with new living arrangements, new transportation, new everything, did not affect only the boys. Ella, too, was learning.

Shortly after they moved into the plumber's 9th Avenue apartment building, she decided to make an apple cake. She hadn't baked since they left Stockach and was looking forward to making homemade sweets again.

She needed baking powder. At the store she found it unusual to find baking powder near household cleaning supplies. Reading the word "powder" on the containers, she was surprised at the varieties of baking powder in America. She said the names to herself as she looked at all the containers on the shelf—Ajax, Babbo, and Comet.

After she made her purchase, she returned home, peeled and sliced some of the apples, and prepared the batter, with Ajax. She baked the cake, and when she removed it from the oven, it appeared quite flat. When it cooled, she cut a thin slice for herself and spat it out. Running up to Mrs. Dinato's, she brought the Ajax with her and explained she had baked with it. Mrs. Dinato laughed loud and long, and almost couldn't stop.

"You tried to bake a cake with cleansing powder!"

"What? Cleansing powder?"

"Yes, this is used to scrub your white porcelain sink," she demonstrated, laughing and shaking the Ajax can so hard some of the powder floated to the floor.

Ella gasped, "Oh no! I'm just glad the oven didn't explode! And I wasted all those apples."

Mrs. Dinato took a cylindrical can from one of her cabinets to show Ella how baking powder was packaged, and added, with a smile she couldn't contain, "You find this in the baking aisle, Ella, with the nuts, sugar, and flour."

"I don't know what I was thinking! Maybe I was just distracted."

"Here, Ella, take some home and make another cake." Mrs. Dinato measured a few tablespoons of baking powder and wrapped it in aluminum foil for Ella.

"Thank you," Ella said as she looked down, embarrassed. She went downstairs and made another cake.

Josef, too, had his own misadventures. More than once he got off at a wrong subway station or bus stop. He created his own words. He called the fire hydrant a "hydrogent" and he referred to "Howard Johnson" as "Johnson & Johnson."

Living around the corner from Madison Square Garden, Ella and Josef planned a special family outing. Over several months, they saved enough money to purchase tickets for all of them to see a Roy Rogers and Dale Evans live show. Ella also bought each boy a cowboy outfit, not only for the show, but to wear until they grew out of them.

"Look at our little cowboys," she said to Josef as she had the two boys show off their outfits—shirts, jeans, hats, boots, holsters, and guns.

On the day of the show, with the boys fully decked out in their cowboy clothing, the family walked to their seats in Madison Square Garden. Josef remembered a conversation he had with Willie. It seemed like a hundred years ago.

They had been playing darts in Willie's shed and drinking more beer than they should have.

"Maybe you are going to be an American cowboy, Josef, just like you see in all the magazines now," Willie had teased.

"Can you see me rounding up cattle somewhere in the Wild West? If I can't catch them I'll just throw my wooden leg at them and stun them!" Josef had replied.

Josef missed his friend.

I will go back to Germany and Poland someday, Josef said to himself as he settled into his seat in the cavernous venue.

He looked at the ring on his finger. He hadn't realized until that moment the initials WM, for Willie Mirz, were the same as his younger son's—Walter Michael. Fingering it, he decided, *Someday, I will give this ring to Walter.*

The lights dimmed in the massive arena, and a spotlight flooded the raised stage. Removing their fake guns from their holsters, the boys stretched their necks, mouths agape, and fidgeted with anticipation. They tightened the straps on their cowboy hats and sat at the edges of their seats like all the other children in the audience. Roy Rogers and Dale Evans rode their beautiful horses, Trigger and Buttermilk, into the spotlight, accompanied by their faithful German Shepherd, Bullet.[52] The crowd, including Ella and Josef, clapped, hooted, and hollered with delight.

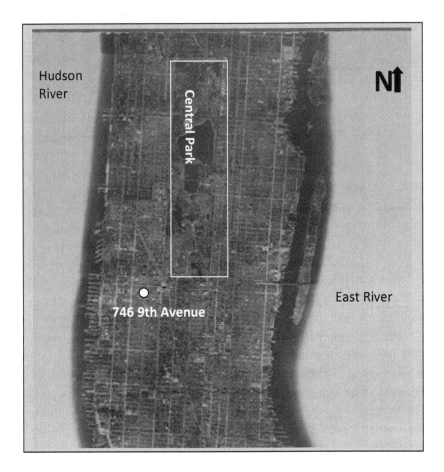

Hudson
River

Central Park

East River

746 9th Avenue

Aerial Map of Manhattan

The plumber-owned apartment building managed by Josef and Ella was located just a few blocks south of Central Park. They moved into the building after spending some time at the DP hotel in Manhattan. Accessibility to the park gave them the opportunity to visit it often. While managing this apartment building, their rent was part of their compensation and they managed to save enough money to purchase their own apartment building in Greenpoint, Brooklyn, in 1958.

Courtesy New York Public Library, Digital Collection; in the Public Domain

34 - Settling In

Living around the corner from Madison Square Garden turned out to be a boon for the boys. They would often hang around the famed arena and sometimes, someone would give them tickets to see a show. They saw the Ringling Brothers Barnum and Bailey Circus several times, a few track meets, and other performances.

The apartment building Joe and Ella managed was old and had a problem with vermin—rats, specifically. The rodents lived in the walls and in the basement, and nothing fully eradicated them. Ella and Josef continued to save as much as they could, hoping to own their own building as soon as possible.

On a Friday night in late December of 1953, Ella had something important to tell her husband. She waited until after she cleaned the supper dishes and the boys had gone to bed.

"Josef, I have something to tell you," she said, as she prepared decaffeinated instant coffee for both of them.

He was reading the newspaper.

Ella placed the mugs of coffee on the holiday poinsettia print tablecloth covering the kitchen table. As she sat across from Josef, she noticed he was still reading the paper. He looked forward to reading it every night.

"Josef, please put the newspaper down; I am talking to you."

Josef folded the paper, and gave his full attention to Ella. "What is it, Mami?" By then, they both had taken to sometimes calling each other "Mami" and "Poppi," just as the children did.

"We are going to have a baby."

Josef opened his mouth in surprise, "Really?"

"Yes, and I hope it is a girl this time."

Josef got up and walked around the table, hugged his wife from behind and kissed the top of her head.

"Our baby will be American, do you know that?" Josef asked.

"Yes, of course I do."

Josef taunted her, "How did this happen?"

"Now stop it, Poppi; every time I get pregnant you ask me how it happened. It happened the same way Walter and Franz happened! You were there, you know."

"I'm just joking with you," he replied with a mischievous grin. "Ella, when do you think we should tell the boys?"

"Maybe when I show more. What do you think?"

"Okay, let's wait until then."

Josef and Ella had used English words like "okay" for a while now. They also uttered "no problem" from time to time.

"When is the baby due, Ella?"

"In July of next year, 1954. That is what the doctor at Polyclinic said. I'm glad the Polyclinic Hospital is just around the corner."

"True," Josef responded, "it isn't far at all."

He cocked his head to the right.

"I want to write to Michael tonight. Will you mail the letter tomorrow, Ella?"

"Yes, of course; please send my love to him and to Stephania."

She continued, "Josef, I forgot to tell you. I opened up a checking account for us. We can pay our bills with it. That way I don't have to go to the post office or any other place to purchase money orders. Also, I sent a check for $15 to Catholic Relief Services, as our first payment for the $300 loan. It was the first check I used. I will send them some money whenever I can."

Josef nodded his head in acknowledgement. *Ella knows how to run a household*, he thought to himself.

"Thank you. I am glad you take care of the finances. You are much better at it than I could ever be."

Ella laughed back, "You just say that so I'll do the bills."

She got up, kissed her husband on the forehead as he wrapped his arms around her waist. She then turned and walked quietly through the boys' bedroom to their bedroom.

Alone in the kitchen, Josef heard the wall clock ticking. It was almost 10:00 p.m. and quiet. He found a piece of white notebook paper, a pen, and an envelope.

Dear Michael,

Some wonderful news for us here. Ella is expecting a baby next July. We both hope it will be a girl.

Things are going well and we work hard; Ella does an excellent job keeping the apartment building clean. My work at the plastics factory is going well, and it is a relief to have a permanent job. I never thought it would be possible, but we are able to save some money and will, one day, own a building, maybe in a Polish neighborhood and near a park. Where we live it is not very green, although there are parks we often visit throughout the city.

We continue to have many friends, some of them very special, like Hanni and Kasimir Zak, who we met on the ship when we came here. She is German, like Ella; and he is Polish, like me. I have more opportunities to speak Polish here with friends we have made among the DPs than I did back in Stockach! I never would have guessed I would be speaking more Polish here in America than in Germany.

I often think of our time together as boys at home in Poland, as well as our years together in Germany. It is my hope we will see each other again here in America or in Poland someday, and I will meet your children and see Pyotr.

337

Until I write again, please send my love to the family, and Ella sends her very special regards to Stephania.

I have enclosed a photograph of the four of us in Central Park. The boys are really thriving and are learning English easily. Do you notice they are dressed like cowboys?

God bless you and keep you well.

Josef

Ella's pregnancy proceeded with some morning sickness, but otherwise, without incident. At almost five months, she and Josef sat in the kitchen with the boys after supper one night.

"Walter, Franz, we have something to tell you," Josef said.

Both boys looked up from their task of dunking dessert cookies into milk.

Josef watched Franz in particular. *I remember when milk almost killed him, and here he is, healthy.*

"Ella, do you want to tell them or should I?"

"I will." She looked at her sons as she smiled, "I am going to have a baby in a few months. You will have a little brother or sister soon."

"Why?" pragmatic Walter asked, licking milk from one of his cookies and then taking a bite of it.

She tried in vain to stifle a smile. "Because your Poppi and I love each other so much and love both of you so much we have some extra love to give to a new baby."

"Where is the baby coming from, Mami?" Franz asked, as he steered a cookie through the air to his mouth.

Josef and Ella's eyes met.

"The baby is inside me, growing, just like you and Walter did."

Franz looked skeptically at his mother. "Where inside?"

Josef had trouble containing a laugh.

Ella told him to come to her, and she placed his hand on her abdomen, and then had Walter do the same thing.

"How does the baby get in there?" Walter wanted to know.

Now both Ella and Josef were suppressing laughter.

"Love puts the baby there," Ella responded.

"How does it come out?" Franz asked.

"That's enough for now, boys," Josef said. "Don't tire your mother. You can play with your toys for an hour before bedtime."

The boys excused themselves from the table and tore at breakneck speed into the parlor, forgetting a new baby was on the way, how it came to be, and how it would arrive into the world.

Josef and Ella remained at the kitchen table, giggling so hard their eyes were tearing.

A few weeks later, Ella and Josef once again spoke with the boys after supper. Much of life happened at their little kitchen table.

"Boys," Ella said. "I have two names in mind for the baby, if it is a girl."

The boys looked up from their dessert.

"Your Poppi and I were thinking of either Monica or Wanda. Wanda is the lady who is going to be the baby's godmother. She is my good friend and sometimes she and I go shopping together. Do you remember her, boys? She sometimes brings you chocolates."

The boys looked at each other, not truly remembering Wanda.

Ella asked again, "Which name do you like better—Wanda or Monica?"

Josef reinforced Ella's question. "Which do you like, Wanda or Monica?"

Walter and Franz looked at each other. Simultaneously they said, "Monica."

"That's the name, then," Ella replied. "If it is a girl, we will name her Monica and her middle name will be Wanda."

"What if the baby is a boy?" Walter asked.

"Yes, Mami, if the baby is a boy, what will be its name?" Franz added.

"We haven't decided on a boy's name yet, have we Poppi?"

"No, we have not. Maybe Pyotr, or Leon, after my father. Do you like those names?"

"They're okay," Franz said.

"But I like Monica better," Walter offered.

"It's settled then. The baby will just *have* to be a girl, won't it Mami?" Josef laughed.

"We'll see," said Ella, hoping the baby would be a girl.

In July of 1954, Franz was seven-and-a-half, and Walter was a month shy of his sixth birthday. Near her due date, Ella's labor began. Josef was still at work, and Ella asked Mrs. Dinato to look after the boys, who climbed the stairs up to her apartment. After the wash-the-kitchen-floor incident, Mrs. Dinato supervised the boys more closely. She offered to walk with Ella to the hospital, but Ella did not think it was necessary. The labor was early and the hospital was nearby. After she wrote a brief note to Josef and left it in a conspicuous place in the center of the kitchen table, she walked alone to Polyclinic Hospital around the corner.

Josef and Ella's daughter Monica was born a few hours later. When Josef came home from work and read the note, he rushed upstairs to Mrs. Dinato to greet the boys, and then walked, alone, to the hospital. Both Ella and the baby were fine, and when he returned home and retrieved the boys, he proceeded to make them supper.

"You boys have a little sister. Her name is Monica—the name you chose."

"When is Mami coming home?" Walter asked.

"She and the baby will be home in about three days. Until then, we'll have to cook for ourselves."

"May we go see Mami?" Franz asked.

"I am afraid not; children aren't allowed in the hospital to visit, but if you want to write your Mami a note or draw a picture, I will give it to her. Now, how would you like some potato soup for supper?"

"Are you going to make it?" Franz asked.

"Yes, I am!"

Josef boiled water and peeled some potatoes; after he cut the potatoes, he carefully dropped them into the boiling water. When the potatoes were cooked, he drained some water and then added milk, salt, pepper and some bacon Ella had cooked the previous day. To thicken it, he tried to make a paste with flour, and burned it.

Franz and Walter had never seen their father cook and they found it amusing, snickering at each other. Josef told the boys to set the table and they sat down to eat.

"What smells, Poppi?" Walter asked.

"I just burned some flour, that's all. Your mother is the cook in the family, so we'll have to make do. It is just we three men for a few nights," Josef said, missing Ella.

The boys had potato soup for three nights, supplemented by some spaghetti and meatballs Mrs. Dinato brought them.

When Josef picked up Ella from the hospital, they walked around the block with little Monica in Ella's arms. Once home, the boys peered at the little intruder and greeted her with welcoming utterances such as "Did it have to be a girl?" and "Are her diapers going to be smelly?" and "Her head looks funny."

Ella closely supervised the boys as they took turns holding their tiny sister, then she placed the baby in the pink and white bassinette.

In the following weeks, the boys grew accustomed to the baby and no longer considered her a stranger. When they returned from daily summer activities, they would always rush to see her, and she was usually asleep. Ella purchased a white

Patricia Walkow

christening dress, and on the day of Monica's baptism, the family walked to Sacred Heart Catholic Church, their local parish.

Josef, Ella, and the boys, along with Monica's godparents, were all dressed up and gathered around the baptismal font.

As the baby girl was christened Monica Wanda, Josef's eyes moistened as the priest read the ritual. His mind drifted to a time and place, not too long ago, when he and Ella were beginning to acknowledge each other in Germany. He remembered the time during the war when he first waved to her from Willie's garden, and she waved back. Now, here he was, almost twenty-nine years old, with three children and a life in America, a steady job, and some money saved. He offered a prayer:

Hail Mary, full of grace, the Lord is with thee. Blessed art thou among women and blessed is the fruit of thy womb, Jesus. Holy Mary, Mother of God, bless my little American daughter, my sons, Ella, and me. Thank you for all your blessings, for good food, for friends. Thank you for peace. Please keep us safe, healthy, and happy. Amen.

When the ceremony was over, the small assemblage headed back to Josef's apartment. A meal of pot roast, string beans, salad, and mashed potatoes was waiting for them. Ella had made it the previous day, and Hanni and Kasimir would be joining them for the celebratory feast. They had become like family.

As they prepared to cross 9th Avenue to return home, Josef turned to Ella, "Give me the baby, Ella. I want to hold her."

Ella tenderly handed Monica to Josef, making certain the infant was well-anchored in his arms before letting go.

"Be careful," she admonished.

"I will," responded Josef.

The entourage waited at the corner. When the light turned green, all but Josef forged across the broad avenue.

When he stepped off the curb, he lifted the baby high above his head and her white dress dangled at an angle above his forehead. He danced cautiously in a circle, sharply aware of every slow step he made in his twirling, prosthesis-led waltz across the busy thoroughfare. When everyone else reached the far side of the street, Ella, the boys, and the godparents turned their heads to check his progress.

"Josef, be careful, please. The baby!" Ella yelled.

But Josef wasn't listening.

The boys giggled and pointed at their father, "Poppi, Poppi!"

But Josef wasn't listening.

The godparents held their hands to their gaping mouths and gasped, "Oh!"at Josef's actions, fearful for the baby.

But Josef wasn't listening.

For a moment he forgot he had only one natural leg.

With Monica held high, he danced proudly and called to anyone, to everyone, "My American daughter! My American daughter!"

Family Portrait from the late 1950s

Back row, from the left: Franz, Ella, Josef, and Walter. Front row: Monica

Courtesy Monica Walkow Dudzkinski

Epilogue

The family flourished in the years following Monica's birth. Josef, Ella, and the two boys became naturalized American citizens in 1957. Having been born in the U.S., Monica was already a citizen.

The plastics factory where Josef worked moved to Brooklyn. In 1958, when they had saved enough money, Josef and Ella purchased a six unit apartment building in the Greenpoint section of Brooklyn. They had searched carefully and found a building across the street from Winthrop Park, an urban oasis full of mature trees. Whenever they looked out their parlor window, they would see green. Greenpoint remains to this day a desirable Polish community, with Polish stores.

When Monica was old enough to go to school, Ella sometimes helped Josef in the factory at busy times and made some money. She applied for a job on the assembly line at Pfizer, a pharmaceutical manufacturer in Brooklyn, and worked the swing shift for many years. The job brought even greater prosperity and excellent health benefits.

In 1963, they visited a friend near Jackson, New Jersey. She was the woman who used to visit her boyfriend in the apartment upstairs from Ella and Josef's, back in Stockach. Near their friend's New Jersey home was an available parcel of land—three acres, tall pine trees, a brook, and a small cottage. They purchased it as a weekend home and, over the years, expanded the cottage by adding a basement and more rooms. They retired there in 1980, after they sold their apartment building in Greenpoint. Josef finally used the axe be brought from Germany.

Josef and Ella made and kept friends easily, and enjoyed going to flea markets and visiting their children all around the country. Ella always retained her love of literature, and kept the house supplied with newspapers, magazines, and books.

Ever the builder and fixer, Josef made a two-story decorative windmill for their New Jersey property, which Ella surrounded with a bed of tulips and daffodils. He repaired motors and gadgets he purchased used, reselling them at a flea market. He ate Lobster Cantonese, his favorite Chinese restaurant dish, whenever he had a chance.

The wind whispering through the pines on their property became the inspiration for calling the place, "Whispering Pines," or, as Ella wrote it on a white, wooden plaque, "Wishpering Pines." Both names seemed appropriate.

Josef never his saw his parents again after that fateful day, early in the war, when he was captured. They remained in what used to be the eastern lands of Poland, which then became part of Ukraine. They died there, of natural causes.

Ella, Josef, and Monica returned to Germany and Poland in 1969 for a visit with family and friends, like Willie, and some of Ella's girlfriends. In the early 1980s, Michael spent a few months with Ella and Josef and met his American niece and nephews and their spouses. In 1993, Josef, Franz, and Walter visited Poland. Josef took a vial with him and filled it with Polish soil. Michael had died by then, but Franz and Walter, now grown men, met their Polish cousins and Uncle Pyotr. In 1995, Walter met his parents in Germany to spend a few weeks with them visiting Ella's family. By then, Josef's colon cancer had metastasized to his liver, and he was undergoing chemotherapy.

Franz, Walter, and Monica are all in long, stable marriages, own their own homes, and have had success in their careers.

On one of the rare occasions when Ella and I talked about her past, she once told me, "You know, Pat, leaving Germany and coming to America, even though there were some very hard years, I look at my children and I know it was the right thing to do. It was worth it. They are my success in life."

She never completely lost her fear of food shortages. Haunted by the hunger years following the war, she lined her basement shelves with rows and rows of green beans, peas, pickles, apricots, peaches, plums, and jams she canned. The first time I saw the larder, she laughed a little nervously, almost embarrassed.

"It's just the war, Pat," she said. "I remember too much."

Josef built a tree house for his two grandsons, Monica's boys, Brian and Andrew. He enjoyed it as much as they did.

When he was with his grandkids, he seemed to revert to his interrupted youth. It was a joy to see.

Hanni and Kasimir became "family" to Ella and Josef; the couples and their children shared many holidays together.

About every ten years, Josef received a new leg from the shop at Lake Constance where the mold of his leg was made after the war. Although Josef tried other legs in the U.S., he found the one from Germany was the best for him, and continued to receive replacements throughout his life.

In October of 1996, Josef and I sat a table in a restaurant at a resort in the mountains of Pennsylvania, and he told me he had decided to stop his chemotherapy. My heart sank, but he didn't want to delay the inevitable any longer, and decided to live the remainder of his life as he wished—enjoying his family and home. That was his choice.

On February 13th, 1997, at the age of seventy-one, Josef died of cancer that could no longer be controlled. At his gravesite, Ella opened the vial of Polish soil he had brought back from Poland and sprinkled it on top of his casket. I had the honor to give his eulogy and spoke about how he was a great fixer of things. He certainly repaired his own life, and he provided a safe place for his children to grow. At his death, cuckoo clocks in various states of repair covered the upper reaches of the walls in the enclosed back porch of his house in New Jersey. Willie Mirz would have been proud.

After suffering from advanced dementia, Ella died on October 1st, 2015, at the age of eighty-nine. About a year before she died, when she still could communicate, however sporadically, I mentioned to her I was writing this story. Her response was, "I hope I don't get in trouble." I told her that her life was an example for many, assured her there was no reason to be in trouble, the war was long over, and she was safe. It seemed to satisfy her. Then she receded, mute, to somewhere I could not go.

Franz, and his wife Janis, Walter, and Monica occasionally visit family in Germany and Poland, and some of their cousins have visited the United States. Social media has helped them all keep in touch frequently.

As of this writing, Stephania, Michael's wife, still reigns as family matriarch. Luzia Rimmele, the daughter of Frau Wilkesmann, Josef and Ella's landlady in Stockach, remains friends with everyone, and lived with Josef and Ella in the U.S. for a while when she was a young woman. She has been to the U.S. since then for several visits, and Walter and I visited her in Stockach.

Every morning, when my husband, Walter Michael, gets dressed, he slips a silver signet ring on his finger. It bears the initials "WM" in fancy script.

Ella and Josef

Ella and Josef Walkow. This photograph was taken between 1988 and 1995. The statue of The Virgin Mary was a gift from Monica, her husband, Paul, and their children Brian and Andrew. Josef kept it in his garden on their property in New Jersey.

Courtesy Monica Walkow Dudzkinski

Author's Notes

My knowledge of World War II increased exponentially as I researched information for this book. It was as though I had discovered the war for the first time, and I realized my understanding of it was limited to what I knew as filtered by the American media in the 1950s.

For the person interested in various aspects of the war, and how they affected individuals of all nationalities, I have included books and articles I found helpful. They are listed in the bibliography.

Regarding the characters in *The War Within, The Story of Josef,* Josef, Michael, Pyotr, Ella, Willie, Frau Zimmerman and Frau Wilkesmann all lived through the war and survived it. Hanni and Kasimir Zak were friends of Ella and Josef's for life. Mrs. Dinato was a real neighbor in the 9th Avenue apartment, and Wanda was a friend of Ella's. Mr. Levy was Josef's employer for many years. The real spelling of Willie's last name is unknown. It was either Mirtz, Mertz, Mirz, or something similar. Fictional characters are Helga, Sonya, Gunter and Hans.

The events experienced by Josef and Ella were gleaned from their own recollections, as well as from conversations with their children. Relatives and friends in both Poland and Germany offered family history and their own remembrances.

For information about additional copies go to:
www.amazon.com or www.barnesandnoble.com

The author welcomes your feedback. You may contact her at:
walkowpc@earthlink.net

Chapter Notes

1. Richard C. Lukas, Editor, *Forgotten Survivors, Polish Christians Remember the Nazi Occupation*, (University of Kansas Press, 2004), as told by Wieslaw Piller), 120

2. Yale Law School Avalon Project, Nazi *Conspiracy and Aggression Volume 1, Chapter X - The Slave Labor Program, the Illegal Use of Prisoners of War*, (www.avalon.law.yale.edu/imt/chap_10.asp)

3. www.fpnp.pl/edukacja/dokumenty_eng.pdf

4. Matthew Hughes and Chris Mann, *Inside Hitler's Germany, Life Under the Third Reich*, (New York: MJF Books, 2000), 50-55

5. Richard C. Lukas, *Forgotten Holocaust, The Poles under German Occupation 1939-1944*, (New York: Hippocrene Books, 1997), 30

6. Alexander Junta, *I Lied to Live, a Year as a German Family Slave*, (New York: Roy Publishers,1994), 222

7. Matthew Hughes & Chris Mann, *Inside Hitler's Germany, Life Under the Third Reich*, (New York: MJF Books, 2000), 126-133

8. Lukas, *Forgotten Holocaust*, 33

9. Discussions with Josef Walkow

10. Lukas, *Forgotten Holocaust,* 38

11. Lukas, *Forgotten Holocaust,* 4,24

12. Lukas, ed., *Forgotten Survivors*, 27-28

13. Junta, *I Lied to Live,* 232

14. Junta, *I Lied to Live,* 213

15. Junta, *I Lied to Live,* 214

16. www.pbs.org/thewar/at_war_timeline_1944.htm

17. Junta, *I Lied to Live*, 221

18. http://www.history.com/news/fooling-hitler-the-elaborate-ruse-behind-d-day

19. www.pbs.org/thewar/at_war_timeline_1944.htm

20. Ibid.

21. www.historyplace.com/unitedstates/pacificwar/timeline.htm

22. www.historyplace.com/worldwar2/timeline/ww2time.htm

23. Ibid.

24. Richard Bessel, *Germany 1945, From War to Peace*, (New York: Harper Collins Publishers, 2009), 116-118

25. Ian Buruma, *Year Zero, A History of 1945*, (New York: Penguin Press, 2013), 292

26. Giles MacDonogh, *After the Reich, The Brutal History of Allied Occupation*, (New York: Basic Books, 2007), 269-277

27. Richard Bessel, *Germany 1945, From War to Peace*, (New York: Harper Collins Publishers, 2009), 205

28. Greg Behrman, *The Most Noble Adventure, The Marshall Plan and How America Helped Rebuild Europe*, (New York: Free Press, a division of Simon & Schuster, Inc., 2007), 51

29. Mark Wyman, *DPs, Europe's Displaced Persons, 1945-1951*, (Ithaca: Cornell University Press, 1998; Previously published by Associated University Presses, Inc., 1989), 44

30. Richard Bessel, *Germany 1945, From War to Peace*, (New York: HarperCollins Publishers, 2009), 169-182

31. Ian Buruma, *Year Zero, A History of 1945*, (New York: Penguin Press, 2013), 54-55

32. Buruma, *Year Zero,* 293

33. Dorothea von Schwanenflügel Lawson, *Laughter Wasn't Rationed, A Personal Journey Through Germany's World Wars and Postwar Years*, (Alexandria, Virginia: Tricor Press, 1999), 387-388

34. Joel Carl Welty, *The Hunger Year in the French Zone of Divided Germany, 1946-1947*, (Beloit, Wisconsin: Beloit College, 1993), 35-36

35. Greg Behrman, *The Most Noble Adventure*, (New York: Free Press, a division of Simon & Schuster, Inc., 2007), 125

36. Giles MacDonogh, *After the Reich, The Brutal History of the Allied Occupation*, (New York: Basic Books, 2007), 520-523

37. Thomas M. Daniel, *Respiratory Medicine, The History of Tuberculosis*, www.sciencedirect.com, November 2006

38. Daniel, *Respiratory Medicine,* www.sciencedirect.com/science/artilce/pii/S095461110600601X

39. Helen Bynum, *Spitting Blood, the History of Tuberculosis*, (Oxford University Press, 2012), 173-175

40. Bynum, *Spitting Blood*, 108

41. Mark Wyman, *DPs, Europe's Displaced Persons*, 1945-1951, (Ithaca: Cornell University Press, 1998), 168

42. *U.S. State Department profile documents* regarding the Federal Republic of Germany

43. Lukas, ed., *Forgotten Survivors*, 25-27

44. Eileen Egan, *Catholic Relief Services, The Beginning Years, for the Life of the World*, (New York: Catholic Relief Services, 1988), 228

45. *Historical Dollar-to-Marks Currency Conversion* www.history.ucsb.edu/faculty/marcuse/projects/currency.htm

46. www.history.ucsb.edu/faculty/marcuse/projects/currency.htm

47. *The Year 1949, www.thepeoplehistory.com/1949.html*

48. Egan, *Catholic Relief Services*, 223

49. *Displaced Person Transports, Cargo of Hope*: www.usmm,org/dp.html

50. *U.S. Naval Records: Ships Manifest: USNS General R.M. Blatchford*

51. *Displaced Person Transportation post World War II*: ww.usmm.org/dp/html

52. www.petcaretips.net/roy_rogers_trigger.html

Bibliography

Primary Sources

Josef Walkow
Ella Stichler Walkow
Franz Walkow
Walter Walkow
Monica Walkow Dudzkinski
Luzia Wilkesmann Rimmele
Józef Walków (lives in Poland, nephew of Josef, listed first)

Books, Articles, Websites

Allied Museum. *Past and Present, 50 Mementos Recall the Western Allied Presence in Berlin 1945-1944.* Berlin: Allied Museum, 1998.

American Merchant Marine at War. *Displaced Persons Transports: Cargo of Hope.* www.usmm.org/do/html.

Behrman, Greg. *The Most Noble Adventure, The Marshall Plan and How America Helped Rebuild Europe.* New York: Free Press, a division of Simon & Schuster, Inc., 2007.

Bessel, Richard. *Germany 1945, From War to Peace.* New York: HarperCollins Publishers, 2009.

Bottome, Phyllis. *The Mortal Storm.* Evanston, Illinois: Northwestern University Press, 1998 .

Buruma, Ian. *Year Zero, A History of 1945.* New York: Penguin Press, 2013.

Bynum, Helen. *Spitting Blood,The History of Tuberculosis.* Oxford: Oxford University Press, 2012.

Clay, Catrine and Michael Leapman. *Master Race, The Lebensborn Experiment in Nazi Germany.* London: BCA, 1995.

Cohen, Gerard Daniel. *In War's Wake, Europe's Displaced Persons in the Postwar Order.* New York: Oxford University Press, 2012.

Crossland, David. *Nazi Program to Breed Master Race, Lebensborn Children Break Silence.* Spiegel Online International.

Daniel, Thomas. *Respiratory Medicine, The History of Tuberculosis.*
www.sciencedirect.com.

Economic Cooperative Administration. *Information on the Marshall Plan for Americans Going Abroad, 1949.* The Office of Information, Economic Cooperative Administration, 1949.

Eder, Angelika. *Polish Life in West Germany After 1945, A Case Study in Hamburg.* www.ruf.rice.edu.

Egan, Eileen. *Catholic Relief Services, the Beginning Years, for the Life of the World.* New York: Catholic Relief Services, 1988.

faculty.washington.edu.

faculty.washington.edu/krumme/german/chronology.html.

faculty.washington.edu.

Friedrich, Jorg. *The Fire, The Bombing of Germany 1940-1945.* New York: Columbia University Press, 2006.

Gilbert, Martin. *The Day the War Ended.* London: Harper Collins, 1995.

Hitler Historical Museum. *German Political & Economic History (Chronology), 1945-1997.* www.hitler.org.

holocaustforgotten.com. *Non-Jewish Holocaust Victims.*
www.holocaustforgotten.com.

Huges, Matthew and Chris Mann. *Inside Hitler's Germany, Life Under the Third Reich.* New York: MJF Books, 2000.

Junta, Alexander. *I Lied to Live, a Year as a German Family Slave.* New York: Roy Publishers, 1944.

Lawson, Dorothea von Schwanenflugel. *Laughter Wasn't Rationed, A Personal Journey through Germany's World Wars and Postwar Years.* Alexandria, Virginia: Tricor Press, 1999.

Lukas, Richard C. *Did the Children Cry? Hitler's War Against Jewish and Polish Children, 1939-1945.* New York: Hippocene Books, 1994.

—. *Forgotten Holocaust, The Poles under German Occupation 1939-1944.* New York: Hippocrene Books, 1997.

—. *Forgotten Survivors, Polish Christians Remember the Nazi Occupation.* Edited by Richard C Lukas. Lawrence, Kansas: University of Kansas Press, 2004.

MacDonogh, Giles. *After the Reich, The Brutal History of Allied Occupation.* New York: Basic Books, 2007.

Mankus, Tony. *Where do I Belong? An Immigrant's Quest for Identity.* Tony Mankus, 2013.

Marcuse, Harold. *Historical Dollar-to-Marks Currency Conversion.* Santa Barbara: www.history.ucsb.edu.

Nagorski, Andres. *Hiterland, American Eyewitnesses to the Nazi Rise to Power.* New York: Simon & Schuster Paperbacks, 2012.

PBS. *Timeline of World War II, 1944.* www.pbs.org/thewar/at_war_timeline.

Porta Polonica. *The Letter "P".* www.porta-polonica.

Samuel, Wolfgang W.E. *German Boy, a Child in War.* Mississippi: University of Mississippi Press, 2000.

Schlesier, Karl H. *Flakhelfer to Grenadier, Memoir of a Boy Soldier, 1943-1945.* United States: Karl H. Schlesier, 2011.

Schmid, Walter. *A German POW in New Mexico.* Albuquerque, New Mexico: University of New Mexico Press, 2005.

Schwartz, Terese Pencak. *Holocaust Forgotten, Five Million non-Jewish Victims.* Westlake Village, California: Terese Pencak Schwartz, 2012.

Smith, Carolyn. *Importance of the Marshall Plan to Economic Recovery in Europe in the Post War Era.* www.articlesbase.co.

Standifer, Leon C. *Binding Up the Wounds, an American Soldier in Occupied Germany 1945-1946.* Baton Rouge, Louisiana: Louisiana State University Press, 1997.

The History Place. *World War II in Europe.* www.history.place.com.

—. *World War II in the Pacific.* www.historyplace.com.

The People History. *The Year 1949 from the People History.* www.thepeoplehistory.com.

U.S. Department of State. *Profile of Germany.* www.state.gov.

Welty, Joel Carl. *The Hunger Year in the French Zone of Divided Germany 1946-1947.* Beloit, Wisconsin: Beloit College, 1993.

Worldology. *Effect of World War II on Each Country.* www.worldology.com .

www.thepeople history.com/1950s/html. www.thepeoplehistory.com.

Wyman, Mark. *DPs, Europe's Displaced Persons, 1945-1951.* Ithaca, New York: Cornell University Press, 1998.

Yale Law School. *Nazi Conspiracy and Aggression Volume 1.* avalon.law.yale.edu.

Made in the USA
Charleston, SC
29 June 2016